D0238697

Lesbian, Gay, Bisexual and Transgender Ageing

15033

of related interest

Reminiscence and Life Story Work
A Practice Guide
4th edition
Faith Gibson
ISBN 978 1 84905 151 4
eISBN 978 0 85700 338 6

Remembering Yesterday, Caring Today
Reminiscence in Dementia Care: A Guide to Good Practice
Pam Schweitzer and Errollyn Bruce
Foreword by Faith Gibson
ISBN 9781843106494
eISBN 978 1 84642 804 3
Bradford Dementia Group Good Practice Guides series

The Psychology of Ageing
An Introduction
5th edition
Ian Stuart-Hamilton
ISBN 978 1 84905 245 0
eISBN 978 0 85700 577 9

Key Issues in Evolving Dementia Care
International Theory-based Policy and Practice
Edited by Anthea Innes, Fiona Kelly and Louise McCabe
Foreword by Professor June Andrews
ISBN 978 1 84905 242 9
eISBN 978 0 85700 503 8

Making Partnerships with Service Users and Advocacy Groups Work
How to Grow Genuine and Respectful Relationships in Health and Social Care
Jackie Martin and Julie Gosling
ISBN 978 1 84905 193 4
eISBN 978 0 85700 608 0

The Activity Year Book
A Week by Week Guide for Use in Elderly Day and Residential Care
Anni Bowden and Nancy Lewthwaite
ISBN 978 1 84310 963 1
eISBN 978 1 84642 889 0

Group and Individual Work with Older People
A Practical Guide to Running Successful Activity-based Programmes
Swee Hong Chia, Julie Heathcote and Jane Marie Hibberd
Illustrated by Andy Hibberd
ISBN 978 1 84905 128 6
eISBN 978 0 85700 317 1

Enriched Care Planning for People with Dementia
A Good Practice Guide to Delivering Person-Centred Care
Hazel May, Paul Edwards and Dawn Brooker
ISBN 978 1 84310 405 6
eISBN 978 1 84642 960 6
Bradford Dementia Group Good Practice Guides series

Lesbian, Gay, Bisexual and Transgender Ageing

Biographical Approaches for Inclusive Care and Support

Edited by Richard Ward, Ian Rivers and Mike Sutherland

Jessica Kingsley *Publishers*
London and Philadelphia

Chapter 6 is adapted from Cronin *et al.* 2011 with permission from Sage

First published in 2012
by Jessica Kingsley Publishers
116 Pentonville Road
London N1 9JB, UK
and
400 Market Street, Suite 400
Philadelphia, PA 19106, USA

www.jkp.com

Library of Congress Cataloging in Publication Data
Lesbian, gay, bisexual and transgender ageing : biographical approaches for inclusive care and support /
edited by Richard Ward, Ian Rivers and Mike Sutherland.
p. cm.
Includes bibliographical references and index.
ISBN 978-1-84905-257-3 (alk. paper)
1. Older sexual minorities--Services for--Great Britain. 2. Social work with older sexual minorities--
Great Britain. 3. Older people--Great Britain--Care. 4. Autobiography--Therapeutic use. I. Ward,
Richard, 1966- II. Rivers, Ian. III. Sutherland, Mike, 1961-
HV1481.G72L47 2012
362.6'9664050941--dc23
2012025297

British Library Cataloguing in Publication Data
A CIP catalogue record for this book is available from the British Library

ISBN 978 1 84905 257 3
eISBN 978 0 85700 537 3

Printed and bound in Great Britain

Acknowledgements

The editors wish to thank the Economic and Social Research Council who funded the seminar series from which this book is taken. We would also like to thank the four universities that hosted the seminars: Queen Margaret University Edinburgh, the University of Glasgow, Robert Gordon University Aberdeen and the University of Edinburgh, and all those who worked so hard to help us stage the seminars at each venue. We would also like to extend our thanks to all the contributors and participants in the seminar series who ensured its success. Particular thanks go to the Equality Network and the Scottish Transgender Alliance for their support throughout. Finally, we are grateful to Caroline Walton at Jessica Kingsley Publishers for her support and patience in the delivery of this book.

Contents

Part III Community Engagement and Support

List of Figures and Tables
Figures

Tables

Introduction

Lesbian, Gay, Bisexual and Transgender Ageing: Providing Effective Support Through Biographical Practice

Mike Sutherland, Ian Rivers and Richard Ward

Putting equality into practice is no mean feat. One of the greatest challenges faced by those who work on the frontline of health and social care services relates to the Equalities Act (2010); while it is clear about the *principles* and *outcomes* for a 'Fairer Britain' it offers few clues as to the *process* of getting there. Having identified that inequalities persist in health and social care in terms of access to services and the appropriateness of the services provided, we are left with the question, how do we take forward an equalities agenda in the hope of creating a more inclusive and egalitarian system for care? In this book we consider biographical practice as one strand of the process of creating fairer provision. Our focus is on the provision of care and support to older lesbian, gay, bisexual and transsexual (hereafter LGBT) service users, an area of practice for which there is currently very limited guidance or evidence to support improvements, and yet every indication of the need for change (Ward, Pugh and Price 2010).

This book is derived from a series of seminars, funded by the Economic and Social Research Council (ESRC) entitled, 'LGBT Lives: The Biographies and Life Course of Sexual/Gender Dissidents'. Over a period of two years, four seminars were held across Scotland that sought to understand the lived experiences of LGBT people, how those lives are themselves represented, and the challenges to the mainstream those lives offer. The seminars attracted international interest and sparked a debate that we have carried forward into this book. Our theme of the life course and the biographies of LGBT people proved incredibly fruitful. It enabled us to begin to understand the diverse ways that LGBT lives can inform working cultures and the delivery of services and, alongside this, the many ways in which biographical practice has been deployed in public services and beyond. Above all, the seminars served to demonstrate that sexuality and gender identity imbue our everyday lives, and rarely are there any points in a person's life at which their sexuality does not shape a connection to the world they inhabit. The success of the seminar series spurred us to share some of what we have learned with a larger audience, and in this book we consider the value of developing biographical practice in working with older LGBT people in health and social care settings.

This book therefore concerns itself with looking beyond a narrow focus on need to consider a life lived and how an understanding of that life might facilitate more effective ways of working with and supporting older people. This book is the first of its kind in a UK context. It is the first to pull together a series of writings that address a range of issues that have affected LGBT people. It is the first to present these issues comprehensively, through the medium of biographical narratives, so that the voices and stories of our older LGBT citizens are heard and understood. It aims to reflect those voices as much as possible allowing the reader to *hear* and *feel* how LGBT people view their old age, 'live' their old age and engage with (or not) health and social care services.[1] Our contributors provide the reader with very good reasons why this approach is a beneficial one in understanding how person-centred care with older LGBT people may be better delivered.

The timing of the publication of this book is apposite, with the introduction, in October 2010, of the UK-wide Equality Act which provides businesses, the private, public and voluntary sectors with a single, streamlined framework for tackling inequality and discrimination. Gender, sexual orientation and gender reassignment are now *protected characteristics* under the Act and it is incumbent upon us all to be mindful of these protected characteristics in terms of service delivery. Soon it will also be unlawful to discriminate against individuals receiving services on the grounds of age. This significant piece of legislation places a requirement on all those providing services to ensure that they are doing everything possible to counter discrimination, including ageism and heterosexism and their insidious presence within large social institutions, such as the welfare system.

---

1   All individual names in the book have been changed to preserve anonymity.

About the book

Research on LGBT ageing is, somewhat ironically, in its infancy, and many of the studies and reports to which our authors refer throughout the book are small in scale in terms of the number of participants and geographic location. This in no means diminishes the value of those studies; they represent the voices of a group of people many of whom are hidden from or overlooked by service providers. Our aim is to achieve depth of understanding, and it is here that the qualitative approaches we advocate have such value and utility.

We hope this book will be of particular interest to a range of people: much of what follows has been written particularly with frontline practitioners in mind, as well as those studying to work in health and social care, but the material gathered here will be relevant and useful for commissioners, service developers and managers, carers, and, we hope, LGBT older people themselves, as well as academics, researchers, and educators in health and social care and/or sexualities and gender studies. Understanding the needs, wishes, and experiences of LGBT people as they grow older is essential to all those delivering support and care and all those who inform that process.

What do we mean by 'biographical practice'?

This book is not a 'how to' manual for biographical methods, although much contained here will stimulate thinking around using such approaches and will provide material for training and awareness-raising for those studying and working in health and social care. Our main intention is to advocate a range of approaches that fall under a 'biographical' heading and demonstrate how they have been used with particular groups and communities. It has long been understood that we should look beyond 'need' in how we think about and organise the provision of care and support, and more recently there has been recognition that fixed categories of identity, applied to service users, are also an inadequate basis by which to tailor support. This applies particularly to work with some minoritised groups where efforts to conjure up 'checklist' responses to inequality have been found ineffectual, and what has been described as an 'add-in and stir' approach to social difference has similarly led to unhelpful and reductionist thinking.

What follows in this book is a series of accounts of various ways in which the lives and biographies of older LGBT people have been used to inform our understanding of ageing and sexuality, and incorporated into the tailoring of support and care. Perhaps the most in-depth of these approaches is the life story method, where as full as possible an account of a person's life is elicited both for its therapeutic qualities and as a framework for the subsequent organisation and tailoring of care and support. Many regard life story work as the gold standard in biographical approaches but, as Ann Cronin and colleagues observe in this book, the value of biographical practice is its inherent adaptability. As such, this book offers insights into various forms of biographical practice in diverse settings and conditions. Central to this is an underlying concern with narrative. For instance, Robin Wright and colleagues demonstrate the power of using a narrative approach when lives take an unexpected turn and we need to 'reconstitute' ourselves in light of these changes. Wright and colleagues demonstrate one of a number of ways in which we can think and practise 'biographically'. This includes anticipatory approaches to understanding how people view the road ahead, as discussed by Rebecca Jones and Stephen Pugh, and the elicitation of more specific narratives that constitute part of a broader life story where particular activities, such as caring for a partner or loved one, provide opportunities to understand how people perform their identities in everyday life – as Ann Cronin and colleagues reveal.

Another crucial strand to the 'portfolio' of biographical approaches for health and social care practice are the benefits attached to thinking more broadly about the life course, as Louis Bailey demonstrates in his chapter on transgender (hereafter 'trans') lives. Life course approaches help us to understand change over time and the cumulative nature of certain types of experience or event. As Jane Traies maps the lives of her lesbian interviewees she explores how identities are negotiated over time and we are shown the contingent and fluid nature of sexual and gender identities. However, what knits together these different approaches is an underlying understanding of the purpose of biographical practice. It is distinct as an approach in health and social care because it stands outside of, and sometimes in stark contrast to the way in which information and insights about service users are usually gathered and understood. Jay Gubrium (1993) captures this distinction as he distinguishes 'life narratives' from 'life histories' in the introduction to his biographical work with nursing home residents:

Life histories are meant to be evaluated according to how accurately they reflect what actually happened in their subjects' lives. The truth of a life history lies less in its formulation than in its subject matter. Ideally, life histories should factually describe the lives they are about. Life narratives, in contrast, are communicated lives. The past, present, and future are linked together to assemble meaning. (Gubrium 1993, p.15)

The notion of communicated lives is woven throughout this book. It underpins the idea that we come into being as we offer narratives of our lives, and this has particular importance for health and social care practice with older LGBT service users. What we are describing as biographical practice is concerned less with the hard facts of a person's life and more centrally with the meanings attached to that life. It is our contention that working with subjective meanings is a far better place to start in the development of inclusive care services than organising care around supposedly objective facts.

The contributions to this volume

The book is divided, we hope usefully, into three parts entitled: (Part I) Growing Older: Diverse Pathways into Later Life; (Part II) Implications for Health and Social Care Practice; and (Part III) Community Engagement and Support.

In Part I we offer some examples of how various biographical approaches have been used with different strands of the LGBT communities. One aim here is to support readers to consider some inter- and intra-group differences and begin to appreciate something of what is distinctive to each. Collectively, these chapters demonstrate that 'LGBT' is very much an umbrella term that covers a broad range of different identities and perspectives. Inevitably perhaps, the closer we look, the more we become aware of the differing perspectives and walks of life that are gathered together under categories such as 'lesbian', 'trans' or 'bisexual'. Taken together, the chapters show the difficulty attached to organising health and social care according to such categories of identity and consequently making assumptions about people's needs on this basis. This is why we are advocating a more biographical focus to practice and provision.

Chapters 1 and 2 are concerned primarily with an *anticipatory biographical approach*; the act of looking forward to an imagined future and the challenges attached to doing this for people whose lives do not fit with the traditional milestones and expectations attached to growing older. Rebecca Jones opens the book with the metaphor of a roadmap as one way to think about what guides us as we age. Using a range of media, participants in her research were asked to consider how they viewed their personal ageing in a context of the relative absence of route-finding techniques. This is the first of a number of chapters to employ spatial metaphors and notions of travel or mobility in order to reframe how we think about the ageing process. Jones invites the reader to think creatively about ageing in order to facilitate different ways of imagining a personal journey into later life. Stephen Pugh similarly takes up the practice of asking people to look ahead, in this case to a more immediate future, where the need for help and care might be on the horizon. He draws upon his doctoral research with a small group of older lesbians and gay men, but speaks also as a practitioner with a career devoted to social work with older people. Thus, he writes from the perspective of a practitioner and educator who has first-hand experience of developing biographical approaches in health and social care and an understanding of their value in supporting older LGBT service users.

Chapter 3 leads the way in outlining a life course model relevant to the trans population in the UK. As far as we are aware, this chapter is the first discussion of trans ageing and the life course to be published in the UK, and Louis Bailey offers a useful synthesis of existing research, in addition to reflecting on his own work as the director of a voluntary sector support network for trans people in the Northwest of England. As Bailey points out, trans ageing is a relatively new phenomenon; those trans people entering old age or seeking to transition in later life have no blueprint or roadmap by which to age. Service providers and policymakers are similarly faced with fresh challenges attached to how best to meet the needs of this group and it is clear that at present very little guidance or evidence exists to support services to work effectively with older trans users. This chapter is very much, then, an opening salvo in what we can only hope will prove to be a fast-growing field of research and emerging good practice.

In Chapter 4, the final chapter in Part I, Jane Traies is quick to ask the pertinent question, why do we not *see* older lesbians? This is the first published account from Traies of a doctoral study that set out to investigate the social and cultural invisibility of older lesbians by drawing on biographical narratives and life histories. Identifying herself as belonging to the 'tribe' she is studying, Traies considers this shared membership to be an important reason why she has had such success in recruiting large numbers of women to her research. Indeed, hers is the largest single survey and investigation of older lesbians to be conducted in the UK to date, and provides readers with a level of insight and detail unmatched by previous research with the LGBT communities, where older lesbians have consistently proved hard to recruit. It seems likely, then, that this study entitled 'Women Like That' will become an important milestone for sexuality studies in the UK, and we have been fortunate to gain some early reflections on the data gathered and their relevance to health and social care practice.

Part II offers instances of research that looks at older LGBT people as users of health and social care services and considers practice issues in the field of HIV, work with informal carers and end-of-life care. Each chapter shows how the narratives provided by older LGBT people can be made central to our ability to understand, provide for and respond to their needs, concerns and wishes.

Employing a biographical narrative approach, Robin Wright and colleagues reveal in Chapter 5 that people living with HIV are another group where ageing represents new territory as a result of the dramatic impact of new therapies. This chapter reveals something of the power of biographical work in supporting people to reconstruct their life narratives in a context where many had previously not expected to see their old age. Here, participants talk of feelings of uncertainty, loss and isolation, but also a sense of resilience and opportunity, and the reader is offered an insight into the therapeutic quality of creating discursive spaces for people to re-evaluate their lives and futures. At the outset of Chapter 6, Ann Cronin and her colleagues warn the reader against the use of arbitrary sexual categories that can become 'fixed' identities for LGBT individuals, likely to elicit a 'fixed', non-personalised mode of caregiving and policy-making. The chapter focuses on biographical narratives, this time in relation to older LGBT carers, and the authors use excerpts from narratives of care to demonstrate their educative quality as well as their potential to provide a basis for decision-making in the provision of help and support. In essence, Cronin and her colleagues assert the need for practitioners to relate to older LGBT people through their individual and joint biographies, as a means to understanding both individual and shared strengths as well as broader connections to a history of oppression.

Part II ends with an examination of end-of-life care issues for LGBT people. In Chapter 7 Gary Stein and Kathryn Almack present the reader with an informative insight into current conditions both in the UK and the United States (US). While not intended to be a comparison between the two, it does afford the reader a glimpse of the differences and similarities in our respective legislative, health and social care systems and provision. The authors focus the reader on particular emerging concerns for LGBT end-of-life care and include narratives of individuals who took part in studies in the UK and the US that offer direct insights into what has to be one of the most vulnerable points in our lives. They reveal that LGBT end-of-life care is an area where current practice lacks an evidence base, and this chapter usefully sets the agenda for future work. Once again, the emphasis here is upon the value of organising care around the lives of service users and the meanings they attach to lived experience.

Finally, Part III explores community engagement and support, work that is either exclusively with or inclusive of older LGBT groups and individuals. The four contributions outline some of the largest and longest-running project work to have been undertaken with older LGBT people in the UK to date. In this section we depart from more academic discourses to hear instead directly from those who have worked with and for older LGBT people and in many instances have achieved significant change and improvements to the delivery of services and levels of awareness. Lindsay River and Richard Ward outline the work of Polari, an organisation that worked for many years specifically with, and campaigned on behalf of, older LGBT people in the UK: Chapter 8 looks back over a series of participatory projects and argues that it is important to consider the biographies of organisations and institutions as well as those of individual service users. In Chapter 9, Sally Knocker and colleagues report on the ongoing 'Opening Doors' initiative run by Age Concern (now AgeUK). In its fourth year now, 'Opening Doors' can lay claim to the achievement of having recruited the largest number, by far, of older LGBT people to any single project. Given what we know of the difficulties that other projects around the country have had in identifying and recruiting older LGBT participants, the advice and experience discussed here is particularly useful. Next, in Chapter 10, Kath Browne and colleagues discuss the Brighton-based 'Count Me in Too' project that worked with LGBT people of all ages. The authors are in a unique position to consider what is distinct to the experiences of older LGBT Brighton residents, but also what continuities and common ground are shared with other age groups. Browne and colleagues emphasise the significance of place and belonging to the lives of older LGBT people through a lens that is rather different from the usual debates in social gerontology on 'ageing in place'. Finally, in

Chapter 11 Roger Newman and Elizabeth Price offer the reader some insights into the challenges attached to setting up a support network for LGBT people affected by dementia. The chapter plots Roger's journey from carer to activist, placing his personal experiences into a wider context of dementia provision where LGBT carers seem to have been overlooked, both at the level of national policy and by practitioners in the field. In contrast to widespread assumptions in healthcare of the importance of statistical evidence derived from surveying large numbers of service users, Roger's auto/biography shows that much that is useful to health and social care can be learned from considering a single life.

Through the narratives provided in this book, we hope that the lived experiences of older LGBT people engaging with health and social care services will be better understood, and that present and future practitioners gain an insight into the fears and concerns of those LGBT people yet to make use of those services. Ultimately, this book provides a starting point for discussions by health and social care providers on how to ensure that they observe the principles and achieve the outcomes outlined by the Equality Act (2010), and that older LGBT people are themselves offered services that are safe, supportive, free from prejudice and above all, meaningful to their lives.

References

Gubrium, J.F. (1993) *Speaking of Life: Horizons of Meaning for Nursing Home Residents.* New York: Aldine de Gruyter.

Ward, R., Pugh, S. and Price, E. (2010) *Don't Look Back? Improving Health and Social Care Service Delivery for Older LGB Users.* Manchester: Equality and Human Rights Commission.

Part I

Growing Older

Diverse Pathways Into Later Life

Chapter 1

Imagining the Unimaginable
Bisexual Roadmaps for Ageing

Rebecca L. Jones

We're all pilgrims on the same journey – but some pilgrims have better road maps. (Nelson DeMille)

Introduction

Life, as the old cliché states, is a journey. We journey into our own ageing but, apart from the end point of our eventual death, most people do not know where they are going to end up or the route they will take to get there. We use roadmaps to guide us into the unknown territory of our futures, roadmaps that give us a representation of the route we might take. These maps usually include major landmarks on the way, which will allow us to check that we haven't got lost and give a sense of predictability and progress to our journey. Conventionally, these major landmarks might be life events such as education, starting paid work, marriage, having children and retirement. We may also navigate by following well-worn roads or, if the path we are following is less travelled, we may follow a trailblazer. While many people's journeys turn out to be different from the ones they had anticipated, whether through unwillingly becoming lost or a more positive choice to change the route, roadmaps for some people's journeys are much more difficult to identify.

This chapter discusses the roadmaps produced by one group for whom traditional roadmaps may be less useful: bisexual-identified adults with a high degree of unconventional life course features. It introduces the particular challenges of imagining bisexual ageing and examines the ways in which using creative methods in an unusual research setting enabled them to overcome this difficulty.

Imagining personal ageing

Gerontologists have noted for many years that people often find it hard to imagine themselves growing old, characterising this failure of imagination as both arising from and contributing toward ageism and the ill-treatment of older people (Bultena and Powers 1978; Bytheway 1995, 2005; Nelson 2005). However, being unwilling to imagine the future and oneself as older can have a variety of negative consequences (Jones 2011), both at a more macro societal level (e.g. inadequate planning and provision of care services [Pickard in press] and environmental degradation and public health problems [Adam in press) and at a more personal level. It is clear that many younger people worry about growing older (Neikrug 2003) and some expect old age to be miserable (Lacey, Smith and Ubel 2006). Lacey *et al.* argue that this expectation can lead to poor decision-making in the present because a future, aged self is not valued, as well as reinforcing inter-generational conflict and misunderstanding. Similarly, Moody (1988) argues that negative visions of old age as a time of tragedy, decline and loss can become self-fulfilling prophecies.

There is a small literature on what happens when researchers ask people (usually school, college and university students) to imagine the future course of their lives into old age. It is clear that, while younger people often have negative and homogenised visions of old age (Kimuna, Knox and Zusman 2005; Mosher-Ashley and Ball 1999; Phoenix and Sparkes 2007; Scott, Minichiello and Browning 1998), they are often able to imagine that their own old age will be more positive (Bulbeck 2005; Patterson, Forbes and Peace 2009). To the extent that people are able to imagine their own ageing, they often draw on older people they know, especially family members, as role models (Hockey and James 2003; Phoenix and Sparkes 2006). They also draw on cultural resources around them, such as films, books and other media (Masters and Holley 2006).

These studies find that imagined future life courses almost always include marriage and having children (Bulbeck 2005; Gordon, Holland, Lahelma and Thomson 2005; Patterson *et al.* 2009; Phoenix and Sparkes 2008). These life course features, while increasingly available to some non-heterosexuals, can be considered aspects of a heteronormative life course, that is to say they valorise heterosexual ways of ageing (Goltz 2008; Warner 1991; Watson 2005).

Imagining queer ageing

In this chapter 'queer' is used as an umbrella term to include all non-heterosexual people and all people whose gender identity does not match well with the gender they were ascribed at birth, or is not simply 'male' or 'female'. Enabling queer people to imagine their own ageing and later life is both particularly challenging and particularly important. Many authors have argued that older queer people are culturally invisible and this means not only that services and resources are often lacking (Fish 2007; Grossman, D'Augelli and O'Connell 2001; Sales 2002; Ward *et al.* 2008), but also that older queer people are rarely available as role models for younger queer people. The commercial gay scene, in particular, is predominantly youth-centred and even hostile to older age, which may be defined as beginning as early as around age 30 (Goltz 2008; Ward *et al.* 2008). Saxey (2008) argues that the prominence given to 'coming-out' stories, which are almost always portrayed as something occurring in earlier life, means that older queer people are also invisible in literature.

Perhaps the most visible figure of an older queer person is the stereotype of an older gay man who is self-loathing, isolated, sexually predatory and closeted (Berger 1996; Hostetler 2004). While research suggests that this bears little relation to most older gay men's experiences, its influence is argued to increase the tendency of young gay men to fear ageing (Goltz 2008). Lesbian communities are generally claimed to be less ageist than gay ones (*ibid.*), but in a previous study we found that many older lesbians reported finding lesbian spaces increasingly unwelcoming and inaccessible as they aged, and lesbian communities largely age stratified (Ward *et al.* 2008). This suggests that younger lesbians may also be lacking in role models for queer ageing.

While a body of research literature now exists on the experiences of ageing for lesbians and gay men (e.g. Heaphy 2007; Heaphy, Yip and Thompson 2004; Pugh 2005; Rosenfeld 2003), there is hardly any empirical work on bisexual, trans or other forms of queer ageing. For bisexual people, Weinberg, Williams and Pryor's paper on mid-life bisexuals suggests some useful starting points (Weinberg, Williams and Pryor 2001) but is not about later life. The age profile of the bi-identified community in the UK (and of those attending the 'Bi-Con' event where this research was carried out), is somewhat older than that of the commercial lesbian and gay scene, but is still relatively youthful with an average age in the mid-30s (Barker *et al.* 2008; Jones 2011).

One empirical piece of research explicitly asked queer people to imagine their own ageing and later life. Goltz (2008) ran a semester-long series of 'generative pedagogical focus groups' for undergraduates at a US university, aimed at imagining queer futures using creative methods such as writing, drawing, making up songs and dancing. Seven people aged between 19 and 29 attended: four were male, of whom three identified as gay and queer and one as queer and attracted to women, and three were women and identified as queer and lesbian or bisexual.[1] Goltz's study asks whether sexuality affects the capacity to imagine a positive later life. He found marked differences between the futures envisaged by the men and the women. The men imagined overwhelmingly negative later lives of isolation, loneliness, bitterness and early death. They did not imagine long-term relationships or having children. The women imagined much happier futures, focused on long-term coupledom and having children but mainly limited to domesticity. Goltz argues that the extent to which the participants were able to imagine happy later lives was dependent on the extent to which they were able to imagine life courses which resembled traditional heterosexual ones.

Goltz's study (2008) suggests that queer people need a roadmap with conventional landmarks in order to imagine their own ageing positively. The 'Imagining Bi Futures' project, while not exactly replicating Goltz's study, was partly aimed at testing this finding.

Methods

The study drew participants from people who attended the main UK annual gathering for bisexual people, BiCon,[2] in August 2010.[3] It is not claimed that either the research participants or people who attend BiCon are in any sense representative or typical of people who identify as bisexual, still less of people who behave bisexually. (For more on the significance of this distinction, see Jones 2010.) As can be seen in Table 1.1, they are an unusual group demographically.

---

1   Goltz unhelpfully collapses these categories in the rest of the paper into 'the gay men' and 'the lesbian women'.

2   BiCon stands for Bisexual Conference and/or Bisexual Convention. See www.bicon.org. uk.

3   With the exception of the six participants in the pilot workshop. This convenience and snowball sample of bi-identified people had, however, all except one person, previously attended BiCon, most of them many times. Several people remarked afterwards that taking part in the pilot workshop had felt like being at a mini BiCon. The visions of the future produced at the pilot workshop are indistinguishable from those produced at BiCon itself in all significant respects. They are therefore included in the analysis.

Table 1.1: Demographic features of participants
in 'Imagining Bi Futures' research

	(n = 33)	Explanatory notes
Age	20–66 (av 37.5)	Participants were in the following age bands: Under 25 — 5 25–34 — 10 35–44 — 11 45–54 — 2 55–64 — 4 65 and over — 1
Bisexual	97% (32)	This figure is a response to a yes/no question 'Have you ever described yourself as bisexual?'
Female	61% (20)	The question about gender identity was free-response and many answers were non-binary. For fuller discussion of how they were coded, see Jones 2011.
Male	18% (6)	"
Trans/genderqueer	21% (7)	"
White ethnicities	76% (25)	The question about ethnicity was free-response. Answers coded 'white' included 'Caucasian' and 'Greek/American'.
Black British	6% (2)	
Mizrahi Jew	6% (2)	One person added '(person of colour)'.
Other	12 % (4)	These were all different and included mixed ethnicities.
Highest educational qualification undergraduate degree or above	82% (27)	
Disabilities	27% (9)	In response to the question 'Do you have any disabilities?'
Currently single	27% (9)	This information comes from a free-response question 'Current romantic/sexual relationships' rather than systematic enquiry, so rates are likely to be an underestimate.
Currently married	15% (5)	"

Cont.

Table 1.1: Demographic features of participants in 'Imagining Bi Futures' research *cont.*

	(n = 33)	Explanatory notes
Currently civil partnered	3% (1)	"
Polyamorous/non-monogamous	58% (19)	This was in response to a question 'Are you poly?' Most people wrote simply 'yes' or 'no' but a few added elaborations.
Currently have children	18% (6)	This was in response to the question 'Do you have children?'
Definitely expect or want to have children	6% (2)	This was in response to the question 'Do you expect or want to have children?'

Thus, it can be seen that participants in this study, in line with people attending BiCon in general (Barker *et al.* 2008), have many life course features which are not found on conventional roadmaps for ageing, such as being bisexual, polyamorous[4] (meaning negotiated, consensual non-monogamy) or transgender/genderqueer and being disabled in earlier life. Taking account of their age profile, relatively few participants had already experienced landmark life events such as getting married and having children. So many people at BiCon display these non-traditional identities and life course features that what is (temporarily) treated as 'normal' differs markedly from broader social norms (Barker *et al.* 2008; Bowes-Catton, Barker and Richards 2011). I argue elsewhere that this was highly salient to the participants' ability to imagine positive non-normative futures (Jones 2011).

Data were collected during three one-hour workshops attended by 33 people in total. Workshops were audio recorded and had a three-part structure which initially focused on negative visions of old age, using the phrase 'When I fear growing older, I imagine…' as a stimulus for discussion. This was followed by a focus on positive visions of old age, including an adaptation of a reading from the book *Growing Old Disgracefully* (The Hen Co-op 1993). Participants were then instructed to make a picture of how they imagined their own old age or later life, using materials supplied – coloured paper, stickers, glitter pens,

---

4   Polyamory (often abbreviated to 'poly'). See, for example, Haritaworn, Lin and Klesse (2006).

glue, felt-tips, scissors, and so on. They were told that it didn't matter whether they created a positive, negative, realistic or mixed picture of their later life. While participants were creating their images I talked to as many of them as I could, asking them what they were representing. When people finished their images they wrote a brief description of what the picture showed and filled in the demographic questionnaire. Finally there was some whole-group discussion.

Figure 1.1: An example of a picture produced during the workshop

The data thus consist of: audio recordings of the whole group discussions and my conversations with people as they were making their images; written descriptions of the images and filled-in demographic questionnaires; and the images themselves. The qualitative data was analysed thematically, looking for patterns in how participants were able to imagine their own futures.[5] An example of one of the pictures created is included above for illustrative purposes but its contents are not analysed here.

The remainder of this chapter discusses the four commonest ways in which participants were able to imagine roadmaps for personal ageing, characterising each theme found in the data as a different kind of route-finding technique. However, the discussion first elaborates on the

---

5   While precentages are sometimes cited, the sample size is small, so all the quantative findings need to be treated as indicative only.

relative absence of the route-finding techniques which have been found by other research into how people are able to imagine their own ageing.

Imagining roadmaps for personal ageing
Relative absence of some common route-finding techniques

As might perhaps be expected from a group with such high rates of current poly practice (58%) and even higher rates of past experience or willingness to consider poly in the future (a further 15%, n = 5), the landmark event of finding 'the one' (Patterson, Forbes and Peace 2009) life partner and settling down to happy monogamy is much less common in this data than in the other studies. Many people imagined poly futures or futures which might be either monogamous or poly – often using the formulation 'my partner(s)'. Imagining a poly future may entail a higher degree of uncertainty about the future than imagining a monogamous future with an existing partner, since the people with whom you will age may not all be known. Given current divorce and re-partnering rates, many people who think of themselves as monogamous will not, in the end, grow older with the person that they imagined they would. But the expectation that they will age with one already known person may make it more possible to imagine their future than someone who may anticipate future change in the number and nature of their partners.

Adding to this a bisexual identity may mean that the gender of future partners is also not known. As Bunny (all names are self-chosen pseudonyms) said of the future partners shown in her picture (see Figure 1.1).

> I deliberately drew that they are a lot less detailed than I am, because I can't imagine other people's futures and I don't know what gender they would have, so I deliberately left them kind of fairly vague, you know, because I didn't think I could specify.

Thus, imagining lifetime continuity through relationships with partners may be less straightforward for some bisexual poly people. Only six participants in this study specified that a current partner would be in their future.

Less than a third (n = 10) of the imagined futures mentioned current or future children. Previous researchers have found clear gender differences in the extent to which people imagine having children (Altpeter and Marshall 2003; Patterson *et al.* 2009), but these were not found in this data. Very similar low proportions of men (33%, n = 2) and women (30%, n = 6) mentioned the possibility of having children. Previous studies have not covered genderqueer/trans people; in this study 29 per cent (n = 2) imagined the possibility of having children. Thus, across all gender categories, around 70 per cent of respondents did not imagine having children.

Other researchers have also found that biological or adoptive family play an important role in providing templates for life courses and ageing (Hockey and James 2003). For example, Phoenix and Sparkes (2006) found that same-sex older family members were a particularly important resource for university student athletes attempting to imagine their own ageing. However, there was very little mention of older family members in this data set.

How, then, did participants manage to construct roadmaps for their own ageing?

1. Navigating by landmarks

While participants in this study predominantly did not use the conventional landmarks of marriage and having children, they did use other types of landmarks, most prominently stereotypes about what older people's lives are like. These stereotypes seemed to function as landmarks on the road ahead, which made later life recognisable and familiar. So, for example, when participants in the first workshop were asked to describe the things they feared about growing older, they very quickly and fluently produced the following list:

- Running out of money.
- Running out of brain, one's mental capacity.
- All my friends dying first.
- Having no control over your life.
- Not being listened to.
- Needing a lot of physical help.
- Feeling vulnerable.
- Not being able to have enough fun, it sounds quite broad, but not being able to do the things that one finds fun or not being able to

do things that one finds fun at that time. Kind of stuck in a nursing home with the telly on and nothing else to do.

- I was thinking of running out of energy.

- Being left out of things.

- Being patronised.

- To bring it right down, elder abuse.

- Not quite understanding what is going on, these young people, what are they doing these days?

These are the kind of fears that many people have about growing old (Neikrug 2003; Nelson 2005) and the participants in this research seemed to be able to imagine that these experiences might be theirs too. While these topographical features are unwanted, they clearly can be imagined and thus they provide landmarks for the future.

Less negatively, some participants drew on the idea of old age as a time characterised by a more home-based life, withdrawn from the hustle and bustle of younger people's lives – a common idea about later life (Patterson *et al.* 2009). For example, Doris was describing and drawing a picture of her imagined future house in the countryside:

> **Doris:** …and the telegraph wires to sort of be connected to the outside and stuff, so it's not completely out in the country.

> **Rebecca:** Is it more on your own in the country than now? Is that something you would envisage?

> **Doris:** I think maybe a little bit more, yes. Or at least there will be more flexibility about, you know, when I want to engage with the wider world. I think I see it as being more of a time of choice rather than a time of sort of necessary engagement, I suppose.

Many gerontologists and organisations working with older people have rejected as an unhelpful stereotype the figure of the frail and dependent older person (Bytheway 1995). Others have rejected the vision of a privatised, consumerist, later life offered by more apparently positive new ways of ageing (Katz 2001–02; Katz and Marshall 2003; Minkler and Holstein 2008). However, this dataset draws attention to the ways in which such stereotyped notions about the characteristics of later life help make it possible for people who are not yet old to imagine that they one day might be so. Evidence of the useful role that stereotypes play in enabling people to imagine the future can perhaps also be seen in two participants' choices of pseudonym: Doris and Pearl. Doris and Pearl sat next to each other in the workshop and imagined futures that included each other. Did playfully giving themselves what I, at least, read as 'old lady' names help them to imagine themselves into a future older persona? It seems possible that it did.

Bodily change is one of the commonest ways in which older age is culturally signified, through markers such as grey hair, wrinkles and stooped posture (Twigg 2007; Ward and Holland 2011). We might therefore expect that the images produced in this study would include representations of visibly aged bodies. However, this was not the case – very few pictures showed bodily changes. One participant indicated that they[6] expected to have put on weight by the time they were older and Rosemary, when explaining her picture to me, said:

Rosemary: And that's my other partner, [name]. I have put glasses on him, he doesn't normally wear glasses.

Rebecca: Okay yes, but this is part of imagining him older?

Rosemary: Yes.

Here, because of our common shared ideas about what happens to people's bodies as they age, I am able to recognise that the glasses signify her partner's ageing and Rosemary confirms my understanding.

Most participants did not represent their own bodies at all, or did so only with a stick figure. The only person to produce a detailed future portrait was Silentium. Their picture of their future self looked remarkably like their present self and their annotations attend to this: 'Still look like I'm only 18...', 'maybe on hormones?' and 'natural white stripes on black hair'. They captioned the whole picture with an underlined 'HARD TO IMAGINE...'. It is tempting to speculate that the absence of representations of bodily change and the generally positive nature of the imagined futures (Jones 2011) are correlated.

2. Avoiding well-known landmarks

An opposite strategy to drawing on stereotypical ideas about later life is to deliberately counter them and position your imagined future in opposition to expectations about life courses and later life. The

---

6   When participants identified as anything other than straightforwardly male or female, I have used 'they' as a singular pronoun where one is needed.

roadmap for ageing can be imagined through the landmarks which are explicitly avoided. For example, a participant in Workshop 1 said she feared 'people calling me grandma even though I have specifically chosen not to have children'. This was the most common strategy used by participants in this study, but is not discussed in this chapter for reasons of space (Instead, see Jones 2011). Clearly, one setting in which roadmaps for unconventional ageing can more easily be imagined is a space such as BiCon which supports the expression and representation of bisexual and other uncommon identities.

3. Following a trailblazer

Although older family members were seldom mentioned as role models for ageing, there was significant mention of older friends who played a role similar to that of a trailblazer in making it possible to imagine non-conventional paths into ageing. This was particularly the case in Workshops 1 and 3, which had the smallest number of participants (six in each, which made more substantial group discussion possible).

Few people knew many older bisexual people, but older people with whom they shared other identity features functioned as role models for some. So, for example, in Workshop 1 Amy said:

> I am a Quaker and I think one of the many, for me, good things about that is that I have got loads of friends who are old and really active still, because that seems to happen to Quakers. I think it is part of just being involved in community, so I have got friends in their eighties who still go hiking in the Peak District.

A few minutes later the following exchange between Amy and Laura took place:

> **Amy:** That's something else I get from Quakers as well, because there are queer people there. I don't know any in their nineties or possibly even eighties, but seventies downwards who I know and who I know are happy, yes, it's helpful.

> **Laura:** I do know one older feminist practice woman who I don't think is, I don't know if she is queer or not, it wouldn't surprise me either way. She has just moved to Hebden Bridge [laughter from group] so that kind of changed the balance of my guess a little, but she is just awesome, she is one of those people that I kind of look at and go 'I want to be like you when I grow

up', she is ex-Greenham Common, a teacher who occasionally teaches workshops in climbing, in locking yourself up trees and things.

Amy: I have a sort of godmother who isn't queer but is an activist. She went on a course last year or the year before on non-violent direct action, and she is 81, I think, now. She says it doesn't matter if she gets a criminal record now!

Here, the participants, unprompted by me, talk about whether or not their role models are queer and orient to this as salient to their ability to map their own future life courses. Trailblazers, it seems, do not need to be exactly like the person who will follow them but just sufficiently similar in important respects.

Laura's childlike formulation 'when I grow up' rather than 'when I grow older' was also used by Lisa in Workshop 3:

I have one role model and that's [name of older LGBT activist, present at BiCon, but not in this workshop] who I just look at and go wow, you are fierce. And, you know, you are completely pagan and out about being SM [sado-masochist] and really activist and you look fantastic, and I just thought yes, you know, I could be you when I grow, I was going to say grow up, I can't bear to say grow older, it's really raw, but that's so precious. [...] [Activist's name] is fantastic and having had the opportunity to be in a space where role models can come together of all ages and they can meet each other [BiCon], it's so precious.

Imagining your own ageing can be highly emotionally charged, even for people with relatively conventional life courses (Neikrug 2003; Nelson 2005), so trailblazers can be hugely significant when people expect their life course to deviate from well-worn paths.

4. Focusing on the traveller

The fourth main way in which participants were able to imagine their own journey into later life was by focusing not so much on the map as on their own characteristics as a traveller. They did this through drawing on the idea of personal continuity. So, for example, Jenny said:

So when I am old I hope that I can still be politically active and that this, like my ideology and political attitude, can be present in my life. They form a background for everything I am doing now and I hope that will be so when I am old and this also represents my wish to be active politically and academically and artistically.

Other participants spoke explicitly about the ways in which their current activities and interests would be maintainable into old age. For example, Rosemary said:

I do indoor rowing and I do, one of the nice things about indoor rowing is that as a sport, I mean we don't just have seniors [...] it's all sorts of ages, and I know somebody called [name] and she is about 85 or something like that. We've actually had somebody who is 99 coming to one of our competitions, wins the 90-plus category! So yes, as long as I can keep going, I want to.

Appropriately, given the analogy of life as a journey, Laura's personal continuity was itself a mode of transport:

Cycling is more or less a kind of identity statement for me so I'd have to be quite knackered not to find, um, be quite physically out of it, not to find some way of operating a bike, um, but yes I think I just tend to assume maybe, I will just find other ways to compensate for the physical ageing process. I already have various, not age related, there are bits of me that don't work quite right and I am so used to working around those, I think I just assume I will find ways to work around whatever else crops up, which as I say might be unreasonably optimistic, but I think I would rather go along assuming that, until something happens to make me not be able to do that.

Here, there is a continuity of cycling still being a major part of her life and also of her own skills in finding ways around physical limitations. The destination and the route of participants' life journeys may be unknown, but by focusing on their own characteristics as travellers they are able to imagine a personal vision of what it might be like to grow older.

Implications

This chapter has used the analogy of a roadmap to discuss some of the ways in which participants in the study were able to imagine unconventional ageing and later life. It has argued that, however much gerontologists and older people themselves might want to resist stereotyped ideas about ageing, stereotypes can provide useful landmarks to enable people to imagine what later life might be like. However, the most prevalent way in which participants were able to imagine their own ageing was by explicitly countering stereotyped ideas about ageing and by asserting their difference from what is usually treated as normative (Jones 2011). Thus, landmarks can function both to provide guidance on the way and as places to be intentionally avoided. The third main way in which participants were able to see the route into their own ageing was by following trailblazers whom they saw as being on a similar life journey to themselves. These trailblazers were mostly not older bisexual people, since few people knew any older bisexual people, but people with whom they shared other identity features such as commitment to feminism, religious practices, and other forms of queer identity. The fourth main way in which participants could imagine their future was by focusing not on the route to be taken but on their own personal characteristics as a traveller. Through drawing on the idea of personal continuity, they were able to project forward and into their own imagined lives. While participants in this particular study identified as bisexual, and unconventional life courses may be more likely for bisexual and other queer-identified people, many heterosexual people also end up having non-traditional life courses. Practitioners need to be careful not to assume either that service users have had traditional life courses or that they imagine or desire them.

I do not conceptualise the futures imagined in these workshops as, in any sense, predictors of what is likely to happen to these individuals, still less to bisexual identified people in general. The accounts produced, and the navigatory techniques employed, are thus understood to be highly context-dependent on the particular social, historical and, especially, temporal–spatial setting. The accounts may, however, themselves influence the future if participants change their behaviours in the light of having taken part in the workshop, as several reported to me subsequently. They also provide evidence that it is possible, for some people in some circumstances, to imagine positive non-normative later life. As other researchers have argued (e.g. Gauntlett 2007), creative methods can free people up to imagine things they would not usually think about or which they may find problematic, such as their own ageing. Simple creative methods, such as drawing and doodling, can be employed by practitioners in everyday contexts in order to help people to articulate their experiences and wishes.

The analogy of a roadmap for ageing has proved fruitful but is it perhaps a rather old-fashioned one? In these days of GPS and route-planning software, travellers may not use maps, and so do not need to envisage their journey more than a few turns ahead. Can we extend the analogy and say that nowadays, when some people's life courses are argued to have become more fluid and less structured (Beck 1992; Giddens 1991; Leccardi 2008), there may be less need for people to be able to imagine where their life is heading? That would be a large claim to make indeed. It is more reasonable to note that focusing on the immediate future is more common in everyday life than thinking about one's own ageing and later life.

References

Adam, B. (in press) 'Future Matters for Ageing Research.' In R.L. Jones and J. Bornat (eds) *Imagining Futures.* London: Centre for Policy on Ageing / The Open University.

Altpeter, M. and Marshall, V.W. (2003) 'Making aging "real" for undergraduates.' *Educational Gerontology 29*, 9, 739.

Barker, M., Bowes-Catton, H., Iantaffi, A., Cassidy, A. and Brewer, L. (2008) 'British bisexuality: A snapshot of bisexual identities in the UK.' *Journal of Bisexuality 8,* 1–2, 141–162.

Beck, U. (1992) *Risk Society: Towards a New Modernity.* London: Sage Publications.

Berger, R.M. (1996) *Gay and Gray: The Older Homosexual Man.* (Second edition.) New York: Harrington Park Press.

Bowes-Catton, H., Barker, M. and Richards, C. (2011) '"I Didn't Know that I Could Feel this Relaxed in My Body": Using Visual Methods to Research Bisexual People's Embodied Experiences of Identity and Space.' In P. Reavey (ed.) *Visual Methods in Psychology: Using and Interpreting Images in Qualitative Research.* London: Routledge.

Bulbeck, C. (2005) 'Schemes and dreams: Young Australians imagine their future.' *Hecate 31*, 1, 73–84.

Bultena, G.L. and Powers, E.A. (1978) 'Denial of ageing: Age identification and reference group orientation.' *Journal of Gerontology 33*, 5, 748–754.

Bytheway, B. (1995) *Ageism.* Buckingham: Open University Press.

Bytheway, B. (2005) 'Ageism and age categorisation.' *Journal of Social Issues 6*, 2, 361–374.

Fish, J. (2007) *Older Lesbian, Gay and Bisexual (LGB) People.* London: Department of Health.

Gauntlett, D. (2007) *Creative Explorations: New Approaches to Identities and Audiences.* London: Routledge.

Giddens, A. (1991) *Modernity and Self-Identity. Self and Society in the Late Modern Age.* Cambridge: Polity.

Goltz, D. (2008) 'Investigating queer future meanings: Destructive perceptions of "the harder path".' *Qualitative Inquiry 15,* 3, 561–586.

Gordon, T., Holland, J., Lahelma, E. and Thomson, R. (2005) 'Imagining gendered adulthood: Anxiety, ambivalence, avoidance and anticipation.' *European Journal of Women's Studies 12*, 1, 83–103.

Grossman, A.H., D'Augelli, A.R., and O'Connell, T.S. (2001) 'Being lesbian, gay, bisexual, and over 60 or older in North America.' *Journal of Gay and Lesbian Social Services 13*, 4, 23–40.

Haritaworn, J., Lin, C. and Klesse, C. (2006) Special Issue on Polyamory. *Sexualities 9*, 5, 515–656.

Heaphy, B. (2007) 'Sexualities, gender and ageing: Resources and social change.' *Current Sociology 55*, 2, 193–210.

Heaphy, B., Yip, A.K.T. and Thompson, D. (2004) 'Ageing in a non-heterosexual context.' *Ageing and Society 24*, 6, 881–902.

Hockey, J. and James, A. (2003) 'Social identities across the life course.' London: Palgrave Macmillan.

Hostetler, A.J. (2004) 'Old, Gay and Alone? The Ecology of Well-being among Middle-Aged and Older Single Gay Men.' In G. Herdt and B. de Vries (eds) *Gay and Lesbian Aging: Research and Future Directions*. New York: Springer.

Jones, R.L. (2010) 'Troubles with Bisexuality in Health and Social Care.' In R.L. Jones and R. Ward (eds) *LGBT Issues: Looking Beyond Categories*. Edinburgh: Dunedin Academic Press.

Jones, R.L. (2011) 'Imagining bisexual futures: Positive, non-normative later life.' *Journal of Bisexuality 11*, 2, 245–270.

Jones, R.L. (in press) 'Imagining Old Age.' In J. Katz, S. M. Peace and S. M. Spurr (eds) *Adult Lives: A Life Course Perspective*. London: Policy Press.

Katz, S. (2001–02) 'Growing older without aging? Positive aging, anti-ageism, and anti-aging.' *Generations 25*, 4, 27–32.

Katz, S. and Marshall, B. (2003) 'New sex for old: Lifestyle, consumerism, and the ethics of aging well.' *Journal of Aging Studies 17*, 1, 3–16.

Kimuna, S.R., Knox, D. and Zusman, M. (2005) 'College students' perceptions about older people and aging.' *Educational Gerontology 31*, 7, 563–572.

Lacey, H.P., Smith, D.L. and Ubel, P.A. (2006) 'Hope I die before I get old: Mispredicting happiness across the adult lifespan.' *Journal of Happiness Studies 7*, 2, 167–182.

Leccardi, C. (2008) 'New biographies in the "risk society"? About future and planning.' *Twenty-First-Century Society: Journal of the Academy of Social Sciences 3*, 2, 119–129.

Masters, J.L. and Holley, L.M. (2006) 'A glimpse of life at 67: The Modified Future-Self Worksheet. *Educational Gerontology 32*, 4, 261–269.

Minkler, M. and Holstein, M.B. (2008) 'From civil rights to…civic engagement? Concerns of two older critical gerontologists about a "new social movement" and what it portends.' *Journal of Aging Studies 22*, 2, 196–204.

Moody, H.R. (1988) *Abundance of Life*. New York: Columbia University Press.

Mosher-Ashley, P.M. and Ball, P. (1999) 'Attitudes of college students toward elderly persons and their perceptions of themselves at age 75.' *Educational Gerontology 25*, 1, 89–102.

Neikrug, S.M. (2003) 'Worrying about a frightening old age.' *Aging and Mental Health 7*, 5, 326–333.

Nelson, T.D. (2005) 'Ageism: Prejudice against our feared future self.' *Journal of Social Issues 61*, 2, 207–221.

Patterson, L.G., Forbes, K.E. and Peace, R.M. (2009) 'Happy, stable and contented: Accomplished ageing in the imagined futures of young New Zealanders.' *Ageing and Society 29*, 3, 431–454.

Phoenix, C. and Sparkes, A.C. (2006) Keeping it in the family: Narrative maps of ageing and young athletes' perceptions of their futures.' *Ageing and Society 26*, 4, 631–648.

Phoenix, C. and Sparkes, A.C. (2007) 'Sporting bodies, ageing, narrative mapping and young team athletes: an analysis of possible selves.' *Sport, Education and Society 12*, 1, 1–17.

Phoenix, C. and Sparkes, A.C. (2008) 'Athletic bodies and aging in context: The narrative construction of experienced and anticipated selves in time.' *Journal of Aging Studies 22*, 3, 211–221.

Pickard, L. (in press) 'Researching the Future with Survey Data: Projections of Family Care for Older People.' In R.L. Jones and J. Bornat (eds) *Imagining Futures*. London: Centre for Policy on Ageing / The Open University.

Pugh, S. (2005) 'Assessing the cultural needs of older lesbians and gay men: Implications for practice.' *Practice 17*, 3, 207–218.

Rosenfeld, D. (2003) *The changing of the Guard: Lesbian and Gay Elders, Identity and Social Change*. Philadelphia: Temple University Press.

Sales, A.U. (2002) 'Back in the closet.' *Community Care 1424*, 30.

Scott, T., Minichiello, V. and Browning, C. (1998) 'Secondary school students' knowledge of and attitudes towards older people: Does an education intervention programme make a difference?' *Ageing and Society 18*, 2, 167–183.

The Hen Co-op. (1993) *Growing Old Disgracefully: New Ideas for Getting the Most out of Life*. London: Piatkus.

Twigg, J. (2007) 'Clothing, age and the body: A critical review.' *Ageing and Society 27*, 2, 285–305.

Ward, R. and Holland, C. (2011) '"If I look old, I will be treated old": Hair and later-life image dilemmas.' *Ageing and Society 31*, 2, 288–307.

Ward, R., Jones, R., Hughes, J., Humberstone, N. and Pearson, R. (2008) 'Intersections of Ageing and Sexuality: Accounts from Older People.' In R. Ward and B. Bytheway (eds) *Researching Age and Multiple Discrimination*. (Vol. 8, pp.45–72.) London: Centre for Policy on Ageing.

Warner, M. (1991) 'Introduction: Fear of a queer planet.' *Social Text 29*, 4, 3–17.

Watson, K. (2005) 'Queer Theory.' Group Analysis 38, 1, 67–81.

Weinberg, M.S., Williams, C.J. and Pryor, D.W. (2001) 'Bisexuals at midlife: Commitment, salience and identity.' *Journal of Contemporary Ethnography 30*, 2, 180–208.

Chapter 2

Care Anticipated

Older Lesbians and Gay Men Consider their Future Needs

Stephen Pugh

Introduction

This chapter focuses on how we as professionals can more effectively care for and support older lesbians and gay men in later life by better understanding the wider context of their lived experience. Through understanding the lives and fears of older lesbians and gay men we can establish a closer fit between the individual and the services that are required to support them. In doing so it is hoped that we can achieve higher levels of satisfaction and improved outcomes at an individual level.

The problem that exists at the moment is that we have very little understanding of how needs for care and support may be different as a consequence of an individual's sexuality. Quite clearly, the basic physiological needs, those for nutrition, hydration, medication or toileting, vary little between people on the basis of their sexual orientation. However, being dependent on others to provide assistance in undertaking some or all of these tasks adds another dynamic to the sense of self. The difference rests with the environment or the atmosphere in which care is provided. An environment that acknowledges and respects difference and which enables the person to live as they wish becomes crucial in the support of the health and social care needs of older lesbians or gay men. Essentially, I am referring to person-centred care – the person at the centre of the care arrangement.

Legislative and policy background

The current emphasis within health and social care practice with older people in general is outcome-focused needs assessment set within the context of the 'personalisation agenda'. This has not emerged as a single, coherent, evidence-based approach with a broadly understood theoretical construct, but rather it is the product of changes in practice that have occurred piecemeal over a considerable period of time.

In the years following the implementation of the National Health Service and Community Care Act (1990) in April 1993, policy developments have emerged which in turn have influenced the current expression of health and social care practice. The current policy documents, following devolution, only apply within an English context, although similar provisions exist in other parts of the UK. The significant documents are:

1. Modernising Social Services (DoH 1998)

2. Putting People First: A Shared Vision and Commitment to the Transformation of Adult Social Care (HM Government 2007)

3. Our Health, Our Care, Our Say: A New Direction For Community Services (DoH 2006).

The direction of Government policy explicitly asserts that having choice and control over the arrangements for care can be transformative for those people in need. Equally, these policies support broader Government policy objectives in respect of health and social care practice and provision, namely the maintenance of independence, social inclusion, high quality service provision, prevention and solutions that are located within communities. However, of key importance for this chapter is that these policies are very clear in articulating the idea that we cannot begin to understand and thereby care and support individual older people in the here-and-now without being able to understand the life that they have lived and their fears for the future. Achieving such an understanding requires the sort of life course or biographical approach advocated here.

Incorporating an anticipatory biographical approach to health and social care assessment

In essence, a biographical approach entails collecting information about the person's life (often) through oral testimony – the spoken word – often conducted in the context of the assessment interview. This approach is essentially a merging of both oral history and biography traditions to produce a text-based product – the story of an individual's life. For this approach to be anything other than an exercise in voyeurism, the taking of the person's life story must inform the outcomes of the assessment for the individual concerned. The support and the services that are appropriate for the person being assessed should reflect how they have lived their life and, significantly, in ways that they feel are meaningful, reflecting their beliefs, values, and fears for the future.

Johnson (1976) introduces into a broader understanding of a biographical approach the idea of a person's life history being viewed as a series of interrelated careers. Johnson's understanding of career includes significant relationships – being a son or a daughter, partner, lover, husband or wife, a mother or a father – as well as employment, education, leisure, etc. This understanding of a career can of course be extended to include how the individual defined and lived their life based on their understanding of their sexuality. Fundamentally, taking a biographical approach involves listening to the life history of the older person, becoming aware of their so-called careers and the way these have shaped their life in the present. However, Johnson further believed that from this process – listening to the older person tell their story – their priorities for later life will emerge, thereby enabling health and social care professionals to see older people as unique individuals. This is supported by Boulton and Gully (1989) who have suggested that the approach is useful in:

• eliciting older people's attitudes

• understanding family relationships

• finding out about relationships between carers and the older person

• discovering kinds of help which would be unacceptable

• relating to and understanding people labelled 'difficult'

• learning how people coped with past difficulty and hardship

• assessing how people might react and be helped in some future crisis.

The key issue in the application of a biographical approach to the assessment process is the ability of this approach to move care provision from generalised, formulaic responses to individualised or person-centred care. 'Knowing the patient' is a valued aspect of humanistic nursing care (Jenny and Logan 1992) and is essential to a patient's feeling of being cared for (Tanner *et al.* 1993). Radwin (1996) highlights that knowing the patient becomes a process of understanding and treating the person as a unique individual.

Anticipation of care needs: My research

As part of my doctoral thesis, between 2005 and 2007, I carried out a series of in-depth life story interviews with three older lesbians and three older gay men in order to gain some understanding of their sense of self as they were growing up and growing older, and their concerns for their future care. These six individuals were:

Ian: born in 1930 in a suburb of a large urban area in the North of England. He joined the Royal Navy in 1948 and served 16 years, leaving in 1964. On leaving the Navy he sought employment in an administrative capacity and had a further three jobs up to the point of his retirement.

Robert: an only child born in London in 1933. Robert retired from employment in 1991 at the age of 58 after 35 years of working with the same employer.

Rachel: born in a large city in the Northwest of England in 1937, the first of two children. She left school at 16 and was employed in various local manufacturing companies, either as an administrator or on the factory floor. Rachel became chronically ill relatively early in life, having experienced but not recognised a heart attack. Today her health is extremely poor as her heart has continued to weaken and she has developed other chronic illnesses. She is now reliant on formal carers whom she views as both intrusive and necessary.

Steven: born in an industrial town in the North of England in 1938, an only child. He undertook professional training and moved into his chosen profession, achieving considerable success until the 1970s when he 'came out' at work, after which his career faltered. Steven took early retirement in 1992 at the age of 54, which he feels was a consequence of his employer's negative reaction to his sexuality. In

2007 Steven collapsed at home and was admitted to hospital where he died after a short illness.

Janice: born in 1943 in a large city in the Southwest of England. At birth she was placed in care and lived in a children's home until she was placed with a foster family in 1956 at 13 years old. Janice's father was a black American soldier in the United Kingdom during the Second World War. She retired when she was 60 in 2003.

Gail: born in 1945, in a market town in the West Midlands of England and is the second of five children. At 18, in 1963, she married a man seven years older than herself and fell pregnant. In the seven years following her marriage she had four pregnancies and gave birth to three children.

These basic facts let us know something about each person – for example, locating them in time, and as part of a particular age cohort, they reflect the type of information we might gather in an assessment situation. Using a biographical approach allows us, as practitioners, to go beyond simple information gathering on someone's life to understanding the meanings they attach to these experiences.

Stories of care anticipated: My findings

Over a series of interviews with each participant I gathered detailed information on their lives, including their own reflections on ageing and sexuality. We discussed both past experiences and what each considered the future held for them. In eliciting future scenarios for care I was particularly mindful of Johnson's suggestion (1976) that in telling their life story a person can reveal much about their priorities for later life. In the discussion that follows I concentrate on these imagined future scenarios as an example of 'anticipatory biographical practice'. In terms of the stories that were told by these six people about their futures, there existed a nuanced interaction between their views on ageing and their views about the arrangements that would be in place to support them in later life. This was particularly notable because at the time only one of the six people who were part of my research was receiving and thereby experiencing support from health and social services. Steven did experience intense support from the health service in the weeks before his death, which occurred within a hospital setting, but this was after our interviews had taken place.

In looking more closely at what each interviewee was saying about needing support, it is striking that all were very negative about prospective formal care arrangements. At that time this was only an abstract issue for five of them, as they were living their lives independently and without the need for support. Ian had asked his partner to ensure that he was never placed in a residential home, commenting:

> ...the only one thing I always said and I used to say to [partner's name] – don't ever put me in an old people's home – I said I don't like it – I used to pass on the bus on the way to work at 7 o'clock in the morning and they were sat in their chairs waiting for their breakfasts – why the hell do they get them up at 7 o'clock in the morning – why couldn't they let them have a lie in – that was one of the things I looked forward to when I retired – I didn't have to get up at the set routine – and I used to say to [partner] don't you ever put me in a nursing home – I have always said that and I will not go into one.

His opinions about care within a hospital setting are starkly contrasting:

> ...if I get the same standard of treatment I don't care who gives it me – whether it is social services people or whoever – I would have no bother about going to hospital – no problem – whether it is a male nurse who is doing something to you or a female nurse – I don't give a damn – they are doing a job – I am a product on their production line type thing – I am quite happy with that situation – if there were any problems – if I felt I was being treated different 'cause of my sexuality then I would be anti – but I have never had and I don't expect it.

In these two comments, Ian is drawing a distinction between residential care and care in a hospital and commenting that he has no objection about the nurses being aware of his sexuality. Whereas time spent in hospital is often short and we can look forward to returning home after recovery, residence in a care home is usually permanent. Gail comments:

> I would think the issues about age are probably no different for a gay woman or a straight woman other than – a total failure to recognise your sexuality and the importance of your past – even if it is not now – but I think that happens to old people anyway – nobody recognises the importance of the past but I

suppose the possible ultimate thing of being in care or being in an old people's home and being the only gay woman – that is quite a daunting prospect that is – because one of the things that is important really isn't it – is remembering things and talking about – do you remember when? – and that is part of how our memories work, isn't it.

Whereas Ian had been concerned with the dehumanising effect of rigid routines in care homes that seemed to erase personal identities, Gail places emphasis on the importance of shared histories. In explaining her fears about entering care she cites the absence of opportunities to openly reflect on these shared histories with others, and the consequent prospect of social isolation. On the subject of residential care, Rachel had two opinions, which were dependent upon her cognitive ability, should such care be required. If unaware of her surroundings, then she is not bothered where her care is offered. However, if she did have an awareness of her surroundings she would emphatically reject residential care as an option, maintaining that she would have nothing in common with the other residents.

Oh no – over my dead body – I know but it is unthinkable for me – for the simple reason is that I would have nothing in common – and I would be in this place with all these old fogies of which I had become one as well – with nothing to talk about – I don't want to hear about what their Jack's had for his tea and how many teeth the grandchild has got – I am not interested, and sitting knitting in the corner – oh no, I don't think so.

By contrast, Robert's emphasis was upon the practicalities of receiving care. He was very clear that he would wish to have support provided by men and not women. Steven was similarly concerned with the more intimate aspects of care and the arrangements that might be in place to support him:

As a gay man the other issue of course is that these intimacies performed by professional strangers who assume you are heterosexual – or whose professional behaviour conditions them to be assuming that you are heterosexual and ignoring your gay things – all these intimacies – I would not be particularly comfortable with women performing intimacies on my body – not while I am conscious.

This issue of envisaging the receipt of 'body work' (Twigg *et al.* 2011) from care professionals was a prominent theme of particular personal significance. It resonates with existing work on LGBT care where the prospect of touch and more intimate forms of care carry particular concerns for both service users and care providers (e.g. Archibald 2010). But what can these comments tell us about the way in which such encounters might be approached? Body work remains an under-researched aspect of the provision of care to older people and yet holds such importance when it comes to how LGBT people envisage the challenges and barriers to accepting care in their own futures.

Steven perceives formal care either at home or in an institutional setting as imbued with assumptions which will affect his care and impact on his sexuality. These assumptions, he feels, present a potentially significant challenge to his identity as a gay man, and he is clear not only that care should be provided without such assumptions, but also that care providers should celebrate his sexuality.

> ...and still in spite of Age Concern and other organisations taking on board the gay concept, if I am in an old folks' home or if I go to the old age pensioners drop-in it will be heterosexually organised, such organizations are rampant with heterosexism in terms of the staff and what they want you to do and what they expect you to do – you know, if two old guys want to go and be together the average forty-year-old woman who chooses to fucking staff these bloody places can't bloody think, etc. [laughing] and that sometimes concerns me but I have enough gay friends my age and younger and a lot younger who are – who will have a regard for me when I am getting older.

Essentially, Steven is talking here about heteronormativity; how the working culture of large-scale organisations serving older people leads to a neglect of those who belong to sexual minorities. But his comments raise the question of what informs such perceptions of provision as people anticipate future care needs, and what might be done to challenge these perceptions. Comments such as this suggest there are grounds for targeted work with older LGBT people that seeks to address their concerns, and above all to demonstrate that care systems have the capacity to adapt and reorganise themselves to better meet the needs of different minority groups.

Rachel, who has direct experience of receiving care, returns to the sensitive topic of body work and the challenges attached to negotiating this aspect of support. After a heart operation, she found being naked in the presence of the female carers embarrassing, and what was worse for her was having to:

> …strip off and be washed by these people and I felt like a piece of meat – lift your arm up – when I first came out of hospital I was very fragile and I couldn't move and I had to learn to walk and talk and feed myself again so I was a bit wobbly – so it was lift your arm up and they would give it a half-hearted wipe not doing all the nooks and crannies and I used to say to them will you make sure that you do me nooks and, crannies 'cause I am fastidiously clean me – I don't do much about glamour but I am fastidious – and they would say oh you are alright – you have not been anywhere – that to me was unacceptable but I had to accept what they gave me – and it was really upsetting – I used to cry when they had gone – it was really upsetting and I have to, it dawned on me – so I thought I am going to have to get used to these buggers and make the most of it.

Rachel is clearly unhappy about these care arrangements but despite these experiences she wants to be able to trust the carers, to develop a relationship with them, for them to listen to her, rather than be frightened of their reaction to her, which includes their acceptance of her sexuality. Rachel has been so unhappy with her circumstances that she resorted to harming herself:

> I started sort of self-harming when I realised that I needed all this help and that I was trapped – that is how I look at – I am trapped in this situation – there is no way for me other than a one-on-one personal assistant or *au pair* – that I would have a continuity with and that I could build up a trust – God that would be wonderful…

These conditions may well apply to anyone facing the need for such support and are not necessarily outwardly concerned with Rachel's sexuality, but it is clear that the turnover of workers supporting Rachel is hardly conducive to her disclosing her sexuality and in this way compounds her anxieties about receiving help and being able to trust her helpers.

What does this mean for the practitioner?

Many practitioners would argue that they do already use a biographical approach in their assessments and at one level this is certainly true. Basic biographical details such as date of birth, next of kin, doctor's details, etc. are collected and entered into assessment forms. These assessments may also identify key life events such as the type of employment a person was engaged in, or their education and significant relationships. This biographical information is intrinsic to any assessment but does not actually tell us much about the person who is being assessed. This is because such information gathering seeks to provide 'the facts' rather than to establish what they mean to the individual concerned. A more thorough biographical assessment requires the practitioner to spend time listening very carefully to the 'storied life' of the person being assessed. It is by hearing what is being said that a much more detailed knowledge and understanding of the person is achieved.

If we take, for example, Rachel's comments about being supported in her own home, we can see that she is deeply unhappy about these arrangements and during interview expresses more than once her fear that her carers might find out that she is a lesbian. In her comments she also gives a very clear statement about what could be done to make things much better for her – she wants to trust her carers and develop a relationship with them, she wants consistency and she wants to be respected. This is not about telling the carers that she is a lesbian so treat her as special, but is about establishing the conditions or foundations such that she in time might wish to tell them herself. She has identified both the problem and the solution that we as practitioners can work on.

Ian has made it very clear that there are certain conditions attached to disclosing his sexuality in a formal care setting – he will only allow professional healthcare workers to know this information within the context of him being treated equally. Robert is also clear that he will only accept care offered by men. For Steven there was a complete rejection of formal care arrangements that would have been an anathema to him. As a consequence any support arrangements would have been about helping the network of friends that surrounded him to care for him.

In each of these examples the individuals have established the conditions under which care and support would be acceptable to them. This was established not by being asked, for example, their date of birth, but by gauging something of the wider context of their lives in order to understand how care might support a degree of continuity in their lives. This applies not only in terms of how they live from day to day but also to more fundamental questions of what they hold dear and the priorities they seek to uphold for themselves.

Conclusion

This chapter has explored the value of using an anticipatory biographical approach with older lesbian, gay and bisexual people who are looking ahead to the use of health and social care services. The importance of this approach rests with the idea that outcomes from care provision are improved, both for the person for whom care is provided but also for the caregiver, if there is recognition of the life that has been lived by the individual, and the fears and concerns they may have about their future care needs. In this respect there exists the potential for higher levels of satisfaction with care arrangements, and for such arrangements to truly reflect the needs of the individual for whom the care is being provided, or will be provided in the future.

Key themes to emerge from the anticipatory biographical work conducted with this small group focused on the importance they invest in the prospect of enjoying meaningful relationships with others in whatever setting they find themselves living or spending time. The potential to build connections with fellow service users based on shared histories was particularly valued. In terms of interactions with providers and caregivers, concerns surrounding the intimacy of touch during the provision of personal care were flagged repeatedly. There is a particular vulnerability attached to being naked in the presence of others, especially when in receipt of care, and the difficulties of envisaging receipt of such body work seemed a particular 'sticking point' for participants as they sought to imagine their future care experiences. As practitioners, we need to consider how care can be informed by these sensitive issues and allay the fears of future service users. It also seems that we need to disentangle notions of sexuality as desire from *sexuality as a social identity* in the context of these intimate, one-to-one caring encounters.

There is however, a much broader structural issue raised for those who commission and plan the care service arrangements, and that is the overarching rejection by participants of the current arrangements of care provision. Based on a clear sense of themselves as lesbians or gay men, they reject the perceived standard service responses to older people who have high levels of dependence. While some place less importance on shorter-term temporary treatment in hospital settings, the fear of living permanently in a care home stems particularly from the imagined lack of respect or consideration for their identities as lesbian or gay. Indeed, some argue that they have little in common with other older people, given that their life experiences differ, and therefore do not wish to share a common care environment.

Whilst their voices about the possibility of being cared for and supported are currently on the whole negative, effective use of biographical approaches with older lesbians and gay men has the potential to change this negativity. My own experiences of eliciting life stories from a small group of older lesbians and gay men revealed just how much more likely one is to find ways forward that are acceptable and identity-affirming for service users when we understand something of the greater narrative of their life and of the trajectory they wish to follow in the future. Listening to the voices of older lesbians and gay men and ensuring that care arrangements reflect the way they view themselves now and in the coming years may then prove transformative, both for the individual concerned and for the working culture that seeks to support them.

References

Archibald, C. (2010) 'A Path Less Travelled: Hearing the Voices of Older Lesbians: A Pilot Study Researching Residential Care and Other Needs.' In R.L. Jones and R. Ward (eds) *LGBT Issues: Looking Beyond Categories*. Edinburgh: Dunedin Academic Press.

Boulton J. and Gully, V. (1989) *Developing the Biographical Approach in Practice with Older People. Project 7*. Buckingham: The Open University.

DoH (1998) *Modernising Social Services: Promoting Independence, Improving Protection, Raising Standards*. Cm4169. London: The Stationery Office.

DoH (2006) *Our Health, Our Care, Our Say: A New Direction For Community Services*. London: The Stationery Office.

HM Government (2007) *Putting People First: A Shared Vision and Commitment to the Transformation of Adult Social Care*. London: Stationery Office.

Jenny, J. and Logan, J. (1992) 'Knowing the patient: One aspect of clinical knowledge.' *IMAGE. Journal of Nursing Scholarship 24*, 4, 254–258.

Johnson, M. (1976) 'That was your Life: A Biographical Approach to Later Life'. In J.M.A. Munnichs and W.J.A. Van den Heuval (eds) *Dependency and Interdependency in Old Age*. The Hague: Martinus Nijhoff.

Radwin, L.E. (1996) 'Knowing the patient: a review of research on an emerging concept.' *Journal of Advanced Nursing 23*, 6, 1142–1146.

Tanner, C., Benner, P., Chesla, C. and Gordon, D. (1993) 'The phenomenology of knowing the patient.' *IMAGE. Journal of Nursing Scholarship 25*, 4, 273–280.

Twigg, J., Wolkowitz, C., Cohen, R.L. and Nettleton, S. (2011) 'Conceptualizing body work in health and social care.' *Sociology of Health and Illness 33*, 2, 171–188.

Chapter 3

Trans Ageing

Thoughts on a Life Course Approach in Order to Better Understand Trans Lives

Louis Bailey

Introduction

The aim of this chapter is to begin to map out life course and ageing issues in relation to the UK trans population. The chapter considers certain key issues facing trans people as they age, and pays particular attention to the health and social care needs of trans people in later life. It is hoped that this preliminary exploration will mark the starting point for further research into trans ageing and, subsequently, the development of social policies and service provision in this area. In the absence of a sustained investigation into the health and social care issues facing older trans people, this chapter will seek to synthesise and interpret existing research drawing on a life course perspective. In addition, it will extrapolate from data pertaining to the penalties and inequalities of being trans as a means of anticipating the long-term impact and consequences in later life. An examination of the intersection of ageing and transgenderism, combined with a study of the dual discriminatory effects of ageism and transphobia, will be central here. It is hoped that the suggestions for good practice, highlighted in the summary section at the end of the chapter, will be of particular use to health and social care practitioners, and policy makers.

Background

Each year, increasing numbers of people are coming out as 'trans' and transitioning from their birth sex towards their felt sense of gendered self. Recent figures show an exponential growth in the number of people who feel that their gender identity differs from the sex they were assigned at birth (Reed *et al.* 2009). 'Trans' is not a monolithic category and instead refers to a wide spectrum of people who have unique and diverse needs. It covers those who have transitioned (socially and/or medically) from male to female (trans women) or from female to male (trans men), as well as those whose gender identity or expression is at odds with conventional understandings of dichotomous sex/gender categories (gender-neutral, polygender or genderqueer). The term also refers to those who cross the gender norms of society by dressing in the clothes of the 'opposite' sex (cross-dresser/transvestite) on either a part- or full-time basis.

Legislative changes and associated gains for trans equality, combined with the development and wider availability of gender reassignment procedures, have made it significantly more viable for people to come out as trans and subsequently transition. The growth of social/support groups for the trans community has made it possible for trans people to locate each other and to find necessary information to assist with their lives. In addition, the rise of the Internet has meant that information about trans issues and support networks is now readily available. As a result, transgenderism is much more publicly visible than it was even just a decade ago.

Within the trans population, a new wave of older people is now emerging – consisting of those who transitioned a number of years ago, as well as those who have decided to transition in later life. This section of the trans population is set to increase significantly in forthcoming years, both as a result of the exponential growth rate of the trans community and as a result of medical progress, which has enabled people to live longer and healthier lives. Although a relatively small proportion of the overall population, the trans population has nevertheless risen significantly in recent years and continues to rise. Current trends show that the number of people who have sought medical care for gender dysphoria is growing at a rate of 15 per cent per annum (Reed *et al.* 2009). During the next decade, health and social care providers will be under immense pressure, both from policy makers and from an increasingly vocal trans community, to meet the unique challenges and issues presented by this growing demographic. However, from a health and social care perspective, there is a lack of research on trans ageing in the UK and every indication of consequently low levels of knowledge and understanding on the part of policy makers and practitioners. This raises the dilemma for practitioners in older people's services of where they should turn for guidance on working with older trans service users.

Trans inequalities over the life course

Despite legal advancements, trans people are among the most stigmatised groups in the UK, enduring comparatively high levels of violence, discrimination and harassment. The socio-economic fallout of coming out as trans is considerable, and trans people are statistically more likely to experience discrimination, harassment, and family and relationship breakdown. In their 2007 survey *Engendered Penalties: Transgender and Transsexual People's Experiences of Inequality and Discrimination* Whittle, Turner and Al-Alami revealed the negative impact of being trans in contemporary British society. They found that 72 per cent of trans people have experienced harassment in public, with the result that 21 per cent avoid going out in public due to fears for their safety. In the realm of employment, 29 per cent of respondents experienced verbal harassment whilst at work. Whilst 41 per cent decided not to transition for fear that they will lose their jobs, 23 per cent transitioned but were forced to change their job. The reasons for the last point could be related to actual or perceived harassment at work, to direct discrimination in the form of forced redundancy, or to a desire to relocate in order to start a new life. In keeping with this, the statistic that 28 per cent of respondents moved house after transitioning could be due to family breakdown (45% within the community), harassment by neighbours (46%) and/or a desire to move in order to live in a new gender (Whittle *et al.* 2007). In being forced to leave their homes and communities, trans people sacrifice support networks and financial security. The emotional cost of such upheaval is considerable but many trans people have little choice as they attempt to protect their dignity and confidentiality.

A survey undertaken by the Scottish Transgender Alliance in 2008 highlights the socio-economic fallout of being trans. The survey found that very high unemployment rates exist within the trans community, with 37 per cent of Scottish respondents living on benefits. However, the same survey found that 55 per cent of respondents have a higher educational degree, meaning that trans people have higher than average rates of education but well below average employment rates (Scottish Transgender Alliance 2008). As such, a significant section of the trans community are on low incomes, and many choose to set up as self-employed. The knock-on effect for pensions and planning in later life is likely to be significant.

As a result of the Gender Recognition Act 2004, trans people can now obtain full legal recognition of their acquired gender, allowing them to change their birth certificate and to marry in their recognised gender. The Act also makes it illegal to disclose a recipient's trans status or history without their explicit consent. However, legislation is only restricted to those identifying as 'male' or 'female'. Within current legislation, if a trans person is already married then they will have to divorce if they wish to obtain gender recognition. This can have enormous consequences for trans people, especially older trans people and those who may have been married for a number of years. It might impact a person's benefits, pension, tax, credit and insurance status. In addition to the financial fallout and laborious amount of paperwork, the divorce process can be extremely distressing for those involved.

Health inequalities

According to a recent survey entitled *Transgender Euro Study – Legal Survey and Focus on the Transgender Experience of Health Care* (Whittle *et al*. 2008), trans people experience health inequalities in the realm of general healthcare and in relation to gender reassignment.

Routine healthcare

A key narrative to emerge from the *Transgender Euro Study* was that trans people avoided accessing routine healthcare because they anticipated inappropriate or prejudicial treatment from healthcare professionals. The survey found that some healthcare professionals either misdiagnose or refuse to treat general health conditions because the person is trans.

It seems that the classification of transsexuality as a mental disorder is a strong factor in the mistreatment of trans people within a clinical setting. A prerequisite of gender reassignment through the NHS is a diagnosis of 'gender identity disorder' or 'gender dysphoria' by a psychiatrist. However, many trans people feel uncomfortable with these labels and the pathologising effects therein, preferring the interpretation of transsexuality as a medical condition rather than a mental illness (Whittle *et al*. 2008). The pathologising of trans identities has, in part, contributed to the negative treatment that trans people experience, or perceive they will experience, within health and social care.

Gender reassignment

It is important to note that some, but not all, trans people opt for medical intervention in order to assist with their transitions. Whilst some may opt for both hormonal and surgical intervention, others may opt for some but not all of the procedures, or none at all.

Funding bodies are forced to engage with the issue of gender reassignment in order to comply with the legal decision of *A, D & G* v. *North West Lancashire Health Authority* (1998), which found blanket bans on gender dysphoria treatment within the National Health Service (NHS) to be unlawful. However, the resulting information is often not disseminated from the funding bodies to general practitioners and, ultimately, patients. This, combined with a lack of training on trans health, means that GPs are often unsure about the appropriate treatment pathways for patients. Patients are often misinformed about what treatments are available and there are few, if any, centralised contacts within health and social care to clarify matters (Combs 2010).

The situation is compounded by widespread misunderstanding and ignorance surrounding trans issues. Some GPs have a negative attitude towards transgenderism and view the treatment of gender dysphoria to be morally and ethically wrong. Some patients report that GPs send them for unnecessary psychological therapy, stall procedures or refuse to act at all (Whittle *et al.* 2008). Even if trans people are lucky to find a GP who is 'on side', waiting times are especially lengthy due to the high demand for services and low clinical capacity, with trans people left unsupported during this time. Gender reassignment is still controversially regarded, resulting in few medical specialists in the area. Battles with primary care trusts (PCTs) over funding are increasingly common (Combs 2010).

Many trans people already wait a significant period of time before first approaching their GP and the delays and stumbling blocks serve to exacerbate their distress. In light of this, it is not uncommon for trans people to go privately, obtaining loans to cover the cost of counselling, hormone therapy and surgery, which can be expensive. This scenario is particularly concerning with regards to older trans people, who might find waiting for gender reassignment difficult, especially if they have delayed transitioning for a number of years already. The low priority of gender reassignment, combined with issues of ageism within healthcare, creates a double barrier for older trans people wishing to obtain gender reassignment treatment. In addition, they might not have access to the relevant information that is often needed in order to 'educate' GPs about transsexuality and the transition process. Often this information takes the form of community hearsay and advice, which can sometimes be unreliable and tends to be found via online forums.

Trans life course and ageing

Although gender reassignment is often incorrectly thought of as a single defining surgical procedure, it is actually a wide-reaching emotional, social and, where appropriate, medical process. Moreover, transition is not a purely medical process. Trans people may change their names, titles and pronouns, alter their documentation and disclose their gender identity to their families, neighbours and co-workers as a first step, or may simply find a new social scene and different way of expressing themselves. Trans people may transition from one binary identity to its 'opposite' or from a gendered state to a non-gendered state (female to gender-neutral, for example).

As well as being a distinctly gendered process, transition also propels people into new age-specific activities and experiences. Trans men and women who undergo hormone therapy (testosterone and oestrogen respectively) enter a second puberty and will experience a range of dramatic changes therein – changes to libido, emotional expression, fat and muscle distribution, hair growth and vocal range, for example (Department of Health 2007). Even those who do not undergo medical intervention also experience some of the joys and frustrations associated with adolescence as they begin to explore life in a new gender – learning or unlearning gender-appropriate behaviours, finding new social networks and experimenting with new clothing, for example.

Trans people may spend years trying to 'catch up' with certain gendered experiences that they initially missed out on in early life. They may also struggle with new social pressures and expectations associated with their new gender role. The disjunction of experiences raises some interesting questions about trans people's experiences of life course and ageing. For instance:

- What are the effects of an enduring (bodily) adolescence in mid or even late adulthood?

- How does this impact on emotional processing and social life?

- How do trans people manage this new life stage, and resulting sets of experiences?

In the absence of any sustained research, we can only begin to speculate about the impact of 'second puberty' within the trans population.

Trans people's conceptualisations and understandings of their gender, as well as their unique experiences of transition, vary throughout their lives and are informed by a complex range of sources: background, relationships, genetics, physicality, professional settings, community ties, etc. These sets of experiences will also be affected by other demographic differences – such as age, race, ethnicity, class, sexuality and geographical area. An individual's experiences of transition will also be shaped by historical shifts in social understandings of gender as well as changing cultural attitudes towards transsexuality, which are, in turn, informed by legal landmarks and medical advancement. For example, Combs (2010) examined how attempts to understand and explain gender are culturally and historically bound, leading to subjective variation within medicalised settings with regards to gender reassignment and consequent interpretations of trans people's identities and lives. Furthermore, someone who is in the early stages of exploring their gender will have very different experiences from someone who transitioned 30 or 40 years ago. Research exploring the nuances of trans life course over time and in relation to these wide-ranging factors is urgently needed in order to understand the sheer diversity, and consequent needs, found within this unique population.

The needs of older trans people

As a relatively new demographic, the needs and experiences of older trans people have yet to be studied in any great depth. From the outset, it is clear that those who transitioned at an earlier stage in their lives will have very different needs and experiences from those who have decided to transition later in life.

Transitioning at an older age

Some trans people may be aware of their gender difference from a young age but it is often social stigma that prevents them from disclosing this information. Trans people may decide to wait until retirement before beginning their transition, possibly because they fear losing their job security and/or social ranking by transitioning during working age. Another trigger point for transitioning in later life could be the recent death of a partner or relative.

Medically transitioning at an older age comes with certain risks. Hormone therapy for both trans men and trans women can come with potential side-effects. Add age to the picture and the risks increase. The older the person, the greater the likelihood of complications during surgery, especially if that person smokes or is overweight, and surgeons may refuse to operate at all. In addition, age increases the likelihood of people developing chronic diseases and other health conditions, which will interfere with both hormone therapy and gender reassignment surgery. It is important to note that some people socially transition into their new gender but do not pursue medical treatment, either out of choice or because they are unable to due to medical complications or other mitigating factors.

The long-term consequences of a medical transition

We are now witnessing the emergence of a generation of trans people who transitioned over 20 to 30 years ago. A growing body of research suggests that there are possible health risks associated with long-term exposure to hormone therapy. There is some evidence that trans women receiving anti-androgens and oestrogen supplements as part of their hormone therapy might be at risk of stroke, arteriosclerosis and liver disease (AgeUK 2010). However, it is not known whether oestrogen protects against heart disease, or increases the risk of developing breast cancer. For trans men who are on testosterone supplements, possible risks include cardiovascular disease and abnormal liver function (*ibid.*). More research is needed to better understand older trans bodies and the long-term impact of medical transition.

Gender confirmation surgeries have come a long way since some of the first forays into sex reassignment surgery during the interwar period. Whilst some of the initial experimental surgery resulted in significant maiming and sometimes death, by contrast today's operations have a very high success rate. However, there are some trans people who underwent surgery at a time when techniques were still being developed and who subsequently are at increased risk of complications as a result of the experimental nature of the procedures.

The social impact of being trans

The stigma of being trans permeates every aspect of day-to-day living – from home and community life, through to housing, education and employment – and has a cumulative effect in later life, potentially leading to decreased quality of life and life expectancy. These factors, combined with difficulties in accessing appropriate healthcare, have a direct impact on the health and well-being of the trans community. In addition, many trans people struggle with the effects of being born into a body that is at odds with their gender, and struggle with the effects of low self-esteem and poor body image. Trans people may be less likely to follow health advice and hence be more likely to develop a range of self-destructive and risky behaviours. Just over a third of trans adults attempt suicide at least once (Whittle *et al.* 2007).

Recent research has found that high rates of alcohol, tobacco and drug consumption exist within the lesbian, gay and bisexual community, and it is reasonable to assume that this trend continues within the trans community owing to the consequences of homophobia and transphobia within British society (Guasp 2011; Hunt and Fish 2008). This is further fuelled by a lack of fitness and leisure opportunities within the trans community, as well as the absence of targeted health work and promotional campaigns. According to the Trans Resource and Empowerment Centre (TREC) *Trans Needs Assessment Survey – North West,* 60.5 per cent of trans respondents do not feel comfortable using sports and leisure facilities (TREC 2010).

Given the absence of research on the long-term impact of being trans, we can only begin to speculate on the challenges that trans people face in later life. As a result of the socio-economic fallout of transitioning, older trans people are more likely to be dependent on health and social care services. However, the question remains, how well equipped are such services to meet the needs of trans people in later life?

There is a real concern that the general lack of awareness around trans health – and the intricacies of trans identities, bodies and needs – means that older trans people are in particular danger of not having their needs met within health and social services. Trans people may present as one gender but their physical bodies may indeed have the health needs associated with the sex of their birth. There is anecdotal evidence to suggest that trans people already avoid having scans of their reproductive and sexual organs due to the incongruence between their felt gender and their birth sex. There are fears around undressing as this could reveal the discrepancies between a person's gender and their birth sex, potentially causing negative reactions and treatment from staff. Given this, trans people are likely to feel especially anxious and vulnerable when accessing home and residential care in later life, fearing ridicule, misunderstanding and abuse. Trans education training in health and social care is essential to meet the needs of this growing population. In addition, trans people may require extra privacy with regards to personal hygiene tasks.

An additional concern that many trans people cite is that they are not taken seriously within health and social care (AgeUK 2010). Add ageing and the prospect of conditions such as dementia to the picture, and this concern multiplies. Trans people may not be 'out' as trans or may have family members who refuse to accept their new gender. Trans people might not be in touch with their families of origin, and as a result may have formed alternative families and support structures. In addition, the experiences of trans people may fall outside of dominant norms, with the result that many trans people may feel marginalised and isolated within a care home environment. Staff need to be aware of these issues when treating trans people in later life.

Trans People's Attitudes towards Ageing Survey

The Trans Resource and Empowerment Centre (TREC) is an independent and trans-led voluntary sector organisation serving as a resource to the trans community in the Northwest of England. TREC delivers services, raises awareness of trans issues, develops opportunities for networking and representation and seeks to promote good practice in other agencies and organisations (see http://transcentre.org.uk/about-trec). A recent survey undertaken by TREC explored trans people's attitudes towards ageing (TREC 2011). This small-scale survey represents an important starting point for more detailed work around trans people's experiences of, and attitudes towards, ageing over the life course.

The survey went live on 11 April 2011 and ended on 11 May 2011. It was advertised to TREC members through the TREC mailing list and Facebook page. A total of 25 responses were received, with ages ranging from 18 to 70 years. Such small numbers mean that we can treat the findings as indicative only and must keep in mind that, in the absence of any broader demographic data on the trans community, it is currently not possible to know the extent to which our respondents are representative of the wider trans community. In answer to the question 'How do you feel about getting older?' the views of the respondents varied, with roughly a third feeling mixed, another third feeling negative and the remaining third feeling positive. Whilst some respondents claimed that they felt apprehensive, depressed or scared at the thought of ageing, others were more neutral and accepted its inevitability. Some worried about the general effects of ageing on their health, mobility and financial security, others were directly concerned about the impact of ageing on their gender transition and *vice versa*, worrying about the physical side-effects of transition and its impact on their ability to 'pass' as their felt gender. Elsewhere, respondents felt positive about ageing, claiming that they were 'making progress' and 'growing old gracefully', and that age had provided 'wisdom and knowledge' and 'the time and opportunity for transition'.

Just under a third of respondents did not feel confident that their health and social care needs would be accommodated in later life, whilst around half were not sure. In addition, just over two-thirds of respondents felt that they would receive negative care in later life because of their trans status. Respondents cited an existing lack of education about trans issues and a consequent lack of understanding about trans healthcare among providers. Respondents based their opinions on previous experiences whilst accessing healthcare and anticipated that they would not be treated with respect in later life, and that their health needs would be ignored or misunderstood. One person felt that 'People may not accept me as the gender I believe I am and abuse me,' while another predicted 'indignity of care when/if I'm not able to speak for myself'. One respondent, however, was keen to point out that 'things are slowly changing', implying that socio-political gains for the trans community might help to improve conditions.

When asked if they felt anxious about the disclosure of their trans status when accessing health and social care services in later life, respondents were divided in their views. Some felt especially nervous:

> Disclosure is always a risk – the more critical the health issue, the more vulnerable I feel. Emergency hospital admittance is particularly fear inducing, because it is a roll of the dice in terms of whether I get someone who is going to be responsive to my explanations of who I am.

Others, however, felt more confident:

> I am female. My 'trans status' is nobody else's business. I do not intend to disclose anything to anyone. My status is already known in my medical records and that is confidential.

Having a binary gender identity and presentation, having already legally and medically transitioned, and being in receipt of a gender recognition certificate – which makes it illegal for a person's trans status or history to be disclosed without that person's explicit consent, and only if it is medically or legally necessary – are all possible reasons for someone to be less anxious about personal disclosure. As one respondent put it:

> I think it depends on how far one has transitioned physically. I think there is still a real struggle with people who are perceived as half and half... I also think the more people know, the bigger the risk of a poor service and discrimination.

In response to the question 'What preparations, if any, are you making for later life?' three respondents stated, shockingly, that they intended to commit suicide before reaching old age whilst one hoped to die before then. Significantly, ten people had made no plans for later life. Of those that had, savings and ensuring that they had a pension were their priorities. Some had talked to loved ones about their specific needs in later life or had active retirement plans. Others, who were in their fifties and sixties, were already, or actively planning on, living somewhere that was accessible and would accommodate their needs if they became more dependent and inactive. One respondent made the 'tough' decision not to undergo medical transition because they had 'concerns over the long-term health implications of doing so.' The following comment raises a particularly interesting issue around longevity in the trans community: 'I need to "put things right" and be in harmony with my body first. Only then will I have a future to think about.'

Eighteen out of the 25 respondents felt that they had friends and/ or family that they could turn to for support, but this figure dropped to just 10 when it came to having someone to rely on in later life. The comments of one respondent sum up the situation: 'I have friends but they would probably have their own families to care about... No support I can count on from my own family.' This phenomenon is teased out further in the following comments: 'Only my trans partner and the trans community will help me, I don't expect anything from my family'; 'I have no contact with siblings or mother (father died in the 1980s). I do have children and that has complicated my transition and continues to influence strong relationships with them, at best it's supportive and at worst it's painful.' With regards to their ideal living situation in later life, 60 per cent of respondents wanted assisted living at home, 16 per cent wanted to be in a care home for LGBT people, while only 4 per cent wanted to be in a mainstream care home, and 20 per cent selected 'other'.

Trans ageing and later life: Guidance for practice

This chapter concludes with some thoughts on best practice that are based upon the work of TREC and feedback from our membership. By no means exhaustive, these pointers are designed to assist service providers in considering the issues, experiences and barriers faced by the UK trans community, as well as in responding appropriately and effectively to the unique health and social care needs of this emerging demographic. Of course, certain issues faced by trans individuals accessing health and social care apply irrespective of age. Many trans people face significant barriers and challenges in health and social care throughout the life course – both in relation to gender reassignment treatment and general healthcare – as a result of a lack of awareness and education about their identities, healthcare needs and lives. The stigma of being trans in contemporary British society is significant, and, as set out in this chapter, trans people are statistically more likely to be victims of hate crime and to experience inequality and discrimination across many areas of public life, resulting in increased rates of poverty, isolation and vulnerability in later life. Such conditions are likely to impact upon well-being and mental health and to shape decisions regarding when or whether to turn to formal services for support and assistance.

At present, we lack research in the UK that specifically addresses the challenges attached to growing older as a trans person and which considers the implications for the welfare services that seek to meet the healthcare and support needs of trans people in later life. Nonetheless, the work of TREC and other trans organisations has shown that trans people anticipate negative treatment within home and residential care services and have particular anxieties about undressing, hygiene tasks, single-sex placements and facilities, and the attitudes of staff. This concern with 'body work' (see for example Twigg *et al.* 2011) echoes findings from existing research with older lesbians and gay men regarding their anticipated support needs in later life, as discussed in this book by Pugh in Chapter 2. It is already clear, then, that there are certain areas of practice where research may usefully begin to focus in order to address these fears, not least because such concerns may otherwise lead to trans people avoiding services and not accessing the help they require.

The following best practice principles apply to the care of trans people in general but provide useful pointers to working with trans service users in later life.

- **Social interactions:** Always address someone according to their gender identity rather than their birth sex; pronouns should match someone's social gender, regardless of their physical bodies.

- **Trans-sensitive service delivery:** Trans people are especially vulnerable within single-sex settings and should be allocated according to their gendered preference. Separate facilities should be used if a trans person does not feel comfortable (or is at significant risk) using particular gendered facilities. Trans people may require extra privacy.

- **Training and awareness:** Staff in older people's services should receive training on trans awareness and health. Information that someone is trans should be handled sensitively and confidentially at all times.

- **Forward planning:** Trans people should be encouraged to make a living will and to write down clear instructions for family and care staff, should they become incapable of caring for themselves. Trans people should also be advised to nominate someone who is sensitive to their needs and best able to advocate on their behalf, should they develop dementia or a similar disorder, this role can be formalised through the use of an Enduring Power of Attorney.

- **Recognising networks:** Trans people may have alternative family and relationship structures, which are often harnessed as a dominant means of support, understanding and connection. These need to be recognised as of utmost significance within trans people's lives, and equal to or, in some cases, exceeding the role played by families of origin.

In their seminal work on gender and ageing the feminist gerontologists Arber and Ginn (1994, 1995) used secondary analysis of survey data to map areas of inequality on the basis of gender at different points in the life course. In particular, they considered the implications for the material, health and caring resources that people have at their disposal in later life. On the strength of this analysis the authors were able to demonstrate how certain disadvantages are cumulative, compounding inequalities in later life. While similarly robust survey data may not yet be available for trans individuals, we have begun to outline a similar pattern for trans people whereby experiences and disadvantages at different points in the life course impact upon the interlocking areas of material, health and care resources in later life. The barriers, exclusion and discrimination that trans people face within the education system, in the workplace, in family relations, housing, leisure and health and social care do not exist in isolation from one another but coalesce and are carried forward as people age. In this chapter we have synthesised data from a number of sources in order to show how the material, health and care resources of trans people in later life are affected as a result. For those who work with and for older trans people it is crucial to understand how many of the disadvantages faced across the life course are compounded in later life, and how this may affect a person's capacity to access the help and support they require. This chapter represents a first and tentative step in trying to map some of these considerations and, it is hoped, will support those working in health and social care to think more broadly about the lives of older trans service users in order to better support and care for them.

References

AgeUK (2010) 'Transgender Issues in Later Life.' www.ageuk.org.uk/Global/Age-Cymru/Information-and-Advice/FS16_Transgender_issues_in_later_life_September_2010_fcs.pdf Accessed on 8 December 2011.

Arber, S. and Ginn, J. (1994) 'Women and Aging.' *Reviews in Clinical Gerontology 4,* 4, 349–358.

Arber, S. and Ginn. J. (eds) (1995) *Connecting Gender and Ageing: A Sociological Approach.* Buckingham: Open University Press.

Combs, R. (2010) 'Where Gender and Medicine Meet: Transition Experiences and the NHS.' (PhD thesis.) University of Manchester.

Department of Health (2007) *A Guide to Hormone Therapy for Trans People.* www.dh.gov.uk/prod_consum_dh/groups/dh_digitalassets/@dh/@en/documents/digitalasset/dh_081582.pdf Accessed on 8 December 2011.

Guasp, A. (2011) *Gay and Bisexual Men's Health Survey.* London: Stonewall. Available at www.stonewall.org.uk/documents/stonewall_gay_mens_health_final.pdf,l accessed on 20 June 2012.

Hunt, R. and Fish, J. (2008) *Prescription for Change: Lesbian and Bisexual Women's Health Check 2008.* London: Stonewall.

Reed, R., Rhodes, S., Schofield, P. and Wylie, K. (2009) *Gender Variance in the UK: Prevalence, Incidence, Growth and Geographic Distribution.* Ashtead: GIRES.

Scottish Transgender Alliance (2008) *Transgender Experiences in Scotland – Research Summary.* Edinburgh: Equality Network.

TREC (2010) *Trans Needs Assessment Survey – North West (2010).* http://transcentre.org.uk/uploads/NWTransNeedsAssessmentReport2010.pdf Accessed on 8 December 2011.

TREC (2011) *Trans People's Attitudes Towards Ageing Survey.* http://transcentre.org.uk Accessed on 8 December 2011.

Twigg, J., Wolkowitz, C., Cohen, R.L. and Nettleton, S. (2011) 'Conceptualizing body work in health and social care.' *Sociology of Health and Illness 33,* 2, 171–188.

Whittle, S., Turner, L., and Al-Alami, M. (2007) *Engendered Penalties: Transgender and Transsexual People's Experiences of Inequality and Discrimination.* London: Equalities Review.

Whittle, S., Turner, L., Combs, R. and Rhodes, S. (2008) *Transgender Euro Study – Legal Survey and Focus on the Transgender Experience of Health Care. Brussels:* ILGA-Europe (International Lesbian, Gay, Bisexual, Trans And Intersex Association). Available at www.pfc.org.uk/pdf/eurostudy.pdf, accessed 8 December 2011.

Further reading

Combs, R., Turner, L. and Whittle, S. (2008) *The 'Gender Identity Services in England' Mapping Project Report.* London: Department of Health.

Cook-Daniels, L. (2006) 'Trans Aging.' In D. Kimmel, T. Rose and S. David (eds) *Lesbian, Gay, Bisexual and Transgender Aging: Research and Clinical Perspectives.* New York: Columbia University Press.

Witten, T.M. and Eyler, A.E. (2007) 'Transgender Aging and the Care of the Elderly Transgendered Patient.' In R. Ettner, S. Monstrey and E. Eyler (eds) *Principles of Transgender Medicine and Surgery.* New York: Haworth Press.

Chapter 4

'Women Like That'

Older Lesbians in the UK

Jane Traies

Over lunch at a graduate seminar, I was chatting to other students. We enquired politely about each other's research. When I said that I was investigating the cultural invisibility of older lesbians, the young woman beside me nodded vigorously, and told a story against herself to illustrate my point. She has two lesbian friends of about her own age, she said, a couple with a young baby. Last time she visited them, they introduced her to two other friends of theirs, a lesbian couple in their sixties. 'And I was shocked,' said my fellow-student, laughing at her own unconscious prejudice, 'because somehow I never thought lesbians could be old!'

The last 50 years have seen an extraordinary shift in attitudes to sexual diversity in Britain – a change which has in many ways 'transfigured the lives of Britain's four million gay people' (Summerskill 2006). Lesbians and gay men have become visible in an historically unprecedented way; but some are more visible than others. Representations of lesbians and gay men in the media remain stereotyped and selective (Cowan and Valentine 2006) and the existence of older non-heterosexuals, especially lesbians, is rarely if ever acknowledged. Representations of older people, particularly women, are equally limited. In Arnold Grossman's words, 'Society is aging. The old are diverse. But society tends to promote images of some aging individuals, while others remain invisible' (1997, p.615).

So why do we not 'see' older lesbians? Monika Kehoe (1986) described them as a 'triply invisible' minority, hidden from view by a particular conjunction of sexism, ageism and hetero-sexism which renders them culturally un-representable. If the popular image of 'lesbian' is a deviant and/or sexualised one, and our picture of the old is asexual; if, as Neild and Pearson (1992) have suggested, every old woman automatically becomes a 'granny' – and therefore heterosexual by default – then old lesbians cannot exist in our imaginations. But it is crucially important, if we are to provide equal services to the whole ageing population, to understand and to challenge the internalised discourses which stop us from seeing some of them. If 'how we are seen determines how we are treated' (Dyer 2002), then those who are not 'seen' will be treated as if they do not exist.

The situation is complicated further if the people we are trying to see are not only hidden, but hiding. The fact that so many older lesbians are still wholly or partially closeted is often given as the reason why so little research into this group exists and why gay men are still more likely to be the subject of such work than lesbians (Heaphy, Yip and Thompson 2003). In their study of LGBT people over 50 in the UK, Heaphy and his colleagues hoped for an equal gender balance in their sample, but recruited only half as many women as men, and only three women over 70. They suggest several possible reasons for this, saying, 'older lesbians may have particular concerns about 'going public' about their sexuality, and experience greater pressures to conceal their sexual identities' (2003, p.6). They imply here that older lesbians are not only made invisible by cultural discourses, but also hide themselves as a protection against social oppression. The authors of the study conclude that further research on lesbians' experiences of old age – and the development of research strategies to access 'this particularly hard to reach' population – are urgent priorities (*ibid.*, p.13).

My current research takes up that challenge, aiming to provide a more comprehensive account of the lives and experiences of older lesbians in Britain today. Using methods drawn from social science, life-history and anthropology, 'Women Like That' combines a large-scale survey by questionnaire with the collection of biographical data through interviews and life-writing. In addition, as an older lesbian myself and so, in effect, an ethnographer of my own tribe, I make use of 'field-notes' from a lifetime of participant observation in the lesbian community.

To recruit as many participants as possible, I emphasised the anonymity of the questionnaire, and made it available by post or email, through a dedicated website and by telephone; it could be completed on paper or online. I followed the usual method for recruiting research subjects from a 'hidden' population, which is chain referral or 'snowballing'. I hoped to tap into lesbian networks which would disseminate my research across the UK, and across barriers of class, education and economic status. The results exceeded my hopes. Carol Archibald (2010) has suggested that older lesbians are more likely to trust a lesbian researcher, and my own older-lesbian identity has undoubtedly been a major factor in the production of such a large response. Three hundred and seventy women over 60 submitted questionnaires, 90 per cent online and the rest by post. About a third of respondents also wrote expressing enthusiasm for a project which, while not 'outing' them individually, could make their existence visible and their views heard.

Demographics

Unsurprisingly, the very large majority of women who responded to the survey are in their sixties. However, 45 of them are aged 70 or over, and nine of these (just over 2% of the whole) are over 80. Although women over 70 form only just over 12 per cent of the sample, they make a significant contribution to a research field in which the LGBT community's 'oldest old' have been so thinly represented.

Respondents come from all regions of Britain except Northern Ireland. A third live in the Southeast of England; 20 per cent in the South and Southwest; 18 per cent in the Midlands; 14 per cent in the North of England; 9 per cent in Scotland and 4 per cent in Wales. Half of these women live in a town or city, and nearly a third in the country; 12 per cent live in suburban areas. Of those who do not fall into any of these categories, some live in substantial villages, one lives a travelling life on a narrow-boat, and one wrote simply, 'small town – a mistake'.

Although the large majority of the women (83%) now describe themselves as 'middle-class,' nearly half were born into working-class families. They have had a wide variety of jobs, from bookseller to bus driver, from bingo-caller to calligrapher; they include artists and antique dealers, company directors and cleaners. Many have had careers in the public sector, as teachers, nurses, social workers or civil servants. Their lives reflect the educational opportunities and social mobility of the post-war generation who make up the majority of my sample; and perhaps also the career patterns and earning power of single and childless women in the second half of the twentieth century.

In all these respects the participants could be said to be fairly representative of the British population, and they certainly demonstrate the heterogeneous nature of the older lesbian community. They are less representative in respect of ethnicity and education, being almost all white, and with higher than average educational qualifications. (This is typical of the 'researcher bias' endemic in snowball sampling, which often produces a sample skewed to reflect the researcher's own characteristics.) Only 1.5 per cent of respondents describe themselves as of mixed heritage; only one is Asian; none identify themselves as Black or Chinese.[1] Six per cent of the sample left school with no qualifications, and another 9 per cent have only school-leaving qualifications, while two-thirds have a university degree or the vocational equivalent. These women were educated in the heyday of the county grammar schools, which raised the educational aspirations of many girls from less privileged backgrounds. The interview data also suggests that many of the women achieved their degree as mature students. In particular those who did not have children (nearly two-thirds of the sample) may have had the time and the resources to extend their education.

I have also collected 32 life-stories, from recorded face-to-face interviews, telephone interviews and written or recorded autobiographies. The subjects come from Scotland, northern England, the Midlands, the Southwest, London and the Southeast. They live in urban, suburban and rural environments and have a variety of economic and educational backgrounds. They are all white; their ages range from 65 to 91.

The database

At the time of writing, the questionnaire survey is still open, and there are nine interviews still to be recorded; information given in this chapter is based on data available at 1 May 2011. The conclusions I draw are therefore preliminary ones, to be refined later.

Health and social care were not my only focus; the data cover a range of topics, including lesbian identity; social life; family relationships; intimate relationships; sex; work and money; community and politics; health; and attitudes to growing older. For the purposes of this chapter, therefore, I have focused on data which illustrate the challenges for professionals working with older adults, and which might suggest ways to improve services. The information is structured to reflect the two theoretical positions discussed above: that older lesbians are both 'hidden' (by social discourses which can unconsciously shape our thinking) and 'hiding' (intentionally concealing or disguising their sexual orientation). So I look first at three factors which might reinforce heterosexist assumptions and form barriers to recognition in those

---

1   For further discussion of the barriers to black and minority ethnic women participating in 'white' research, see Bakshi and Traies (2011).

providing services to older lesbians: marital status, motherhood, and sexuality. I then consider the extent to which older lesbians conceal or reveal their sexual identities, using data on 'outness', friendship networks, and attitudes to health and social care.

Mistaken identities: Marriage and motherhood

An older woman is introduced to you as 'Mrs X'. What do you know (or think you know) about her? For most people the word 'Mrs' will reinforce their unexamined assumption that Mrs X is (and always has been) heterosexual. Once this heterosexist assumption has been made, if no (male) partner is in evidence, then it will follow that Mrs X must be either widowed or divorced, and hence alone. In fact, 52 per cent of respondents in my survey have been married (2% still are). In the over-80 age group, that figure rises to 63 per cent. Although all of them now identify as lesbians, and 42 per cent of them are currently in physical/sexual relationships with other women, many still use their married names. To complicate the matter further, while over a third say that they married because 'it was the expected thing', a quarter say that they were in love with the person they married. These figures challenge popular stereotypes of old women and of lesbians; they also challenge essentialist assumptions about the nature of sexual identity, pointing to the fluidity in women's sexual orientation suggested by Moran (2008). Motherhood can be another cultural barrier to recognition: as one interviewee's mother said when her daughter told her she was a lesbian, 'You can't be! You're a married woman with children!' However, 42 per cent of the women in my survey have had children. In the over-80 age group, this rises to two-thirds (67%).

And if 'Miss X' rather than 'Mrs X' is introduced? The lesbian identity of older women who (like almost half my participants) have remained legally single can be obscured by a different set of cultural assumptions. Not far from the surface of our collective consciousness lie ancient but still potent stereotypes of the unmarried woman: old maid, frustrated spinster, the one who has never been kissed. Images of the lone woman carry other implicit assumptions too: that 'singleness is not the norm; that no-one would be single if they could avoid it; and that single women need to act in a way that overcomes other people's hostility or indifference' (Reynolds 2008, p.6). In deciding whether to 'come out,' therefore, single lesbians are choosing between two stigmatised identities. Interview data indicate that many lesbians keep their married names as a way of retaining what they see as a socially respectable status.

More than one in ten of the women who married say that they did so because they wanted children. For most of those who formed their lesbian identities early in life, and never married or entered into heterosexual partnerships, having children was simply not an option. Until comparatively recently, choosing a lesbian lifestyle almost inevitably meant forgoing motherhood. More than half (58%) of women in this survey have not had children. This is three times more than in the female population at large (Rendall and Smallwood 2003). In their old age this may be a more significant social difference than either sexual orientation or marital status: an old woman who cannot talk about her grandchildren is at the same kind of disadvantage as a man who is not interested in football. In our culture, childlessness is construed as a misfortune, a tragic condition to be medically corrected or, failing that, courageously borne. The identity of 'childless older woman' is a deficit identity, to the extent of being defined by what one is not, and can lead to invisibility in the female life-cycle (Reynolds 2011). A childless woman may also have had far fewer contacts with health services; may be less accustomed to physical examination by a doctor, and therefore may be reluctant to present with physical symptoms. If she is also a lesbian, there is only a 50 per cent likelihood that she has disclosed the fact to her GP (Hunt and Fish 2008).

Sexuality

There are still 'huge cultural roadblocks' to the idea of older people as sexually active (Barker 2004). We shrink from the idea of our parents as sexual beings. How difficult, then, to imagine our grandparents in a sexual liaison; and almost impossible to imagine our grandmother making love with another woman. Nonetheless, the small amount of data available (Kehoe 1988; Adelman 1991) shows that lesbians over 65 do remain sexually interested and active, though evidence for those aged 70 or more is 'extremely skimpy' (Barker 2004). My survey supplies new data for this age group.

Respondents were asked how often in the past year they had been physically sexual with another woman. One in five women reported having sex monthly or more often, and one in ten said they had sex once a week or more. Asked about the importance of sex, 84 per cent said it was the main part or an important part of a relationship when they were younger; 67 per cent rated sex as still being an important part of a lesbian relationship after age 60. Just under half (47%) had not been sexually active at all; of these, four out of ten said it was not by choice.

Well over half the women in the survey (57%) are currently involved in an intimate relationship with another woman. This per centage decreases somewhat with age, but 43 per cent of women over 70 and 33 per cent of those over 80 reported being in such relationships. The data also suggest that women continue to form new sexual partnerships into old age: one in ten of current relationships reported are two years old or less. Interview data provides further evidence that lesbians go on finding new partners well into their seventies and even their eighties. They also go on experiencing the pain of relationships ending; more than one interviewee over 70 has described a recent break-up and the emotional distress it caused.

When older lesbians do become visible, then, they present a number of challenges to current assumptions and practices, one of which is that (like older people in the mainstream) they are still loving, sexual beings.

'Outness'

For practitioners in health and social care, one of the main barriers to recognising an older lesbian is still that she is unlikely to reveal herself (in fact she has probably spent many years perfecting an unobtrusive but highly effective camouflage). Even if she wants to tell you (and 13% of respondents say they want to be 'more visible as a lesbian than [they are] now'), she may struggle to break the taboo of a lifetime. Angie's story[2] is not an uncommon one:

---

2   All the names used in this chapter are pseudonyms.

> Angie and Pam hid their relationship from their families and work colleagues, taking extreme measures to conceal even the fact that they shared an address. They had an active social life within the lesbian community, but kept the different parts of their lives strictly segregated, making sure that friends, family and work colleagues never met each other. When Angie died suddenly, Pam had to tell Angie's family for the first time that she and Pam had been lovers for over thirty years and had recently registered their civil partnership.
>
> There was no mention at Angie's funeral of the relationship which had been the centre of her life for so long.
>
> (field-notes, 2009)

Change is slow. The survey shows that older lesbians are more open about their sexual identities than they were 30 years ago; but they are still more likely to be out to friends than to family, and less likely to be out to their neighbours or other people. In reply to the question 'At the time of filling in this questionnaire, who knows you are a lesbian?' 81 per cent said that most of their friends know they are lesbians; only 2 per cent said that none of their friends know; 74 per cent said that most of their family know about their sexual orientation, and another 14 per cent that some of their family know; but *nearly one in ten said that no one in their family knew, or knows now, of their lesbian identity.* Outside the circle of trusted friends and family, respondents exercise even more discretion. A third said that most of their neighbours know they are lesbians, and another third said some neighbours do. However, more than a quarter said that none of their neighbours know. Older people who have not shared their sexual identities with family members or neighbours may be reluctant to disclose it in a care situation, for fear it will be revealed to them.

Health professionals and social services receive about the same level of trust as neighbours, with about a third (37%) of respondents reporting that they are out to 'most' health professionals and another third (32%) saying they are out to 'some'. Nearly a quarter (22%) say they are not out to any health professionals, and 9 per cent ticked the 'not applicable' box, which suggests they have no contact with health professionals at all. Forty-two per cent say that their doctor does not know they are lesbian, a slightly lower figure than the 50 per cent recorded in a general survey of lesbian health (Hunt and Fish 2008). The same per centage say they have never felt able to discuss sexual matters with a health professional.

The results for social services show the lowest levels of disclosure. About a third of the women have some contact with social services, and of these more than a third say they are out to 'most'. A further 10 per cent say they are out to 'some'; but *half of service users (49%), including all of those over 80, say they are 'out to none' of these professionals*. The positions illustrated by these figures can be entrenched ones. Over 80 per cent of respondents either agreed or agreed strongly with the statement 'My sexual orientation is nobody's business but my own'; and in answer to the question 'Would you like to be more or less visible as a lesbian than you are now?' 84 per cent said they were 'happy with the current situation'. However, as Billie's story shows, a closeted identity is never entirely free of anxiety.

> Billie died peacefully in hospital in her eightieth year, mourned by the lesbian social group which had formed her friendship circle and 'family of choice' for many years. The secretary emailed the group to ask whether they felt it would be proper to attend her funeral. An agitated debate ensued.
>
> Billie had always concealed the fact she was gay, from an absolute conviction that it would cost her both job and career; the habit of concealment never left her. Her friends naturally wanted to attend her funeral, but some were worried that their presence might 'out' her against her wishes. Others argued that Billie had no surviving family, and that it was important that there should be real friends there, not just a handful neighbours.
>
> Then one member pointed out that it is not unusual for elderly women to have single women friends of the same age, so it would perhaps not look suspicious if a few of them attended on behalf of the whole group; and that was what they did.
>
> (field-notes, 2009)

'Coming out' is an ongoing, dynamic process. Every unfamiliar person and place (such as a hospital or nursing home) demands yet another decision about disclosure. Many things will affect that decision, not just the attitudes (or perceived attitudes) of staff and of other patients or residents; but also the expectations, based on past experience, which the individual brings to the situation.

Friendship networks

The fact that the large majority of older lesbians in the survey are out to 'most' of their friends must be qualified by the fact that most of their friends are also lesbians. In many cases these friendships operate within a close-knit group and have lasted for many years. Fifty-eight per cent of respondents say 'Most of my closest friends are lesbians,' and nearly half say that they see their closest friends once a week or more often. Eighty-one per cent say 'Most of my closest lesbian friends are within ten years of my age.' Kehoe (1988), Kimmel *et al.* (2006) and Barker (2004) have remarked on the importance to older lesbians of friends and families of choice; the idea that 'my friends are my family' is still often heard in older lesbian conversation. These friendships are often formed and maintained through membership of an organised local or regional social group. No fewer than 82 per cent of respondents have belonged to such a group at some time; 44 per cent still do. Some of these groups started as branches of Kenric, (the first social organisation for lesbians in Britain, founded in 1963); others were formed by a handful of friends looking for like-minded others. More or less invisible to mainstream society, some of these 'informal, local and "hidden" networks' (Heaphy *et al.* 2003, p.6) have survived for 30 years or more and have been a lifeline for many women.

The isolated minority

We know that older lesbians are likely to live longer than (gay) men, to be less well off in later life and to make greater use of health and social care services. Archibald (2010) points out that their chances of requiring long-stay care are therefore greater than those of gay men. Although so many older lesbians are well supported by partners or friends, there is also a minority who lack such support, and who may be the group most likely to need social care services in old age. Half of the women in this survey currently live alone. A third have health problems which restrict their activities. Two per cent said none of their friends know they are lesbian. Six per cent said none of their family know, three per cent see their closest friends 'rarely'. Eleven per cent describe themselves as 'rather unhappy' or 'very unhappy'. Women in all these categories are less likely to be in a relationship, and more likely to be without family and to rate their own emotional health as 'poor'. While they are the most likely to need social care in the future, they are also least likely to be 'out' to health and care professionals.

Shaz [aged 65] was born into a struggling working-class home in an industrial city and was diagnosed with epilepsy at ten years old. She identified as 'gay' from the age of 12, and 'came out' while still at school, frequenting gay bars with older friends. At seventeen she ran away from home, was brought back, and spent the next four years in a mental hospital. At 21, she became pregnant. She married the baby's father, mainly to get away from her parents and despite the fact that 'every time he came near me, I just used to freeze up. I had to be drunk to get pregnant.' Two of her four children died in infancy. She had her first lesbian relationship a year after her marriage. Eventually she left her husband, and met her long-term lesbian partner. They stayed together for 12 years. It was a comparatively stable period for Shaz, but when her partner died suddenly, she suffered from another bout of mental illness and became homeless. Haunted by memories in the place where they had lived together, she decided to return to the town where she was born. She lodged in a hostel for the homeless until referred to a local housing project, where she found a temporary home, emotional support and unconditional acceptance of her lesbian identity from the project workers. One of these workers is a lesbian herself. Shaz was encouraged not only by this woman's friendship but by the way in which her sexual orientation was clearly accepted by all her colleagues. Shaz had been re-housed just before I met her. She neither hides nor advertises her sexuality to her neighbours, though she thinks they have probably guessed. But she is pleased that all the housing association staff know she is a lesbian and are so positive about it.

(summary from interview, November 2010)

Attitudes to services for older people

The overt culture of acceptance demonstrated by the service providers who helped Shaz was crucial in overcoming her sense of exclusion. Archibald (2010) suggests that older lesbians will approach health and care services 'in ways that differ from younger lesbian women and from their heterosexual peers', and my survey shows that many have a deep distrust of what they see as the heterosexist assumptions and attitudes of services for the elderly. This belief is illustrated by the responses to questions about two later-life scenarios: retirement communities and care homes. The women were asked to rate four possible types of retirement community (not all of which currently exist in the UK): lesbian-only; lesbian and gay; women-only; and (the current norm) a mixed/heterosexual community. 'Lesbian-only' and 'women-only' were both given positive or very positive ratings by three-quarters of respondents (72% and 75% respectively), while 'lesbian and gay' had positive ratings from 62 per cent. However the mainstream, heteronormative scenario produced only 22 per cent positive ratings, and a negative or very negative response from 78 per cent of respondents. Negative experiences serve to reinforce such beliefs. Maureen (aged 69) tells how she and her partner were driven out of their flat in a retirement complex by homophobic bullying and by what they saw as the unwillingness of housing association staff to acknowledge or deal with it:

> Our plans for retirement have been thoroughly destroyed... We feel we can never live in sheltered accommodation again while both of us are alive, and [are] very nervous that such a thing might happen again. (Autobiography, written April 2011)

Even an 'out' interviewee (aged 67) who is happy in her sheltered accommodation would prefer

> somewhere where gay people could live together. You know, like you get these complexes, like here — it would be nice to have one which was gay... Because all the people here know I'm gay, I make no secret of it, but it's still not the same as having people living around you, is it, who are gay? (Bobby, interviewed December 2010)

When respondents were asked to think about residential care, the negative response to a mixed/heterosexual context was even more pronounced. Two-thirds or more gave positive ratings to lesbian-only and women-only homes, while lesbian/gay homes scored almost as well, but 83 per cent responded negatively or very negatively to the standard 'heterosexual' model. One interviewee (aged 73) explained:

> If I had to go into care…I wouldn't want to go on living, I don't think…I wouldn't mind so much if there were other people that were gay. But what conversation would I have with anybody? And I certainly don't want to go where they're being really patronising. 'Oh, you never got married then?' or something like that, you know? I really don't want it. I'd want to say, 'No, perhaps I didn't get married! But I've had really nice relationships with women, and I don't regret a life like that.' But I won't be able to say that… Bad enough, you know, if they have someone coming in here, to care for me…and I couldn't have a decent conversation with them, and say, 'Oh, my friends are coming round,' you know, and it's 'Oh, they're not married then?' I don't need it. I didn't like it when I was younger, and I certainly don't want to have to lie now about my sexuality… I would think that if I was in a residential care home and I came out with, 'I'm gay, you know, and I've had lots of girlfriends,' they would watch me! And think that I'd be pinching their bottoms, something like that, and then they'd have nasty talks about me, in the staff room. (Ronnie, interviewed May 2011)

Ronnie's fears are based on earlier experiences of homophobic prejudice. The large majority (80%) of women in the survey said they had been discriminated against because of their sexual orientation, and feel that lesbians generally suffer from discrimination. These negative expectations present a huge challenge to service providers.

Conclusions and ways forward

Older lesbians are more likely than some other groups to have need of services designed to support older people, but they are resistant to the idea, fearing prejudice and discrimination. These fears, together with their wholly or partially closeted lives, present particular challenges to service providers. Overcoming their reluctance to engage with health and care services is an urgent priority if such services are to be truly inclusive.

After nearly sixty years of marriage, Edith [aged 89] and her husband bought a bungalow in a sheltered retirement community. Edith had been blind for some years, and her husband was suffering from heart disease. A couple of years after they moved there, Edith's husband died. As time passed, it was obvious to care staff that Edith was becoming more, rather than less, distressed. After sympathetic encouragement from the resident warden, Edith disclosed to her that she was a lesbian. She was certain of it, even though she had never had a physical relationship with a woman, having chosen duty to her husband and family over the offer of lesbian love many years before. She had concealed this secret while her husband was alive, but now, aged 85, felt an overwhelming need to 'come out'.

The warden did some research and found an appropriate counsellor/therapist for Edith to talk to. The therapist contacted the local lesbian social group, asking if they could help. Women from the group visited Edith, listened with empathy to her story, brought her lesbian/feminist talking books, and supported her through the ordeal of 'coming out' to her children and grandchildren. Edith is now over ninety, still living independently within the retirement community, and has a group of lesbian friends whom she sees regularly.

(Summarised from interview, July 2009)

There are encouraging examples of effective non-discriminatory practice with older LGBT people, such as the stories of Shaz and Edith given here. But there is clearly a need for a far wider recognition of sexual difference, and particularly of the existence of older lesbians, on the part of those who work in services for older people. To achieve this, it is necessary to:

- challenge current social assumptions about both sexuality and ageing, by identifying and acknowledging the heteronormative imperatives and practices which shape our thinking

- gain a more contextualised understanding of the lives of older women who identify as lesbian – one which takes into account their personal and community histories and the long years of oppression and concealment that many have experienced

- reinforce non-discriminatory practices, including challenging inappropriate behaviour in others, whether professionals or service users. People who expect prejudice will not recognise acceptance or goodwill unless it is overt and lived out.

Equality of provision is a moving target, troubling categories and challenging prevailing discourses; reflective practice means constantly re-examining our own assumptions. A final caution: the aim is not to make old lesbians 'come out' (though that may be one indicator of success); it is to develop care services which are truly inclusive, and professional practice which allows every individual to feel valued, knowing that her relationships and lifestyle are validated by those who care for her.

References

Adelman, M. (1991) 'Stigma, gay lifestyles, and adjustment to aging: A study of later-life gay men and lesbians.' *Journal of Homosexuality 20*, 3–4, 7–32.

Archibald, C. (2010) 'A Path Less Travelled: Hearing the Voices of Older Lesbians: A Pilot Study Researching Residential Care and Other Needs.' In R.L. Jones and R. Ward (eds) *LGBT Issues: Looking Beyond Categories*. Edinburgh: Dunedin.

Bakshi, L. and Traies, J. (2011) '"Come Out, Come Out, Wherever You Are": The Problem of Representativeness and BME "participation".' Unpublished conference paper presented at the 18th Lesbian Lives Conference, University of Brighton, 12 February 2011. Available at: www.helensandler.pwp.blueyonder.co.uk/womenlikethat/ComeOutWhereverYouAre.pdf. Accessed on 11 May 2012.

Barker, J. C. (2004) 'Lesbian Aging: An Agenda for Social Research.' In G.H. Herdt and B. De Vries (eds) *Gay and Lesbian Aging: Research and Future Directions*. New York: Springer Publishing Company.

Cowan, K. and Valentine, G. (2006) *Tuned Out: The BBC's Portrayal of Lesbian and Gay People*. London: Stonewall.

Dyer, R. (2002) *The Matter of Images: Essays on Representation*. London: Routledge.

Grossman, A.H. (1997) 'The Virtual and Actual Identities of Older Lesbians and Gay Men.' In M.B. Dubberman (ed.) *A Queer World: The Center for Lesbian and Gay Studies Reader*. New York: NY University Press.

Heaphy, B., Yip, A. and Thompson, D. (2003) *Lesbian, Gay and Bisexual Lives over 50*. Nottingham: York House Publications.

Hunt, R. and Fish, J. (2008) *Prescription for Change: Lesbian and Bisexual Women's Health Check 2008*. London: Stonewall.

Kehoe, M. (1986) 'Lesbians over sixty-five: A triply invisible minority.' *Journal of Homosexuality 12*, 3-4, 139–152.

Kehoe, M. (1988) *Lesbians Over 60 Speak for Themselves*. New York and London: Haworth Press.

Kimmel, D., Rose, T., Orel, N. and Greene, B. (2006) 'Historical Context of Research on Lesbian, Gay, Bisexual, and Transgender Aging.' In D. Kimmel, T. Rose and S. David (eds) *Lesbian, Gay, Bisexual, and Transgender Aging: Research and Clinical Perspectives.* New York, Chichester: Columbia University Press.

Moran, C. S. (2008) *Mid-life Sexuality Transitions in Women: A Queer Qualitative Study.* Southern Connecticut State University, Connecticut, MA.

Neild, S. and Pearson, R. (1992) *Women Like Us.* London: Women's Press.

Rendall, M.S. and Smallwood, S. (2003) 'Higher qualifications, first birth timing and further childbearing in England and Wales.' *Population Trends* 111, Spring issue, 18–26.

Reynolds, J. (2008) *The Single Woman: A Discursive Investigation.* London and New York: Routledge.

Reynolds, J. (2011) 'Childless older women: Combating a deficit identity?' International Society of Critical Health Psychology 7th Biennial Conference, University of Adelaide.

Summerskill, B.E. (2006) *The Way We Are Now: Gay and Lesbian Lives in the Twenty-first Century.* London and New York: Continuum Press.

Further reading

Gay and Grey in Dorset (2006) *Lifting the Lid on Sexuality and Ageing.* Bournemouth: Help and Care Development Ltd.

Lesbian Identity Project (2011) *Lesbians on... Living Our Lives.* Bradford: Lesbian Identity Project.

National Lesbian and Gay Survey (1992) *What a Lesbian Looks Like: Writings by Lesbians on their Lives and Lifestyles.* London and New York: Routledge.

River, L. (2006) *A Feasibility Study of the Needs of Older Lesbians in Camden and Surrounding Boroughs.* London: Polari.

Smailes, J. (1994) '"The Struggle has Never been Simply about Bricks and Mortar": Lesbians' Experience of Housing.' In R. Gilroy and R. Woods (eds) *Housing Women.* London: Routledge.

Turnbull, A. (2002) *Opening Doors: The Needs of Older Lesbians and Gay Men. A Literature Review.* London: Age Concern England.

Part II

Implications for Health and Social Care Practice

Chapter 5

'I'm Older than I Ever Thought I Would be'

The Lived Experience of Ageing in HIV-positive Gay Men

Robin Wright, Gareth Owen and Jose Catalan

Introduction

We are now in the fourth decade of the HIV epidemic. The Health Protection Agency (Health Protection Agency 2010) estimates that the number of adults aged 50 or over accessing HIV care in the UK has almost doubled in less than ten years from one in ten to almost one in five. This increase is attributed to: improved survival since the introduction of highly active antiretroviral therapy (HAART); new diagnosis in older people; and continued transmission. Until recently there has been little research on HIV in older people, and ageing with HIV remains largely uncharted territory.

Background

Medical research is now investigating the influence of chronic HIV infection and HIV therapeutics on ageing processes, although the extent of this relationship remains uncertain (Deeks and Phillips 2009; Pratt, Gascoyne and Cunningham 2010). Some of the effects of HIV, including cognitive, metabolic and hormonal changes, mimic those more generally associated with ageing (Myers 2009); other diseases associated with ageing such as coronary artery disease, dyslipidemia, metabolic syndrome, diabetes, osteoporosis and dementia, are more likely to develop earlier in people living with HIV (hereafter abbreviated to PLHIV).

Social research has started exploring the lived experience of ageing with HIV. Siegel, Raveis and Karus (1998) found that older PLHIV considered ageing to have advantages, such as increased wisdom, patience and contentment, and disadvantages, such as physical deterioration, social isolation and lack of sympathy from others. Shippy and Karpiak (2005) found that 40 per cent of older PLHIV considered their social support network inadequate because stigma and isolation had disconnected them from traditional, informal support networks. Similarly Emlet (2006; Emlet, Tozay and Raveis 2010) found that although many PLHIV over the age of 50 expressed resilience, the 'double jeopardy' of ageism and HIV stigma produced experiences of discrimination, stereotyping, rejection and social isolation. In Canada, Robinson *et al.* (2010) found 'differences in the experience of ageing between long-term survivors and older men diagnosed with HIV later in life' (p.109). The long-term survivors often struggled with both the interruption of their imagined life trajectory and feelings of confusion from surviving beyond expectation. By contrast, those diagnosed more recently felt less connected to the struggles of the early epidemic and focused instead on concerns about HIV disclosure, the prospect of life foreshortened and the physical–emotional burden of starting treatments. In this chapter we aim to explore some of the issues facing older HIV-positive gay men.

Methods

Our research draws on interviews with ten London-based HIV-positive gay men aged 50 or over. We adopted a biographical narrative approach (Wengraf 2001) to create space for participants to describe their experience using stories from their personal biographies. This method draws on the idea that 'in order to understand and explain social and psychological phenomena we have to reconstruct their *genesis* – the process of their creation, reproduction and transformation' (Rosenthal 2004, p.49). Participants were asked: '*Please tell me the story of your experience of getting older as a HIV-positive gay man.*' The interviewer then asked follow-up questions to clarify the narrative and encourage a collaborative co-construction of meanings (Holstein and Gubrium 1995). Interviews took between two and five hours and were digitally recorded, anonymised and fully transcribed. Participants were invited to review their transcript and engage in an ongoing analytic email dialogue to improve the credibility of our interpretative analysis.

Findings

The experience of ageing with HIV was relatively unproblematic for some, while others struggled with the long-term social and medical consequences of getting older with a chronic illness. We found that attitudes to the prospect of ageing with HIV were particularly influenced by:

- the lived experience of HIV infection on personal health
- emotional proximity to AIDS-related bereavements
- an individual's narrative interpretation of the history of the epidemic.

Analysis began by identifying the main themes that emerged across the sample. Each interview was examined for the overall form in which the participant told their story and the moral concerns underlying the narration. Gergen and Gergen (1988) suggest that one way of analysing biographical narratives is to identify the general direction taken in relation to the individual's valued life objectives: thus 'progressive' narratives tell of a movement towards valued life goals, while 'regressive' narratives indicate a drifting away from valued goals.

Applying Gergen and Gergen's analytic device to our data, *regressive* narratives tended to be characterised by storylines describing the ongoing biographical disruption of HIV (Bury 1982; Carricaburu and Pierret 1995). These ambivalent narratives spoke of being trapped by past experience of HIV and expressed greater fear and anxiety about the prospect of ageing. Participants talked about the trauma of multiple AIDS-related bereavements and described the unexpected burden of loss as an experience of premature ageing. For these participants, the introduction of HAART tended to be interpreted as the continuation of an irresolvable life-long struggle with HIV.

> **Tom (61):** So old age was always a fearful future but I protected myself with friends. We were all in it together. But then in the mid '80s they all dropped dead around me. It was as if I had been catapulted from being young to being 70 in the space of a couple of years... So when I look to the future I don't see much. I'm very concerned about being old on my own in a big city without the support and structure that used to be in the HIV world... I think when they downgraded HIV from being a terminal condition to a chronic condition and everyone kind of packed up their briefcases and moved onto the next cause, that's

when I felt really lost. Now I can't understand my life situation, because this isn't how I planned it because AIDS took the plans away and left me in a world I hadn't expected to be in and I don't know how to resolve that.

Regressive narratives were more commonly found in participants who had: (i) a close emotional connection to the early epidemic; (ii) social networks damaged by AIDS-related bereavements; (iii) diagnosis prior to HAART when HIV was regarded as a potentially terminal condition; and (iv) interrupted careers, often leading to dependency on state benefits and financial hardship.

By contrast, *progressive* narratives were characterised by storylines moving towards valued life objectives where living with HIV tended to be defined by a normalising discourse of HIV as '*just* a chronic treatable illness'. These narratives demonstrated an orientation to the present rather than the past and contained fewer anxieties about the prospect of ageing with HIV.

Steve (53): We never expected this to happen. Perhaps that's one reason why I hadn't thought a great deal about getting older and I still think, in a way, I'm not going to get old. I don't think my mind's in any kind of different state than it would have been if I hadn't had HIV, I don't think it really makes any difference – other than having made me sort of evaluate what I'm getting out of life. But it certainly doesn't make me worry about what I might face in the future… I think at the time we didn't realise what a miracle it [HAART] was, but looking back it is absolutely a miracle… And I suppose what I am trying to say is that from then on I've felt very optimistic.

Progressive narratives were more commonly found in participants who: (i) were more recently diagnosed; (ii) interpreted HAART as an opportunity to proceed with a 'normal' life course towards old age; (iii) had working lives uninterrupted by illness; (iv) were less dependent on state benefits; (v) had fewer AIDS-related bereavements; and (vi) had social networks not organised around HIV support services.

With these two general storylines in mind we: (i) developed an examination of the lived experience of ageing with HIV; (ii) considered how the narratives were used to construct identities in relation to a 'moral imperative' to age well with HIV; and (iii) explored the possibility of building supportive communities which are sensitive to the needs of older HIV-positive gay men.

1. The lived experience of ageing with HIV

Several themes emerged within the diversity of experience described by participants which can inform practitioner understanding of the needs of older HIV-positive gay men.

UNCERTAINTY

Uncertainty has always been part of the experience of living with HIV (Brashers *et al.* 1999). Before the introduction of HAART it was often attributed to the life-threatening potential of HIV but is now also experienced in association with anxieties about the effect of HIV on the 'normal' ageing process. The boundary between morbidities associated with HIV infection and those of the 'normal' ageing process are not easily distinguished (Nixon 2012). These uncertainties were mentioned as a source of anxiety for many of the participants in this study:

> **Nathan (57):** They are quite sort of nebulous issues and my difficulty is knowing…how much is changing because I'm HIV-positive or just getting older. How can I know?

> **Gordon (60):** I said to my doctor, tell me; am I feeling tired because I've got HIV, am I feeling tired because of the side-effects of the drugs for HIV, am I feeling tired because I've got Type 2 diabetes, or is it because of the drugs that I take for Type 2 diabetes, or is it because of the other medication I take, is it because I've got a very stressful job, or is it because I'm 60? And he said yeah, I don't know which it is.

Those who had been diagnosed after HAART had transformed HIV from a life-threatening to a chronic illness, tended to cope with these uncertainties using a temporal orientation of 'living with a philosophy of the present', which Davies (1997) identifies in her research on long-term HIV-positivity as an effective adaptive strategy for living with uncertainty:

> **Steve (57):** I live very much for the present and that may be part of adjusting to living with HIV. I tend not to think too much about what I'm going to do in the future…or when I get old and need care.

Some participants expressed their orientation to the present by describing how HIV has been 'normalised' to background noise:

Thierry (52): I can't say I think that far ahead, what might or might not happen in the next five or ten years' time. People really do work themselves into mental disorders about it. I think I've enough to worry about in the present... I think there are issues around ageing but for me they're not HIV-specific. HIV is just part of the mix but it's not a particularly important part of the mix because it's not a particularly difficult condition to deal with. So it's in there but sort of just background noise really.

AMBIVALENCE

While the introduction of HAART was a cause for optimism in some, it also created additional anxiety for those who felt burdened by their long involvement with HIV. These participants were more likely to have had interrupted careers and be dependent on welfare benefits. They expressed more ambivalence and weariness at the prospect of living longer with the extended uncertainties of HIV in the post-HAART era:

James (57): That was defining, not great joy, it was fear, because I'd already accepted that's how it was. Then all of a sudden it was like, well, there's hope now and you're improving. And it was awful and really hard because...I didn't know who I was supposed to be now... I haven't told anybody this, but sometimes I feel disappointed that my HIV hasn't moved on. It's not wishing to be unwell, it's thinking, 'Oh God, here we go again' – it goes on and on, and every day the pills, for ever and ever.

The introduction of HAART in 1996 was a key moment in the social history of HIV. It was followed in 1997 by the end of ring-fenced government funding for HIV, which led to a gradual reduction in funding for third sector organisations and a reduction in available support services. In this climate of change some participants were left struggling:

Charles (60): So it wasn't an easy process, coming to terms with the fact that you've got to start thinking about your future again when you felt previously it had been closed off to you... It's almost like you missed opportunities to make the best plans for future old age... And the other thing is, you've got to give yourself reasons for going on because the paradox here is that while you've been given the means of living on, in a lot of cases the reasons – the rationale, has been taken away.

LOSS AND TRAUMA

For some participants who had experienced HIV as a life-threatening illness, ageing with HIV seemed inextricably linked with a sense of regret and loss. Participants described an experience of premature ageing after losing so many friends in a relatively short space of time:

> **Nathan (57):** I think it's relatively unusual to have lost a large group of friends when you're in your 40s, all within the space of five or six years. So that has had a big impact on me. It stopped me from developing those relationships, so there's not enough people I can enjoy being a grumpy old man with.

Several participants described the difficulty in repairing their damaged social networks:

> **Carl (54):** I don't have a circle of friends like I used to. They all went, all of them. I never replaced them.

Other participants describe how they had escaped close personal involvement with the trauma of the early epidemic:

> **Thierry (52):** I missed the worst of it because I was living away, coming back and forth, but not really being very involved. And even though I knew those who died, I missed their deaths. I didn't see them die. And then when I actually became positive it was very late and treatments already existed. So you'll have a group of people who went through the whole HIV thing with the discovery and all the deaths and political stuff, and then there's the post-treatment generation who have a different view and completely different needs.

2. Moral identities and 'successful ageing'

The experience of ageing and living with a chronic illness has a moral dimension arising from the social expectation to demonstrate independence and resilience to adversity. Since disease is often associated with stigma, illness narratives are frequently told as moral tales where the individual claims the right to participate as a valued citizen of society (Blaxter 2004; Frank 1997). According to Giddens (1991) identity is a 'reflexive project of the self, which consists in the sustaining of coherent, yet continuously revised, biographical narratives' (p.5). In the discursive space offered by the biographical interview method, participants in this study worked to construct moral identities in relation to the circulating discourses about successful ageing and living with HIV.

RESILIENCE AND OPPORTUNITY

Participants' assertions of being empowered, independent PLHIV were more difficult to sustain where life trajectories had been significantly diverted from the traditional life course by the biographical disruption of HIV. Emotive moral tales of careers interrupted by illness and state benefit dependency emerged as progressive–regressive tensions in these narratives. For example, in drawing a comparison with people who had been more recently diagnosed, Carl was concerned that his painful experience of 'going backwards' should be understood as a consequence of his traumatic experience of HIV related losses:

> **Carl (54):** They [recently diagnosed] are coming in with psychological armour undented so they can go to work and have as normal a life as possible... But can I get any kind of life back now? As hard as I try to keep it together I'm not getting any younger. Money isn't going to come in to wipe out the debts – I know everyone is feeling it, but I'm not even standing still anymore, I'm going backwards because there is no way out of anything.

Despite feeling trapped by the disadvantages of his situation, Carl demonstrates his continued engagement with the moral identity work of 'trying to keep it together' but feels his sense of self-efficacy has been compromised. By contrast, Stuart's narrative suggests a more progressive engagement with the ageing process:

> **Stuart (57):** In '*Chicago*', there is that great line, '*I'm older than I ever thought I would be*' which is a great truism. As a kid I worked on the basis that every time you had a birthday your biological clock ticked you up one year, so you became older and more sensible. But it doesn't work like that, the youth stays inside and the outside ages. If you want to be an old person then be an old person but that's just fitting into what society dictates you should be.

Stuart demonstrates self-efficacy and claims the right to define his own narrative of successful ageing in opposition to other narratives of decline. Ong and Bergeman (2004) argue that belief in self-efficacy is a key component of resilience and therefore has a positive impact on the long-term health and well-being of older people.

EMPLOYMENT, BENEFITS AND RETIREMENT

Financial security emerged as a prominent theme, not least in identifying tensions in relation to moral concerns around work, benefit dependency, and being valued as productive contributors to society. Gordon believed his 'strong financial position' had contributed greatly to his relatively positive attitude to ageing with HIV. Other participants, advised to retire and prepare for life-threatening illnesses in the pre-HAART era, expressed considerable fear and guilt about their dependence on disability benefits for financial security:

> **James (57):** I mean I couldn't do a full-time job now. I know I couldn't do that. And there's this tension – you are terrified you're going to lose Disability Living Allowance – and there is this guilt thing for claiming benefits as well.

According to Prince (2008) claiming a disability benefit is a contested field in which the social citizenship of claimants is positioned between 'passive victims living in the kingdom of the sick' and 'deserving beneficiaries' of state support (p.30). This tension is mirrored in the moment when the dominant discourse of 'HIV as a life-threatening crisis' was to some extent normalised to 'HIV as *just* a chronic treatable illness'. As a consequence society now requires the PLHIV to abandon the 'sick role'. Adjusting to having '*just* a chronic condition' has been a difficult transition for some interviewees, particularly long-term survivors who experienced significant losses and trauma in the earlier phases of the epidemic. Research on the stigmatisation of HIV within gay communities finds that 'older and longer diagnosed positive men were described as being situated at the lowest rung of a contemporary gay social hierarchy' which 'resented and rejected those who were classed as "dependent on the state"' (Dodds 2006, p.447).

These tensions were replicated within our sample, as illustrated by this comment from a more recently diagnosed participant:

> **Thierry (52):** I know some people who've made themselves into real victims. And they're on benefits and it's their whole life. As soon as they were diagnosed they stopped working, they went on all the benefits they could, almost with relish because

at one point you could get quite a lot. Very nice thank you very much, for the British taxpayer [laughs]. I'm sure it's not like that anymore.

The effect of benefit dependency stigmatisation was painfully expressed by a participant diagnosed prior to the advent of combination therapy:

Carl (54): Everybody makes you feel guilty for everything [in tears]. They make you feel guilty about wanting hospital appointments, make you feel guilty because you don't have a GP, make you feel guilty because you won't fit in the box, feel guilty about benefits...and as part of the guilt process you think, well, could I go back to work, am I being pathetic? But [my attempt] last year taught me that, no, I couldn't.

These moral narratives suggest that those whose 'psychological armour' has been dented by the biographical disruptions of HIV can feel stigmatised and can struggle to construct positive identities as older HIV-positive gay men.

3. Building supportive communities

The possibility of building supportive communities to protect against social isolation in older age emerged as a recurring theme in this study.

LONELINESS, AGEISM AND SEXUAL IDENTITIES

Tom (61): ...an emotional barrenness... I miss the touch, I miss affection, I miss the passion...

Several participants expressed a growing sense of isolation as a consequence of past trauma and bereavement:

Tom (61): The older gay HIV-positive people I know – living on their own and not in a relationship – are pretty fearful of the future...and don't want to live too long.

Other participants described their fear of loneliness specifically in relation to being single and growing old without a partner, or being removed from the workplace before the usual retirement age:

Nathan (57): I do feel quite isolated, especially since I don't get out and about to meet people very often now. One of the impacts of not working is you don't interact with people on a regular basis.

Some participants with progressive-orientated narratives actively challenged ageism by arguing it was a social construct, and, while acknowledging that ageism was more prevalent in the gay scene, were less likely to feel excluded. Whereas Tom spoke of feeling increasingly 'invisible' in the generally youth-oriented commercial gay venues:

Tom (61): I think the gay scene was always very much about youth and beauty...and suddenly you find yourself as an older gay man quite invisible.

One participant pointed to the potential for triple discrimination:

Carl (54): It's hard for all older people. Older people feel left out. Now add to that being gay. And then add to that HIV...

Disclosure of status was still problematic for some, and appeared to become more difficult to negotiate with age:

Nathan (57): Meeting other people is always difficult and particularly letting them know you're HIV. I feel I've got to the age where I can't be bothered explaining, so would rather not bother meeting at all.

For gay men, sexual interactions have traditionally played an important role in building social networks. For those identifying strongly with the gay community a loss of libido with age could also add to the sense of isolation:

Charles (60): As a gay man, my primary mode of meeting people and consequently forming friendships has been through sex. Without a partner, I fear the loneliness of old age – and then you hear the whistle as the train with your libido departs and there really is nothing much you can do!

INDEPENDENCE AND SUPPORT

Diverse social groups both within and beyond gay cultural life were valued by participants as important sources of mutual support. Most participants were still active or had long histories of involvement as volunteers within HIV community organisations. Some mourned a sense of camaraderie from the early days of the crisis:

> **James (57):** Even though we were unwell people pulled together…there was a lot of understanding even in the gay community… I don't think there appears to be so much now.

Maintaining independence and social networks is an issue for many older people. The prospect of increased isolation in older age and the need to protect against this by building supportive communities and developing mutual support was a recurring theme in this study. With his long history of activism and voluntary HIV community service, Tom calls for the renewal of grassroots communities that can respond creatively to the challenges of social isolation for gay men in later life:

> **Tom (61):** One thing which would reduce my anxiety about getting older is getting into a supportive community. Obviously a bit of the old hippie in me and a kind of romantic idea maybe, but a big rambling house with a nice big kitchen and a place where we can eat together but have our own areas too.

RESIDENTIAL CARE

Several participants felt that older people's sexual identities are ignored in health and social care policy. There were underlying concerns that mainstream retirement and nursing homes might not affirm non-heterosexual identities.

> **Tom (61):** Should the day come that I need a nursing home, how am I going to fit in as an openly gay man? Because my generation is probably the first generation of being openly gay. Who's going to understand my life reminiscences?

Some participants suggested the need for residential and nursing homes specifically for the LGBT community, but this idea was not appealing to all participants:

Gordon (60): I have absolutely no desire to end my days in a nursing home of whatever colour and the idea of an OAP gay ghetto is repulsive to me.

Some participants expressed anxieties about declining quality of life and dependency by considering the possibility of suicide.

Gordon (60): However, a life of dependency is not for me and when such a situation becomes inevitable, other measures are available.

HIV SPECIALIST CARE

Most participants identified the HIV specialist clinic as the cornerstone in their management of ageing with HIV. For the more isolated it was a 'safe harbour' and an important element of their social network:

Tom (60): I feel so privileged by the care I get, particularly at the hospital. I mean I just feel they're like my family.

The trust in HIV specialists was often contrasted with a lack of confidence in primary care services:

Nathan (57): Most of the HIV professionals acknowledge the validity of my observations and have been willing to explore matters which I bring to their attention, using their knowledge and resources to test and examine the possibilities. The GPs on the other hand are usually well out of their depth and are quite open about that.

With the complexity of co-morbidities and co-infection in the HIV ageing process, participants identified the need for closer liaison between HIV specialist services, primary care and gerontology.

Key points for practitioners

In developed countries the remarkable social history of the HIV epidemic spans three decades: from the first reports of a killer disease affecting gay men; through a period of multiple losses and uncertainty as HIV emerged as a highly stigmatised life-threatening condition; to the 'HAART moment' in 1996 and the transformation of HIV to chronic treatable illness; and now, approaching the fourth decade, the uncertainties facing a newly emerging cohort of ageing PLHIV.

The main finding of this exploratory study is an illustration of how the experience of growing older with HIV is influenced by an individual's biographic relationship to the history of the HIV epidemic. These narratives suggest that some gay men diagnosed in the pre-HAART era may experience greater challenges to growing older with HIV than those diagnosed in the post-HAART era. Therefore, following Arber and Ginn (1998) 'we need to be sensitive to the relationship between structural inequalities and health among older people, in particular how material and social resources in later life...have been fashioned by earlier phases of their personal biography' (p.151).

In summary, the findings suggest that practitioners need an understanding of the following issues which affect the experience of ageing with HIV.

UNCERTAINTY

Despite the success of HAART, HIV can still be a life-threatening condition and uncertainties about the long-term effects of treatment remain. The effect of HIV on the normal ageing process is also very uncertain. These uncertainties are experienced in the context of funding challenges and the wider reorganisation of healthcare services, which may further impact on their ability to visualise a future.

AMBIVALENCE

It is important to be aware of possible feelings of HIV-related ambivalence, particularly in some long-term survivors who may feel silenced by a dominant positive discourse of HIV as 'just a chronic treatable illness'. Unacknowledged ambivalence could undermine motivation and resilience, adherence to anti-retroviral therapy and wider engagement with care services.

RESILIENCE AND OPPORTUNITY

The experience of surviving HIV demonstrates resilience and can be experienced as a positive aspect of ageing with HIV. Where morale and self-motivation is low, practitioners could encourage older HIV-positive gay men to use their experience and acquired wisdom to strengthen their communities.

EMPLOYMENT, BENEFITS AND RETIREMENT

With loss of employment and careers interrupted by illness, those economically disadvantaged by HIV need access to financial advice to maximise economic resources in mid-life before entering retirement. It is important not to overlook that dependency on welfare benefits can be a considerable source of guilt and stigmatisation.

LONELINESS, AGEISM AND SEXUAL IDENTITIES

There is a need to ensure that support is available to address the effects of loneliness and ageism, which can accentuate the effects of social isolation for some HIV-positive gay men entering later life.

INDEPENDENCE AND SUPPORT

Although many older gay men are integrated in diverse and well developed social networks, our findings suggest that some HIV-positive gay men become increasingly socially isolated as they grow older. The Office for National Statistics (2005) reports that never-married older men are more likely to enter institutional care because they lack a spouse or children who could care for them. Following Heaphy and Yip (2006), policies for the future care of older HIV-positive gay men need to go beyond the 'heterosexual assumption' to ensure that non-traditional life styles, identities and ways of living can be supported within the health and social care system.

HIV SPECIALIST CARE

As patients age with HIV there will be a need for closer integration between primary and secondary care. Recognising the pivotal role of the HIV specialist clinic, the provision of care would also benefit from greater clinical and research collaboration between gerontology and HIV medicine. To retain patient confidence, an identifiable healthcare professional should have overall responsibility for coordinating patient care within developed clinical pathways, to facilitate a seamless transition between service providers as different needs arise.

LOSS AND TRAUMA

It is particularly important to recognise the impact of the biographical disruption of HIV diagnosis and, in particular, unresolved grief and loss of social and support networks. Some older HIV-positive men feel their historical battle with the epidemic through illness, polypharmacy and multiple bereavements is misunderstood, ignored or forgotten.

Andrews (2009) argues that we need to hear 'multiple narratives to assist us in building our own models of successful ageing' (p.81). With the dominant discourse of ageing well with HIV tied to its post-HAART transformation as 'just' a chronic treatable illness, it is important that we continue to listen for more ambivalent narratives like Tom's that remind us of the traumatic history of the epidemic:

> **Tom (61):** You can't talk about that ambivalence to most people; they don't want to hear. You keep those feelings to yourself because people say things like, 'Oh you've got to embrace life: you must fight on and relish life.' And I do to a degree, but the memory of the life that was, compared to the life that is, makes it hard to embrace the present... And there's only some of us left who have the complete story of what happened – this precious story – and it has to be remembered because it was unbelievable... And yeah, I feel I am the one who has been left to turn the light out at the end of the party.

Providing opportunities to retell the AIDS story creates possibilities for 'post-traumatic growth' (Neimeyer 2005) and affirming the connection between who one is in older age and who one has been in the years leading up to that time will help PLHIV preserve a sense that this challenging journey is worthwhile.

References

Andrews, M. (2009) 'The narrative complexity of successful ageing.' *International Journal of Sociology and Social Policy 29*, 1–2, 73–83.

Arber, S. and Ginn, J. (1998) 'Health and Illness in Later Life.' In D. Field and S. Taylor (eds) *Sociological Perspectives on Health, Illness and Health Care.* Oxford: Blackwell.

Blaxter, M. (2004) 'Life narratives, health and identity.' In D. Kelleher and G. Leavey (eds) *Identity and Health.* London: Routledge.

Brashers, D.E., Neidig, J.L., Cardillo, L.W., Dobbs, L.K., Russell, J.A. and Haas, S.M. (1999) '"In an important way, I did die": Uncertainty and revival in persons living with HIV or AIDS.' *AIDS Care 11*, 2, 201–219.

Bury, M. (1982) 'Chronic illness as a biographical disruption.' *Sociology of Health and Illness 4*, 2, 1451–68.

Carricaburu, D. and Pierret, J. (1995) 'From biographical disruption to biographical reinforcement: The case of HIV-positive men.' *Sociology of Health and Illness 17*, 1, 65–88.

Davies, M.L. (1997) 'Shattered assumptions: Time and the experience of long-term HIV positivity.' *Social Science and Medicine 44*, 5, 561–71.

Deeks, S.G. and Phillips, A.N. (2009) 'HIV infection, antiretroviral treatment, ageing and non-AIDS-related morbidity.' *British Medical Journal 338* (26 Jan.), a3172.

Dodds, C. (2006) 'HIV-related stigma in England: Experiences of gay men and heterosexual African migrants living with HIV.' *Journal of Community and Applied Social Psychology 16*, 6, 472–80.

Emlet, C.A. (2006) '"You are awfully old to have this disease": experiences of stigma and ageism in adults 50 years and older living with HIV/AIDS.' *The Gerontologist 46*, 6, 781–90.

Emlet, C.A., Tozay, S. and Raveis, V.H. (2010) '"I'm not going to die from AIDS": resilience in aging with HIV disease.' *The Gerontologist 51*, 1, 101–11.

Frank, A.W. (1997) 'Illness as moral occasion: restoring agency to ill people.' *Health 1*, 2, 131–148.

Gergen, K.J. and Gergen, M.M. (1988) 'Narrative and the Self as a Relationship.' In L. Berkowitz (ed.) *Advances in Experimental Social Psychology*. San Diego: Academic Press.

Giddens, A. (1991) *Modernity and Self-identity: Self and Society in the Late Modern Age*. Cambridge: Polity.

Health Protection Agency (2010) *HIV in the United Kingdom: 2010 Report*. London: Author.

Heaphy, B. and Yip, A.K.T. (2006) 'Policy implications of ageing sexualities.' *Social Policy and Society 5*, 4, 443–51.

Holstein, J.A. and Gubrium, J.F. (1995) *The Active Interview*. Thousand Oaks, CA: Sage Publications.

Myers, J.D. (2009) 'Growing old with HIV: The AIDS epidemic and an aging population.' *JAAPA 22*, 1, 20–24.

Neimeyer, R.A. (2005) 'Re-storying loss: Fostering Growth in the Posttraumatic Narrative.' In L.G. Calhoun and R.G. Tedeschi (eds) *Handbook of Posttraumatic Growth: Research and Practice*. Mawha, NJ: Lawrence Earlbaum.

Nixon, E. (2012) 'Triaging Patients Attending Unwell.' In N. Ault *et al.* (eds) *Advanced Clinical Practice in HIV Care: A NHIVNA Handbook for Nurses, Midwives and other Healthcare Practitioners*. London: Routledge.

Ong, A.D. and Bergeman, C.S. (2004) 'Resilience and adaptation to stress in later life: empirical perspectives and conceptual implications.' *Ageing International 29*, 3, 219–46.

Office for National Statistics (2005) *Focus on Older People: 2005 Full Report*. Norwich: HMSO.

Pratt, G., Gascoyne, K. and Cunningham, K. (2010) 'Human immunodeficiency virus (HIV) in older people.' *Age and Ageing 39*, 3, 289–94.

Prince, M.J. (2008) 'Claiming a Disability Benefit as Contesting Social Citizenship.' In P. Moss and K. Teghtsoonian (eds) *Contesting Illness: Processes and Practices*. Toronto: University of Toronto Press.

Robinson, W.A., Petty, M.S., Patton, C. and Kang, H. (2010) 'Ageing with HIV: Historical and Intra-community Differences in Experience of Aging with HIV.' In J.T. Sears (ed.) *Growing Older: Perspectives on LGBT Aging*. London: Routledge.

Rosenthal, G. (2004) 'Biographical Research.' In C. Seale, G. Gobo, J.F. Gubrium and D. Silverman (eds) *Qualitative Research Practice*. London: Sage Publications.

Shippy, R.A. and Karpiak S.E. (2005) 'Perceptions of support among older adults with HIV.' *Research on Aging 27*, 3, 290–306.

Siegel, K., Raveis, V. and Karus, D. (1998) 'Perceived advantages and disadvantages of age among older HIV-infected adults.' *Research on Aging 20*, 6, 686–711.

Wengraf, T. (2001) *Qualitative Research Interviewing: Biographic Narrative and Semi-Structured Method*. London: Sage Publications.

Chapter 6

Categories and Their Consequences

Understanding and Supporting the Caring Relationships of Older Lesbian, Gay and Bisexual People[1]

Ann Cronin, Richard Ward, Stephen Pugh, Andrew King and Elizabeth Price

Introduction

This chapter addresses one aspect of the lives of older lesbian, gay and bisexual (LGB) people – the reciprocal, ever-changing and carefully negotiated caring relationships in which many are involved, and the ways in which these are understood by health and social care policy makers and practitioners. Our aim is to show that through narratives of care and caring relationships practitioners are not only provided a broader biographical context in which these caring relationships unfold, but can gain an understanding of the meanings that people attach to their identities and how these identities are performed in everyday living.

At the heart of this chapter is an attempt to explore what we consider to be a primary tension involved in working with older people who belong to a minoritised group. That is, how do practitioners tailor and personalise support at an individual level while understanding and recognising the broader inequalities that particular minorities face, and the impact such inequalities may have upon their relationship with service providers?

We are particularly interested in exploring how being 'lesbian', 'gay' and 'bisexual' shapes the way practitioners respond to the needs of those older service users. The chapter presents findings from research

---

1   This chapter is an amended version of a paper that originally appeared in the journal *International Social Work* (Cronin *et al.* 2011)

that demonstrate how using biographical narrative approaches in engagement with older LGB people may enable practitioners to develop appropriate assessment and intervention strategies.

Thinking beyond sexual labels

LGB people do not simply constitute one easily defined, homogenous social group whose needs are similar by virtue of membership. We would suggest that using arbitrary labels to define, or group together, diverse populations is problematic in both practice and policy contexts, as there is a tendency to see these categories as both fixed and unchanging; and that this presupposes a similarly fixed range of health and social care 'needs'. There is a danger that 'generalities' may replace 'complexities' in the assessment of, and intervention in, LGB people's lives (Meyer 2001).

A tendency to conflate sexual minority identities into convenient groupings (e.g. 'LGB') may have little relevance in terms of people's lived experience. When we refer to LGB people as one seemingly homogenous group, we risk missing important differences that should inform practice and the development of policy. Treating groups of people as if they have unitary and fixed needs is contrary to the contemporary 'person-centred' focus of health and social care policy. It is these issues, rather than the fact that the person may identify with a particular social grouping, that may determine what their needs are in any given context.

Ward and Jones (2010) warn, however, that focusing only on individual contexts may also mean that wider social inequities are not addressed. It is, therefore, equally important to identify wider social influences that shape LGB people's experiences, particularly in the health and social care arena. While it is important to recognise diversity, it is also necessary to acknowledge the ways in which identifying as a member of a sexual minority can colour people's experiences. There are elements of LGB people's lives that serve to forge a sense of community with others – 'stigma, prejudice, legal inequality, a history of oppression, and the like' (Weeks 2000, p.183). Thus LGB people share a history of oppression that may invalidate more obvious social divisions (Coon 2003). In the context of health and social care, these social conditions are particularly telling; they impact upon access to and standards of care, including the potential for 'culturally sensitive' care and the selection of research priorities (Meyer 2001). As Eaglesham (2010) notes, however, health and social care services should not perceive LGB categories as prescriptive, rather these categories are connected in only loose ways and may, or more significantly, may not be the starting point for considering an individual's needs.

For practitioners it is important to consider individual difference, whilst acknowledging how this difference may relate to experiences of oppressive social systems for individuals. One way of doing this is to work within a paradigm which recognises that a 'caring encounter', be this in formal or informal contexts, constitutes part of a life *story* which is constructed by each individual. The following section illustrates this, drawing on the integrated findings from two qualitative studies of older LGB adults conducted by two of the authors (Cronin 2004; Cronin and King 2010, King and Cronin 2010).

Caring narratives and ageing sexualities

The first study focused on older lesbian-identified women and was exploratory in nature. The second and more recent study, funded by an inner-city local authority, investigated the experiences and needs of its older LGB residents. A total of 36 adults – 12 men and 24 women, aged between 50 and 78 years, were interviewed across the two studies. Twelve men and 13 women lived in the Southeast of England; the remaining 11 women lived in the United States (US). Data from the US interviews do not appear in this chapter. All participants identified as White, apart from one man who identified as Mixed White/Black African-Caribbean. Participants represented a range of socio-economic statuses. Twelve of the women and two of the men had been married, but were now divorced. Of these, all had children except one man and one woman. In both studies snowball sampling was used to recruit participants. Initial contact was made with individuals, relevant organisations and, in the case of the second study, organisations working specifically with older people, as well as health centres and other public organisations in our chosen location.

A narrative analysis approach was used to both collect and analyse participants' biographical stories. Writing about narrative analysis, Riessman (1994, p.114) notes that storytelling is a universal practice, which enables the teller to construct and identify significant events in their everyday lives, and in doing so link 'the past and present, self and society' as part of a story of someone's life: what has happened, what is happening and what may happen. Instead of regarding an individual account as representative of 'real life', it is posited that such an account is the outcome of a process in which people engage in 'story telling' (Plummer 1995) and in doing so produce narrative-like accounts of their lives. We will go on to consider the implications of this understanding of biographical narratives for health and social care practice shortly.

Existing research suggests that older LGB adults' experiences of caring will be shaped by the heteronormative nature of social relations (Cronin and King 2010). By this we mean that heterosexuality is often prioritised (implicitly and explicitly) in the course of everyday social interactions. Certainly care giving and receiving amongst the older LGB population differs from the general population, in relation to both gender and care practices (Kurdek 2005; MetLife 2006). Studies of caring amongst older LGB adults also highlight the importance of non-familial relationships – 'families of choice' (Weeks, Heaphy and Donovon 2001) or 'friendship families' (Dorfman et al. 1995) – and that roles of caregivers and care receivers may be fluid, interchangeable and context-dependent (Manthorpe and Price 2005; Northmore, Ball and Smith 2005).

Caring for others – parents

A number of participants told stories of caring for their parents. These stories emphasised not only how caring for parents was framed in terms of 'heteronormative' social relations, but also how these experiences had significantly impacted on their own experiences of ageing and their sexuality. Sandy, a 64-year-old lesbian, for example, explained that her relationship with her mother had been difficult for most of her adult life, largely because her mother could not accept that she was a lesbian. Sandy was now in a situation where she was expected by other members of her family to care for her mother, to the detriment of her own happiness and lifestyle:

> I feel tied by her at the moment. I do have a brother but it's all change really. His family have moved over to [country] so he's spending more and more time there so I've got sole care of my mother now really. She [her mother] lives in [town in Eastern England]. And she's in sheltered housing but she needs quite a lot of care. I have to go up there twice a month and all over Christmas because the carers aren't working... I think I've spent all my life trying to stay as free as I could and not tied down and

> I come to my old age and I'm really feeling tied down by my mother. (Sandy, 64)

Whilst Sandy's narrative made clear that she was unhappy about her current situation, others embraced the role of carer but still noted its restrictions on their lives. Peter, a 58-year-old bisexual man, had been the principle carer for his mother until her death, three years prior to the interview. Peter explained that this had impacted on his possibilities for finding a partner, both at the time and subsequently:

> Terribly selfish I know, but for years I cared for my elderly mother who was in a wheelchair and while that was going on, obviously, I couldn't have a partner so I just got out of the habit as it were. (Peter, 58)

Caring for his mother also fitted into a more general story Peter provided about care: he was a volunteer for several charities that provided support and care to people with mental health problems, and for older people with disabilities. Peter indicated that these experiences had affected his decision to care for his mother. Therefore, despite the limitations in his own life, his care practices 'made sense' within his biography and the place of care in that context.

The importance of biographical context was made especially clear by William, a 56-year-old gay man, who made regular trips to visit and care for his father, who lived some 50 miles away. Like Sandy, William explained that his siblings expected him to care for his father because he had fewer 'responsibilities' i.e., he did not have children and was not, at the time, working full-time. The stress of travelling and caring for his father had a significant impact on William's mental and physical health, particularly his HIV status. William became depressed and stopped taking his own anti-retroviral medication. He also withdrew from his wider network of friends and stopped participating in the gay community, something that William regarded as central to his identity. The turning point in William's story was the deterioration of his father's health to a point where he was admitted to residential care. This enabled William to 'get back to [his] old life' and reconstruct his sense of self. While we recognise that many of these issues are not specific to older LGB adults, they have to fit their experiences into biographies that are shaped by a heteronormative framework. This is particularly evident in the way in which some of our participants talked about their concerns about receiving care, either in their own homes or in residential settings.

Receiving care

George was a 74-year-old gay man who led a very active life. When asked about the possibility of receiving care at home, he reflected the concerns of many of our participants in that, while he did not relish the thought, he had accepted it with a degree of inevitability:

> It's a thought that would scare me; I don't like the idea of other people visiting where I live... I think the thought is something I wouldn't be happy with but on the other hand, if it had to happen, I think I'd probably be very philosophical about it. I wouldn't like it. (George, 74)

Peter (introduced earlier), who had experience of caring for others, emphasised how thoughts about receiving care are framed in a biographical context that acknowledges culturally dominant understandings of sexuality:

> Hopefully, I will just be a client to any professional carers, as far as they're concerned, when it happens. I am just a person who needed care regardless of my sexuality. (Peter, 58)

A particular concern for some of our participants related to a fear that receiving care, either in the community or in a residential setting, would result in their having to go 'back into the closet' as they grew older. For example, Donna, who talked about the possibility of ending up in residential care, voiced concerns about being unable to maintain friendships with other gay adults or to maintain a relationship with a partner. This, coupled with generalised feelings of social isolation due to having either little in common with residents or a fear of hostility from others, made the prospect of ending up in residential care a very bleak one:

> What happens if you need assisted living or long-term care? Unless you're in a lesbian or lesbian–gay centre, you're stuck with listening to other hets talk about their spouse – dead or alive – and their lives together, but you cannot do the same with a feeling of safety and without a fear of repercussion (such as being totally shunned, which would be a horror, since you're stuck there and have no other options). Worse yet, if you were lucky enough to room with your partner in an assisted living centre there would be NO privacy such as the het partners have

and that part of your life would be regulated. In other words, NO SEX LIFE!!! (Donna, 65)

Previous studies (e.g. Fannin *et al.* 2008) have suggested that one coping strategy adopted by LGB people is to desexualise their home environment. Several of our participants made reference to this, particularly with regard to certain signifiers of sexuality such as magazines and 'smutty fridge magnets' (William, 56). William held a strong sense of belonging to the LGB community, and suggested that becoming housebound could have a significant effect on his self-identity, in terms of becoming isolated from the gay community. He suggested that having a gay carer could be beneficial here:

> Even someone to come round and have a camp chat. [...]I don't know that you could specify when you need someone to come round that it would be a gay man rather than anybody else, or whether you should even be able to, but actually that's probably one of the things that would be missing from your life if you are in your own home and can't get out, you know, gay company. (William, 56)

Indeed, this raises interesting questions about the personalisation agenda that is currently being promoted by the Department of Health in England and similar departments in other parts of the UK, and the importance of tailoring services to the needs of individuals rather than a general model of care. It suggests that taking narratives of ageing and sexuality into account could have significant policy implications.

Untold stories: Making sexuality visible in health and social care practice with older people

In this section we turn to consider how caring narratives, such as those outlined above, might be used to enhance health and social care practice with older LGB service users. We outline why a focus upon such narratives or stories, rather than an orientation toward categories of identity, might better support practitioners to respond appropriately to the needs of older LGB people. Our argument here is that narrative or story work has particular benefits and significance to policy, research and practice.

In advocating the use of biographical narratives in health and social care practice, we do so from a critical perspective on how sexuality is currently made visible in work with older people. For instance, in dementia care sexuality is considered largely under the banner of 'behaviour' (and not as an identity), consequently any form of sexual expression by the person with dementia is treated as problematic in care settings (Ward *et al.* 2005). There are no spaces within dementia care for sexuality to be expressed positively, let alone embraced as a viable social identity, and this has specific implications for LGB service users who may be ostracised and vilified (Archibald 2006) and for carers who find their support needs poorly met (Price 2008; Ward 2000). Using biographical narratives means taking into account the 'social worlds' of older LGB service users and, in the case of caring relationships, shows how such stories provide a context in which ageing sexualities are expressed and practised. Such narratives can support a shift away from treating service users' sexuality as an 'already-given' where they 'come packaged as fixed types' (Hicks 2008).

In a helpful review of narrative approaches in social work, Riessman and Quinney (2005) note there is a dearth of published accounts of their use by practitioners. This is especially so in relation to working with older LGB service users (Cronin and King 2010). Nonetheless, the benefits of taking into account biographical contexts when working with older LGB individuals are supported by existing literature in health and social care. For instance, Pugh (2005) highlights the importance of understanding past experiences in the way older LGB individuals negotiate access to care services and their fear arising from the role played by the state in policing homosexuality throughout much of the last century. Similarly, Bayliss (2000) has argued that life story work with older lesbians supports an understanding of a life history of oppression. Quam (1997) recommends using case studies drawn from biographical material in order to raise awareness with practitioners and share good practice, while Jones (2009) has developed fictional narratives of bisexual characters in order to support a better understanding of the fluid nature of bisexual identities over time. We would add that eliciting narratives from older LGB service users promotes an understanding of their lives and identities, and shows how different constraints and life events are responded to, often very creatively within caring relationships, supporting a 'strengths-based' model of assessment.

Incorporating caring narratives into social work practice

There is no formula for how or when to elicit and incorporate biographical narratives in practice. The value of narrative approaches lies in their flexibility and adaptability. We argue that there are potential benefits not only to service users but to practitioners working with older LGB people, given that their lives and personal histories have often been hidden and hence practitioners have limited prior understanding upon which to draw.

Nonetheless, it is important to take a critical stance on biographical approaches, recognising their limitations as well as appreciating how context and situation can influence their use. For instance, Hicks (2008) argues that sexuality should be considered not so much as a personal attribute but more like a 'discursive production' (a form of self-presentation). Furthermore, practitioners should be mindful of ways in which certain social and story-telling conventions may shape the way biographical information is told. For example, the 'coming out narrative' is one discursive formula that may in fact constrain the telling of an individual's experience. However, it should not be assumed that service users will be able to articulate their view of their own identity in a coherent fashion. Indeed, Hicks (2008) further cautions practitioners (in this case social workers) to critically examine the 'accounts' they construct of the stories told to them, avoiding heteronormative judgements as they draw upon biographical material in their practice.

Often, it is the case that the practitioner gains biographical insights and accumulates information over time in an informal way. There is an inherent danger here that such insights may be lost due to staff turnover or when service users transfer from one service to another. A more structured approach to gathering narratives may help avoid this and, at the same time, provide greater control for the service user concerned in terms of the type and level of knowledge that is recorded and shared. For instance, practitioners may choose to use life story work as an intervention that captures biographical detail before it becomes less accessible – this may be particularly useful in working with people in the early stages of dementia. In other contexts, biographical narratives may be used to support collaborative working with service users, providing a context that helps tailor support in a person-centred fashion. Furthermore, jointly elicited narratives may offer a better understanding of the interdependent nature of some caring relationships among older LGB caring dyads (Cronin and King 2010).

There will be situations in which working with biographical narratives is less appropriate. For instance, in her discussion of practice issues in dementia care, Mackenzie (2009) argues that biographical work can 'feel intimidating (for LGB couples) as it exposes details of loving relationships which may have been concealed for many years' (p.19). The author's advice is to ensure that the individuals or couple concerned are given the lead in constructing their autobiographies, maintaining control over the level of detail shared.

Using narratives of care in practice allows us to ask how both sexual and age-related identities operate in particular 'theatres of life' (Gubrium 2005). It is important that we do not fall back upon assumptions that identity categories or labels influence the lives and relationships of older LGB people in ways that are stable, cutting across all domains of everyday living. Eliciting biographical narratives helps us to understand what it means to be older and gay, lesbian, or bisexual, and that these identities have differing implications for different areas of day-to-day living. Narratives underline the inadequacy of identity categories as organising 'tools' for health and social care practice. It is our view that using biographical narratives with older LGB service users is an important addition to the 'portfolio' of relationship-based approaches available to practitioners. Ultimately they promote personalised and person-centred forms of practice, but need to be approached in ways that help to address, rather than downplay, the broader social and historical context of inequality and oppression.

Conclusion

In this chapter we have problematised the way in which categories of identity can shape health and social care practice and prove unhelpful to service users. For older LGB people accessing welfare services there is a danger that they will be amalgamated into a catch-all sexual category that does little to acknowledge their personal biographies and life experiences, even when such practices are well-meaning and claim to be 'LGBT-friendly'. Indeed, there is currently little recognition of the fact that some users prefer not to be categorised at all. We have also attempted to show that 'person-centred' approaches can sometimes be inadequate in terms of grasping the broader social and historical context of inequality and oppression that many older LGB people have collectively experienced.

For those working with older LGB people receiving or providing care in various contexts, we suggest a model for practice that takes LGB people's lived experience as a starting point for assessment and intervention. The narrative approach we propose stems from an appreciation of the importance of biography and life experience, which enables the service user and practitioner to engage with each other from a perspective that acknowledges and respects cultural, historical and social contexts as well as the personal contexts of individual lives. In so doing, the variety of older LGB people's lives may be appreciated and acknowledged for what they are – unique and individual. We would argue that engaging with service users in this way generates a true expression of the concept of 'personalisation' and 'person-centred' practice in health and social care.

References

Archibald, C. (2006) 'Gay and lesbian issues: Learning on the (research) job.' *Journal of Dementia Care 14*, 4, 21.

Bayliss, K. (2000) 'Social work values, anti-discriminatory practice and working with older lesbian service users.' *Social Work Education 19*,1, 45–53.

Coon, D. W. (2003) *Lesbian, Gay, Bisexual and Transgender (LGBT) Issues and Family Caregiving.* San Francisco, CA: Family Caregiver Alliance. National Center on Caregiving.

Cronin, A. (2004) 'Sexuality in Gerontology: A Heteronormative Presence, a Queer Absence.' In S.O. Daatland and S. Biggs (eds) *Ageing and Diversity: Multiple Pathways and Cultural Migrations.* Bristol: Policy Press.

Cronin, A. and King, A. (2010) 'A Queer Kind of Care: Some Preliminary Notes and Observations.' In R. Jones and R. Ward (eds) *LGBT Issues: Looking Beyond Categories.* Edinburgh: Dunedin.

Cronin, A., Ward, R., Pugh, S., King, A. and Price, E. (2011) 'Categories and their consequences: Understanding and supporting the caring relationships of older lesbian, gay and bisexual people.' *International Social Work 54*, 3, 421–435.

Dorfman, R., Walters, K., Burke, P., and Hardin L. (1995) 'Old, sad and alone: The Myth of the ageing homosexual.' *Journal of Gerontological Social Work 24*, 1-2, 29-44.

Eaglesham, P. (2010) 'The Policy Maze and LGBT Issues: Does One Size Fit All?' In R.L. Jones and R. Ward (eds) *LGBT Issues: Looking Beyond Categories.* Edinburgh: Dunedin.

Fannin, A., Fenge, L.A., Hicks, T., Lavin, N. and Brown, K. (2008) *Social Work Practice for Older Lesbians and Gay Men.* Exeter: Learning Matters.

Gubrium, J. F. (2005) 'The Social Worlds of Old Age.' In M. Johnson (ed.) *The Cambridge Handbook of Age and Ageing.* Cambridge: Cambridge University Press.

Hicks, S. (2008) 'Thinking through sexuality.' *Journal of Social Work 8*, 1, 65–82.

Jones, R.L. (2009) 'Troubles with Bisexuality in Health and Social Care.' In R.L. Jones and R. Ward (eds) *LGBT Issues: Looking Beyond Categories.* Edinburgh: Dunedin.

King, A. and Cronin, A. (2010) 'Queer Methods and Queer Practices: Re-examining the Identities of Older Lesbian, Gay, Bisexual (OLGB) Adults.' In K. Browne and C. Nash (eds) *Queer Methodologies in Social and Cultural Research*. Aldershot: Ashgate.

Kurdek, L. (2005) 'What do we know about lesbian and gay couples?' *Current Directions in Psychological Science 14*, 5, 251–254.

Mackenzie, J. (2009) 'The same but different: Working with lesbian and gay people with dementia.' *Journal of Dementia Care 17*, 6, 17–19.

Manthorpe, J. and Price, E. (2005) 'Lesbian carers: Personal issues and policy response.' *Social Policy and Society 5*, 1, 15–26.

MetLife (2006) *Out and Aging: The MetLife Study of Lesbian and Gay Baby Boomers*. Westport, CT.: MetLife Mature Market Institute. Available from URL www.asaging.org/networks/lgain/OutandAging.pdf. Accessed on 4 February 2008.

Meyer, I.H. (2001) 'Why lesbian, gay, bisexual and transgender public health?' *American Journal of Public Health 9*, 16, 856–859.

Northmore, S., Ball, S. and Smith, A. (2005) 'Multiple identities in older age: A re-examination.' Paper presented at the 2005 National Council for Voluntary Organisations 11th 'Researching the Voluntary Sector' Conference, University of Warwick, 31 August to 1 September 2005.

Plummer, K. (1995) *Telling Sexual Stories*. London: Routledge.

Price, E. (2008) 'Pride or prejudice? Gay men, lesbians and dementia.' *British Journal of Social Work 38*, 7, 1337–52.

Pugh, S. (2005) 'Assessing the cultural needs of older lesbians and gay men: implications for practice.' *Practice 17*, 3, 207–218.

Quam, J.K. (ed.) (1997) *Social Services for Senior Gay Men and Lesbians*. New York: Haworth Press.

Riessman, C.K. (1994) *Narrative Analysis*. London: Sage Publications.

Riessman, C.K. and Quinney, L. (2005) 'Narrative in social work: A critical review.' *Qualitative Social Work 4*, 4, 391–412.

Ward, R. (2000) 'Waiting to be heard: Dementia and the gay community.' *Journal of Dementia Care 8*, 3, 24–25.

Ward, R. and Jones R.L. (2010) 'Introduction.' In R.L. Jones and R. Ward (eds) *LGBT Issues: Looking Beyond Categories*. Edinburgh: Dunedin.

Ward, R., Vass, A.A., Aggarwal, N., Garfield, C. and Cybyk, B. (2005) 'A kiss is still a kiss? The construction of sexuality in dementia care.' *Dementia 4*, 1, 49–72.

Weeks, J. (2000) *Making Sexual History*. Cambridge: Polity Press.

Weeks, J., Heaphy, B. and Donovan, C. (2001) *Same-sex Intimacies: Families of Choice and Other Life Experiments*. London: Routledge.

Chapter 7

Care Near the End of Life

The Concerns, Needs, and Experiences of LGBT Elders

Gary L. Stein and Kathryn Almack

Introduction and background

LGBT individuals have often been invisible in elder care, services, and research, leading to major gaps in knowledge about end-of-life care issues for older lesbian, gay, bisexual and trans[1] people (hereafter referred to as "LGBT elders"). While LGBT and heterosexual elders share the normative psychosocial and physical aspects of ageing and end-of-life care, LGBT elders have the added dimension of social vulnerability and anxiety related to status as a sexual minority. "Many have experienced a lifetime of marginalization at best, and abuse and rejection at worst" (Stein, Beckerman and Sherman 2010, p.423). For example, LGBT elders may be reluctant to disclose their sexual orientation because of fears of discrimination. Trans people may have particular needs regarding privacy or may encounter difficulties in living (and thus dying) in their preferred gender, because of risks to their family relationships. This chapter examines leading studies and reports from the UK and the US that address end-of-life issues facing the LGBT community.

Most significantly, the HIV/AIDS epidemic has had a profound impact on the LGBT community in dealing with and thinking about life-threatening illness. Over the past 30 years, the community has faced relatively high numbers of HIV-related illnesses and deaths, and has served as family caregivers and providers to the ill. As a result of more effective, life-extending treatments for HIV/AIDS, an increasing number of older adults have the disease—almost 25 percent of HIV/

---

1   In the UK, 'trans' is the preferred term within trans communities to describe anyone who is intending to have, is having or has undergone gender reassignment treatments or has a cross-gender identity.

AIDS cases in the US are among adults age 50 and over (National Institute on Aging 2009). Many of these individuals will require elder care services, including palliative and end-of-life care.

Data from a survey of 800 non-heterosexual cancer patients in the UK highlight concerns about respect and dignity (Department of Health 2010). Research suggests that LGBT people may receive suboptimal care at end of life due to assumed heterosexuality, lack of provider awareness and homophobia, and gaps in knowledge (Almack 2007; Seymour and Bellamy 2010; Stein *et al.* 2010; Higgins and Glacken 2009; Green and Grant 2008; Röndahl, Innala and Carlsson 2006; Stein and Bonuck 2001a, 2001b). At a policy level, commissioned work has highlighted needs and concerns, including gaps in evidence.

Examples from the UK include:

- An NHS guide highlighting the specific needs of trans people in planning for end of life, including bereavement (Whittle and Turner 2007).

- A Welsh Assembly commissioned literature review (Davies *et al.* 2006), which reported discrimination and subsequent impact on services for LGBT people.

- The English End of Life Care Strategy Equality Impact Assessment (DoH 2008) noted a dearth of evidence but concluded from consultations with LGBT groups that in terms of quality of end-of-life care, LGBT people were *most* at risk of discrimination.

In the US, examples include:

- *Still Out, Still Aging: The MetLife Study of Lesbian, Gay, Bisexual, and Transgender Baby Boomers* (MetLife Mature Market Institute 2010), which surveyed the concerns and experiences of 45–64-year-old individuals on issues related to aging, retirement, caregiving, and healthcare.

- Comprehensive analysis and recommendations in reports of the National Gay and Lesbian Task Force Policy Institute (Grant 2009), and the LGBT Movement Advancement Project and SAGE (2010), which document discrimination against LGBT elders in access to health services, financial benefits, housing, and other services.

- A 2011 report of the Institute of Medicine of The National Academies calling for more data and research on the health needs of LGBT populations of all ages.

LGBT elders have experienced prejudice, discrimination, and past criminalization of their sexual activities (Heaphy, Yip and Thompson 2003; LGBT Movement Advancement Project and SAGE 2010). Past experiences have an impact on current attitudes towards healthcare and social services (MetLife Mature Market Institute 2006; Pugh 2005; Stein and Bonuck 2001b), which can have consequences for end-of-life care. For example, LGBT elders may be hesitant to disclose their sexual orientation, thereby diminishing the possibilities of receiving care that acknowledges and respects their sexual orientation and families of choice. In addition, their needs may be exacerbated by later life vulnerabilities such as ill-health, a partner near the end of life, or fragility (Almack *et al.* 2010). Evidence suggests that LGBT elders are more likely to live alone in old age, with fewer links with younger generations, thereby increasing their risk of isolation (Adelman, Gurevitch, de Vries and Blando 2006; Brookdale Center on Aging 1999; Heaphy *et al.* 2003; New York City Department of Health and Mental Hygiene 2008). Therefore, they are likely to require formal sources of care and support, yet may be more hesitant to approach healthcare and social services.

Beyond similarities linked to sexual orientation, individual biographies may uncover a multitude of needs, concerns and experiences (Cronin *et al.* 2011) that impact on end-of-life care. Some will have been married and have had children. Some may not identify with or wish to use labels such as "lesbian," "gay," "bisexual," or "trans." Examining the LGBT community by other demographic and cultural factors, such as race, religion, ethnicity, and disability, may reveal further diversity. Although the commonly used acronym "LGBT" includes bisexual and transgendered people, there is a particular dearth of literature that meaningfully explores end-of-life issues for these groups.

Emerging concerns
1. Disclosure of sexual orientation
Many LGBT elders, by necessity, lived "closeted" lives. Unlike many of today's "baby boom" generation and young adults who are comfortable being open about their sexual orientation, older LGBT people grew up at a time when coming out resulted in serious negative repercussions. Those who came out often faced job discrimination, family disapproval, psychiatric interventions, criminalization, and various other forms of bigotry. As a result, most were open about being gay with only their most

trusted family members, friends, and colleagues. Some married members of the opposite sex and had children through these relationships (LGBT Movement Advancement Project and SAGE 2010).

Many LGBT elders fail to disclose their sexual orientation due to fears of negative or discriminatory reactions from their providers. In Stein and Bonuck's (2001b) New York metropolitan area survey of 575 respondents,[2] most (of all ages) report that disclosure is essential to their healthcare—"to increase honesty and improve understanding," because "health care is better if the provider knows," and "to avoid unnecessary questions and procedures." Seventy percent (70%) of respondents disclosed their sexual orientation, even though they report that less than a third of physicians (28%) inquired about their orientation. Among the 30 percent who failed to disclose, many (47%) worried about negative reactions or bad treatment (Stein and Bonuck 2001b). Other studies found comparable rates of disclosure (Eliason and Schope 2001; Klitzman and Greenberg 2002).

Provider-initiated discussions are necessary to address barriers to disclosing sexual orientation and to relieve patients of the burden of bringing up these topics themselves. Yet questions regarding sexual orientation are not commonly asked during intake or the delivery of services in most healthcare facilities, as noted by one participant:

> **Molly:** In the carers' assessment form, there was nothing about sexuality at all, not even a choice of whether you want to say or not—and that's the same through the whole assessment. It makes you feel invisible. (Study 1)[3]

As one gets older, and particularly in end-of-life care settings, the likelihood of requiring more contact with health and social care services increases, which in turn can make it more difficult to conceal living arrangements and personal circumstances. LGBT elders may have particular fears about heterosexism and homophobia:

> **Mark:** I have to think very carefully about the possible repercussions when I let each doctor know, because I have been discriminated against and worse. (Study 2)

---

2   Stein and Bonuck's 2001 analysis included lesbians, gay men, and bisexual individuals; transgendered individuals were excluded from the analysis due to very small numbers.

3   Pseudonyms are used throughout for focus group participants and for people they refer to in the quotes. Quotes are from both authors' published studies – Study 1: Almack, Seymour and Bellamy 2010; Study 2: Stein, Beckerman and Sherman 2010.

Eileen: People don't come in with an open mind, they come in with assumptions. We've got a friend who has to think twice if somebody's coming in, like the cleaner or a carer, of putting away the photographs with her and her partner in a lovely embrace or something like that. (Study 1)

2. Familial and support networks

Research in end-of-life care is primarily focused on family relationships, with an emphasis placed on the importance of family support and care, coupled with a predisposition towards families constructed by marriage and blood ties (Manthorpe 2003). Sexual orientation can influence the social supports available to individuals at the end of life. LGBT elders may have experienced little support from families of origin, or even hostility and rejection, leading some to rely on alternative networks for support. This indicates a need to examine other important social relationships in end-of-life practice. Young, Seale and Bury (1998) note, for example, the wider neglect of the role of friendship and informal social networks. LGBT research has described alternative LGBT networks, often referred to as "families of choice" (Weeks, Heaphy and Donovan 2001; Weston 1997, first published 1991). Exploratory data suggests a complex picture where networks of LGBT elders are a diverse mix of families of origin and families of choice, including biological and social ties.

Eileen relates how, due to ongoing health problems and frequent falls, she moved from a large city to a town on the other side of the country to be near two long-standing friends—her ex-partner Sue and Sue's current partner. Her story encapsulates the notion of "families of choice":

I had a partner, Sue, for 15 years, that was 17 years ago, but she's my best friend, her partner too. I've no other family, they are my family and they sorted out my moving so I was closer to them. They both look after me if I have to go into hospital, they do everything for me, she tells me off, leaves me notes on the wall. Sue even calls me "sis" sometimes. (Study 1)

It is not uncommon in LGB narratives for families of choice to include ex-partners and the current partners of ex-partners, as in Eileen's case. Eileen reports how Sue calls her "sis" sometimes; elsewhere she says, "we are like sisters," providing a reference to the "family-like" bond of these relationships.

> **Richard:** Since my late partner died, his family has been absolutely fantastic in terms of providing ongoing support and so on. So I've become very conscious of those bonds and certainly I do consider them family in every sense of the word. We haven't got a word for those relationships, have we? (Study 1)

Richard has been bereaved, but he has strong ongoing relationships with the family of origin of his deceased partner. This account provides insight into new and complex understandings of personal networks that challenge the traditional meanings of family involving blood or marital relationships. Some of these configurations are so new that language fails to include them. For example, Richard went on to express the difficulty in knowing how to refer to his late partner's daughter and her children in a way that conveys the importance and closeness of those relationships. This illustrates the need for healthcare and social services professionals to listen to stories to gain a whole picture of who are important in their patients' and clients' lives.

BEREAVEMENT

Being unable to disclose one's sexual orientation or having limited support networks can have a profound impact during times of bereavement. The full strength and importance of relationships which may fall under the "umbrella" term of friendships may not be recognized, which can lead to disenfranchisement occurring prior to and after the death of a partner or close friend. This concept was initially developed by Doka (1989), who defines disenfranchised grief as: "the grief that persons experience when they incur a loss that is not or cannot be openly acknowledged, publicly mourned or socially supported" (p.4).

Those involved in non-traditional relationships may be excluded in a number of ways, such as not being able to have an active role in the care of the dying, or by not having their grief acknowledged (Walter 1999). For example, Jeremy discussed how he and his partner (David) had not disclosed their relationship to anyone. When David died, his family made the funeral arrangements in which Jeremy had no say:

> I knew he wanted burial and he wanted to be buried next to his mother. He ended up being cremated the other side of (city) and cremation was totally against his religion... I couldn't stop them

but it was like strangers organising his funeral; I was his family… But he never wanted it to be known that he was gay. (Study 1)

Another participant recalled a friend who did not get compassionate leave when his partner died, and very little recognition of his loss other than from close friends:

Michael: I went to his funeral and the family were none too happy with the situation, I don't think they wanted people knowing their son, brother was gay. And my friend who was grieving, he's been with his partner for years, he never got a mention from the vicar, not one. (Study 1)

These accounts provide examples of disenfranchisement: the exclusion of one group or person by another group or person, such that their relationship with the deceased and their grief goes unrecognized. Even for LGBT elders who have been open about their relationships, the strength of their relationships may not always be recognized and therefore a person may not be supported through bereavement.

3. Advance care planning and surrogate decision-making

Events of the past three decades have highlighted the special significance surrogate or proxy decision-making policies and practices have for the LGBT community. In a landmark legal case, Karen Thompson fought for legal guardianship of her partner Sharon Kowalski, who was severely brain damaged and quadriplegic following a 1983 car accident. Although the women had a long-term, committed relationship, Ms. Kowalski's father was appointed as her guardian, and both of her parents excluded Ms. Thompson from visitation and decision-making. Ms. Thompson engaged in an ultimately successful seven-year battle in the Minnesota courts and the media to gain guardianship rights for her partner (Lewin 1991).

As this case was making its way through the legal process, some gay men discovered they had no legal rights to visit or make healthcare decisions for their incapacitated partners with HIV/AIDS (Levine 1990). Following their partners' deaths, many men also faced challenges from their deceased partners' families in burying their partners or inheriting their estates. William Rubenstein of the American Civil Liberties Union stated, the "[Thompson-Kowalski] case, and AIDS, have been the defining events...in this area. [They've] underscored why we need legal protection, and created a terrific incentive to fight for these kinds of marital rights and recognition of domestic partnership" (Lewin 1991).

Community advocacy for partnership and marital rights during the 1990s led to social recognition of lesbian and gay relationships during the 2000s. There are large discrepancies across the US in the level of legal recognition for same-sex relationships. As of July 2011, six states and the District of Columbia allow gay couples to marry, and nine states offer civil unions or broad domestic partnerships (Lambda Legal 2011). Equally important for surrogate decision-making, 29 states in the US have constitutional amendments defining marriage as being between a man and a woman, and 12 states have laws banning recognition of same-sex marriage (Schwartz 2011). In the UK, the Civil Partnership Act of 2004 became effective in December 2005 and provides same-sex couples with the rights and responsibilities identical to civil marriage. Internationally, same-sex marriage is allowed in ten countries, including Canada, the Netherlands, Spain, Sweden, and South Africa (Fastenberg 2010). Many other countries provide for unions that grant same-sex couples all the legal rights of marriage without allowing use of the name.

In jurisdictions where same-sex marriages, unions, or partnerships are legal, partners are usually treated as spouses for surrogate decision-making, and thereby are assumed to be decision-makers for their incapacitated spouses/partners (Murphy 2011). In the majority of states in the US that do not legally recognize same-sex relationships, it is critical that coupled individuals appoint their partners or other trusted individuals to serve as their healthcare proxy. If they fail to do so, partners may have no legal rights to make medical decisions and visit their partners in intensive care, no matter how long their relationship (Castillo et al. 2011; Murphy 2011). And for same-sex couples living in the UK, as well as in those states that provide legal recognition for same-sex relationships, it remains important to protect one's rights in complex health systems through advance care planning, especially (in the US) when travelling in less gay-affirming locales.

Advance care planning is vital to assure that one's preferences, values, and interests are protected when one lacks capacity to make medical decisions. Furthermore, using legal means to document one's preferences and wishes at the end of life may be particularly important for LGBT individuals where recognition of caregivers may be contested by healthcare professionals or families of origin. In the

US, such planning is formalized through durable powers of attorney for healthcare (or healthcare proxies) to appoint someone to make medical decisions in times of incapacity, and through living wills to specify one's wishes regarding life-sustaining treatments in the event of a terminal condition or permanent unconsciousness (Sabatino 2010). In the UK, under the terms of the Mental Capacity Act 2005, formalized outcomes of advance care planning might include one or more of the following:

- advance statements of preferences and values to better inform subsequent medical decisions made by others during times of incapacity
- advance decisions to refuse treatment that are legally binding if valid and applicable to the circumstances at hand
- appointment of Lasting Powers of Attorney ("health and welfare" and/or "property and affairs"). (NEOLCP 2011; General Medical Council 2010).

Stein and Bonuck's (2001a) New York survey examined community knowledge, document completion rates, and provider discussions regarding advance care planning. Overall, most respondents were knowledgeable about appointing healthcare proxies (72%) and living wills (90%), but were much less likely to complete them (healthcare proxy, 42%; living will, 38%). Most (77%) reported that their providers had never asked who should make medical decisions if they were unable to do so themselves. Unsurprisingly, people over 60 years of age were much more likely to know about and execute advance directives than their younger cohorts (Stein and Bonuck 2001a).

4. Long-term care

Little is known about the experiences and concerns of LGBT elders living in residential care facilities. Although LGBT elders have certainly been residents of facilities such as skilled nursing homes and assisted living, community members are generally unknown to staff and other residents. "This may result in failure to receive adequate services; unaddressed needs for emotional, social, and cultural support; failure to acknowledge and respect partners and close friends; and isolation from the wider residential community and other social support networks" (Stein et al. 2010, p.422). Unfortunately, institutions rarely attempt to identify gay elders, staff members may not be trained to serve the community, and other residents may be ill-prepared for LGBT roommates or acquaintances.

In a 2005 Washington State study of gay men and lesbians of all ages, 73 percent of respondents believed that discrimination occurred in "retirement care" facilities, and one-third (34%) would "go into the closet" if they entered such a program (Johnson *et al.* 2005). Stein *et al.* (2010) conducted focus groups with LGBT elders living in the community, as well as with gay men living in residential care, regarding their thoughts, concerns, and experiences about being a gay senior in residential settings, their comfort level regarding residential care, and how providers could be more responsive to the community. Participants at both settings expressed the universal challenges of aging, such as loss of hearing, physical frailty, chronic illness and debilitation, and increased dependency. In addition, elders living in the community expressed fears about being openly gay in long-term care, being abused or neglected by healthcare professionals and aides, and not receiving equal or safe treatment.

> **Sam:** There's no reason to feel I'll be treated with respect after a lifetime of being mistreated. (Study 2)

> **Paul:** I'm afraid to have a stranger in my home, someone who may be very anti-gay, and then what if they find out about my life and now they're in my home regularly, and could somehow take advantage or mistreat me? (Study 2)

These findings are also reflected in UK research. A study into the needs, wants, fears, and aspirations of older lesbians and gay men found that when thinking about residential and nursing care, the greatest number, 38.5 percent, wanted gay-friendly homes, and over three-quarters wanted their sexuality to be taken into account (Help and Care Development 2006). However, some were concerned that gay exclusivity would be counterproductive:

> Although exclusively gay care sounds appealing, it is not a good thing in that it isolates older gay people from the community rather than integrating them into a society where homophobia is not tolerated. (Help and Care Development 2006, p.29)

Other comments showed that people felt strongly about being accepted by gay or gay-friendly carers in their own homes:

> My main concern would be that my carer would understand and respect my sexuality. (Help and Care Development 2006, p.29)

Residents in long-term care talked about experiences shared by all: staff not talking directly to them; loss of energy; fear of not receiving care; and staff determining mealtime socialization patterns and other activities. They also expressed many challenges of being gay men in long-term care, voicing fear of being neglected or abused because of their sexual orientation. Already feeling physically vulnerable and separated from their emotional supports, they reported feeling at higher risk for maltreatment and ostracism from healthcare providers, as well as from other nursing home residents. They expressed three major concerns: the fear that one's sexual orientation would result in less than equal care; the fear of having to deal with roommates or others who disliked gay people ("bullies from the past"); and the fear of having to be careful not to offend others for being gay and so "hiding their lives."

> **Max:** I'm sure I am safer if nobody knows that I lived with my life partner for 40 years. It would only make matters worse for me if others knew, and so I can't speak about my life at all, can I? (Study 2)

Again, similar themes emerged from UK research. One participant talking about his concerns about going into a care home said:

> **Eric:** These things take generations to disappear... The discrimination will come from your peer group in there who'll say, "Well, he's a poofter."... You might be in there with people your age whose opinions haven't shifted. (Study 1)

Regarding health providers, residents made distinctions between physicians and nursing care. There appears to be less anxiety about anti-gay physicians, and more anxiety about daily physical care and assistance with activities of daily life. They feared there was more anti-gay bias among those they needed the most help from to get through the day safely:

> **John:** It's a terrible feeling to be dependent, and needing their help to get to the bathroom, and being afraid they would be unkind if they knew. (Study 2)

Moreover, gay residents voiced many psychosocial concerns, including loneliness, isolation, and loss. They worried they would be at risk for discussing their lives, their partners, and their grief following their partners' deaths. On the other hand, some participants in Almack *et al.*'s (2010) study had had a more positive experience in reality:

> **Andrew:** When I was caring for my partner, when he had to go into a care home we decided that right at the very start we would be out; and that was a very brave decision for [my partner] because he hadn't come out before. And actually I couldn't fault the place; they got it right. (Study 1)

However, while anticipatory fears and concerns will not always be carried through into actual reality, they are, nevertheless, real concerns that providers must address.

LGBT elders had suggestions for improving residential care. First, facilities could be made more "gay-friendly." Such programs would have staff who don't assume that residents are heterosexual, and who treat them with "respect," "dignity," and "non-judgmentally." One gay elder noted the importance of "cultural visibility—photos, books and art which are crucial to identity, and therefore self-esteem" (Help and Care Development 2006, p.29). Second, staff would be trained to promote respect and acceptance, and to support intimate relationships. Finally, living arrangements and services could be redesigned. Although residents preferred not to live in a "gay ghetto," most would feel safer on a separate floor for gay residents. They desired the option to share a room with their partners. And they preferred having gay or gay-friendly health providers, in addition to gay bereavement and support groups (Stein *et al.* 2010).

Model training programmes are available to address these concerns. Projects such as "No Need to Fear, No Need to Hide," created by SAGE and the Brookdale Center for Aging in New York (2004); "Project Visibility," created by the Boulder County, Colorado Aging Services (2006); and "Opening Doors," created by Age Concern England (now AgeUK) in London (2001) offer guidance and principles of good practice for staff working with older LGBT people, including how to develop an inclusive organization into a lesbian- and gay-affirming one through specific or adapted services, training, and consultation. Furthermore, in the US, several communities have developed senior housing specifically for LGBT elders in an effort to address their unique psychosocial needs.

Koskovich (2009) found eight LGBT-targeted housing communities in existence, and an additional 20 in various planning stages. Unfortunately, there are few comparable options for LGBT-specific care in most areas of the UK and the US. Most LGBT elders requiring long-term care will rely on mainstream providers. Given the concerns voiced above, there is an immense need for services, institutional policies, and staff training informed by community perspectives (Stein *et al.* 2010).

5. Issues for trans people

Trans people may identify as heterosexual or LGB in their preferred gender. Many will have issues in common with LGB people, as addressed in the previous sections. However, there are additional complexities to address and there is still a great deal of hostility, prejudice and ignorance of trans issues in our society:

> Little is known about what life and health will be like for trans people in later life. We are only now seeing the first generation of trans people who have taken hormone therapy for 30 years or more, and who are living with gender reassignment surgeries performed using the very different techniques of the 1960s and 1970s. (AgeUK 2010, p.12)

In the UK, the Gender Recognition Act 2004 provides recognition of a person's acquired gender for all legal purposes (there is no equivalent federal law in the US). Surgery or any other gender reassignment treatment (hormone therapy, for example) is not a prerequisite for a person to obtain a gender recognition certificate. This has implications for the delivery of health and social care at the end of life and through to death and bereavement for older trans people. For example, there will be concerns about bodily care and being treated with dignity—as noted by an NHS guide on bereavement:

> In plain terms, health and social care professionals as well as coroners, pathologists, mortuary staff and undertakers will now be in contact with deceased who are legally men without penises and with a vagina and some people who are legally women with penises. (Whittle and Turner 2007, p.9)

The Gender Recognition Act also safeguards trans people's right to privacy. Anyone who acquires knowledge in their professional capacity of a trans person's history must keep the information totally confidential, unless they have explicit permission from the trans person to pass on information. The only exception is when a trans person is unable to give consent and disclosure to a colleague may be required for medical purposes. This underlines the importance of advance care planning, as discussed in a previous section.

The importance for a trans person to write down preferences and wishes in the event of becoming confused or losing capacity in old age extends beyond issues of privacy. Trans people may have particular concerns if they require care services relating to managing their bodies. The AgeUK Factsheet (2010) includes wider issues such as noting clothing preferences. What should happen for example, if a trans man has size 4 feet and the service provider says they can only find women's slippers in that size? Noting a preference for boys' slippers rather than women's slippers might be relevant to ensure that staff act in the best interests of the trans person, maintaining dignity as well as privacy.

Family arrangements of trans people may appear unorthodox—arrangements may require particular sensitivity when talking to a trans person's partner, friends, and family towards end of life and into bereavement. A trans woman may, for example, have maintained a relationship with the woman she married prior to transition. In such a case, a gender recognition certificate may not have been applied for, as it would render the marriage void. They may live their relationship as a same-sex couple or understand it in different ways—requiring tact and sensitivity from any care providers. Others may be estranged from families of origin, who may never have known the trans person in their preferred gender; some research suggests that rates of relationship breakdown with birth family are very high (Whittle, Turner and Al-Alami 2007). After death, this may raise issues about dealing with a trans person's status, balancing the family's response (for example, they may refer to the deceased by their former gender), and the rights of the deceased and those close to the deceased person. These are just some of the issues to consider; there is an urgent need for more research in this area.

6. Issues for bisexual people

Assumptions that bisexual people are either heterosexual, lesbian or gay can hinder both the ability to be open about sexual orientation and people's understandings of bisexuality. Some people who have had relationships with men and with women would not use the label "bisexual." Some may have more than one partner, but that can also be a stereotype of "bisexual" that many will not fit into. End-of-life research has yet to address the implications of these and other issues in both the UK and the US and, indeed, there is hardly any empirical work on bisexual ageing, although some work on mid-life bisexuals suggests some useful starting points (Weinberg, Williams and Pryor 2001).

Jones (2011) suggests that in terms of "imagined futures," bisexual older people's life course experiences may vary greatly and are more likely to include "non-normative life course features" (also see Chapter 2). For example, they may have male or female partners and social networks that encompass both. Responding to concerns of bisexual older people relating to end-of-life care may in part be addressed by the same principles of good practice that would apply for the wider LGBT population, as discussed above. However, this is another area where further research is needed to develop the evidence base of bisexual people's concerns, experiences, and needs relating to end-of-life care.

Conclusion

Being LGBT profoundly matters in the delivery of healthcare and services, including those near the end of life. Sexual orientation and identity may be linked to one's unique family and informal support networks, relationships of trust, and perspectives about healthcare and services. To ensure that one's wishes for care are respected, it is beneficial for LGBT people to appoint their preferred decision-makers and document their wishes regarding end-of-life care. Further, LGBT people should be acknowledged and respected by the healthcare providers, administrators, and institutions. This will require the healthcare community to become more culturally proficient with respect to the LGBT community, as well as developing further research into community perspectives. Although it may have been possible for elder care practitioners and researchers to overlook the community in the past, new generations of LGBT elders will expect and demand recognition of their needs, issues, and relationships.

References

Adelman, M., Gurevitch, J., de Vries, B. and Blando, J. (2006) 'Openhouse: Community Building and Research in the LGBT Aging Population.' In D. Kimmel, T. Rose and S. David (eds) *Lesbian, Gay, Bisexual, and Transgender Aging: Research and Clinical Perspectives.* New York: Columbia University Press.

AgeUK (2010) *Transgender Issues in Later Life: Factsheet 16.* London: AgeUK.

Age Concern England (2001) *Opening Doors: Working With Older Lesbians and Gay Men.* London, UK: Age Concern England. Available at: www.ageconcern.org.uk/AgeConcern/Documents/Opening_Doors_resource_pack.pdf. Accessed on 31 March 2010.

Almack, K. (2007) 'Palliative care and end-of-life care for the non-heterosexual community.' *End-of-life care for Nurses 1,* 2, 27–32.

Almack, K., Seymour, J. and Bellamy, G. (2010) 'Exploring the impact of sexual orientation on experiences and concerns about end-of-life care and on bereavement for lesbian, gay and bisexual elders.' *Sociology 44,* 5, 908–924.

Boulder County, Colorado Aging Services (2006) *Evaluation of Project Visibility Training: Outcome and Satisfaction.* Boulder, CO: Boulder County Aging Services. Available at: www.bouldercounty.org/cs/ag/programs/Project_Visibility/PV_Training_Evaluation.pdf. Accessed on 31 March 2010.

Brookdale Center on Aging (1999) *Assistive Housing for Elderly Gay, Lesbian, Bisexual and Transgender Elders.* Washington, DC, US: National Gay and Lesbian Taskforce Policy Institute.

Castillo, L.S., Williams, B.A., Hooper, S.M., Sabatino, C.P., Weithorn, L.A. and Sudore, R.L. (2011) 'Lost in translation: The unintended consequences of advance directive law on clinical care.' *Annals of Internal Medicine 154,* 2, 121–128.

Cronin, A., Ward, R., Pugh, S., King, A. and Price, E. (2011) 'Categories and their consequences: Understanding and supporting the caring relationships of older lesbian, gay and bisexual people.' *International Social Work 54,* 3, 421–435.

Davies, M., Addis, S., MacBride-Stewart, S. and Shepherd, M. (2006) *The Health, Social Care and Housing Needs of Lesbian, Gay, Bisexual and Transgender Older People: Literature Review.* Cardiff: Centre for Health Sciences Research, Cardiff University.

Department of Health (2008) *End-of-life Care Strategy: Promoting High Quality Care for all Adults at the End of Life: Equality Impact Assessment.* London: Department of Health.

Department of Health (2010) *National Cancer Patient Experience Survey Programme 2010: National Survey Report.* London: Department of Health.

Doka, K. (1989) *Disenfranchised Grief.* Lexington, MA: Lexington Books.

Eliason, M.J. and Schope, R. (2001) 'Does "don't ask, don't tell" apply to health care? Lesbian, gay, and bisexual people's disclosure to health care providers.' *Journal of the Gay and Lesbian Medical Association 5,* 4, 125–134.

Fastenberg, D. (2010) 'A brief history of international gay marriage.' *Time.* Available at: www.time.com/time/world/article/0,8599,2005678,00.html. Accessed on 21 July 2011.

General Medical Council (2010) *Treatment and Care Towards the End of Life: Good Practice in Decision Making.* London: General Medical Council. Available at: www.gmc-uk.org/End_of_life.pdf_32486688.pdf. Accessed on 26 July 2011.

Grant, J.M. (2009) *Outing Age 2010.* Washington, DC, US: National Gay and Lesbian Task Force Policy Institute. Available at: www.thetaskforce.org/downloads/reports/reports/outingage_final.pdf. Accessed on 21 July 2011.

Green, L. and Grant, V. (2008) 'Gagged grief and beleaguered bereavements: An analysis of multidisciplinary theory and research relating to same-sex partnership bereavement.' *Sexualities 11*, 3, 275–300.

Heaphy, B., Yip, A.K.T. and Thompson, D. (2003) *Lesbian, Gay and Bisexual Lives Over 50.* Nottingham: York House Publications.

Help and Care Development (2006) *Lifting the Lid on Sexuality and Ageing.* Bournemouth: Help and Care Development.

Higgins, A. and Glacken, M. (2009) 'Sculpting the distress: Easing or exacerbating the grief experience of same-sex couples.' *International Journal of Palliative Nursing 15*, 4, 170–176.

Institute of Medicine (2011) *The Health of Lesbian, Gay, Bisexual, and Transgender People: Building a Foundation for Better Understanding.* Washington, DC, US: The National Academies Press. Available at: http://books.nap.edu/openbook.php?record_id=13128. Accessed on 21 July 2011.

Johnson, M.J., Jackson, N.C., Arnette, J.K. and Koffman, S.D. (2005) 'Gay and lesbian perceptions of discrimination in retirement care facilities.' *Journal of Homosexuality 49*, 2, 83–102.

Jones, R. (2011) 'Imagining bisexual futures: Positive, non-normative later life.' *Journal of Bisexuality 11*, 2 and 3, 245–270.

Klitzman, R.L. and Greenberg, J.D. (2002) 'Patterns of communication between gay and lesbian patients and their health care providers.' *Journal of Homosexuality 42*, 4, 65–75.

Koskovich, G. (2009) 'LGBT Retirement Housing.' Unpublished table prepared for the LGBT Aging Issues Network (LAIN) of the American Society on Aging, available in the LAIN subject files at the GLBT Historical Society, San Francisco, CA.

Lambda Legal (2011) 'Status of same-sex relationships nationwide.' New York: Lambda Legal. Available at: www.lambdalegal.org/publications/articles/nationwide-status-same-sex-relationships.html. Accessed on 21 July 2011.

Levine, C. (1990) 'AIDS and changing concepts of family.' *Milbank Quarterly 68*, 1, 33–58.

Lewin, T. (1991) 'Disabled woman's care given to lesbian partner.' The New York Times, 18 December, p.A26. Available at: www.nytimes.com/1991/12/18/us/disabled-woman-s-care-given-to-lesbian-partner.html?scp=1andsq=tamar+lewinandst=nyt. Accessed on 21 July 2011.

LGBT Movement Advancement Project and SAGE (2010) *Improving the Lives of LGBT Older Adults.* NY: LGBT Movement Advancement Project and SAGE. Available at: http://sageusa.org/uploads/Advancing%20Equality%20for%20LGBT%20Elders%20[FINAL%20COMPRESSED].pdf. Accessed on 21 July 2011.

Manthorpe, J. (2003) 'Nearest and dearest? The neglect of lesbians in caring relationships.' *British Journal of Social Work 33*, 6, 753–768.

MetLife Mature Market Institute (2006) *Out and Aging: The MetLife Study of Lesbian and Gay Baby Boomers.* Westport, CT, US: MetLife Mature Market Institute. Available at: www.lgbtagingcenter.org/resources/resource.cfm?r=31. Accessed on 5 April 2012.

MetLife Mature Market Institute (2010) *Still Out, Still Aging: The MetLife Study of Lesbian, Gay, Bisexual, and Transgender Baby Boomers.* Westport, CT, US: MetLife Mature Market Institute. Available at: www.metlife.com/assets/cao/mmi/publications/studies/2010/mmi-still-out-still-aging.pdf. Accessed on 26 July 2011.

Murphy, T. (2011) 'Surrogate health care decisions and same-sex relationships.' *Hastings Center Report 41*, 3, 24–27.

National End of life Care Programme (2011) Capacity, *Care Planning and Advance Care Planning in Life-limiting Illness: A Guide for Health and Social Care Staff.* Leicester: NEOLCP. Available at: www.endoflifecareforadults.nhs.uk/assets/downloads/ACP_booklet_June_2011__with_links.pdf. Accessed on 26 July 2011.

National Institute on Aging/National Institutes of Health (2009) *Age Page: HIV, AIDS, and Older People.* Bethesda, MD, US: National Institute on Aging. Available at: www.nia.nih.gov/HealthInformation/Publications/hiv-aids.htm. Accessed on 21 July 2011.

New York City Department of Health and Mental Hygiene, Bureau of Epidemiology Services (2008) *Community Health Survey.* New York: New York City Department of Health and Mental Hygiene.

Pugh, S. (2005) 'Assessing the cultural needs of older lesbians and gay men: Implications for practice.' *Practice 17,* 93, 207–218.

Röndahl, G., Innala, S. and Carlsson, M. (2006) 'Heterosexual assumptions in verbal and non-verbal communication in nursing.' *Journal of Advanced Nursing 56,* 4, 373–381.

Sabatino, C.P. (2010) 'The evolution of health care advance planning law and policy.' *The Milbank Quarterly 88,* 2, 211–239.

SAGE and Brookdale Center on Aging (2004) *No Need to Fear, No Need to Hide: A Training Program About Inclusion and Understanding of Lesbian, Gay, Bisexual and Transgender Elders for Long-term Care and Assisted Living Facilities.* New York: SAGE and Brookdale Center on Aging. Available at: www.sageconnect.net/intranet/resources/uploads/documents/titlepagecreditsoverview.pdf. Accessed on 21 July 2011.

Schwartz, J. (2011) 'After New York, new look at Defense of Marriage Act.' *The New York Times,* 27 June. Available at: www.nytimes.com/2011/06/28/us/politics/28doma.html? r=1andscp=4andsq=defense%20of%20marriage%20actandst=cse. Accessed on 26 July 2011.

Stein, G.L., Beckerman, N.L. and Sherman, P.A. (2010) 'Lesbian and gay elders and long-term care. Identifying the unique psychosocial perspectives and challenges.' *Journal of Gerontological Social Work 53,* 5, 421–435.

Stein, G.L. and Bonuck, K.A. (2001a) 'Attitudes on end-of-life care and advance care planning in the lesbian and gay community.' *Journal of Palliative Medicine 4,* 2, 173–190.

Stein, G.L. and Bonuck, K.A. (2001b) 'Physician–patient relationships among the lesbian and gay community.' *Journal of the Gay and Lesbian Medical Association 5,* 3, 87–93.

Walter, T. (1999) *On Bereavement: The Culture of Grief.* Buckingham: Open University Press.

Weeks, J., Heaphy, B. and Donovan, C. (2001) *Same-sex Intimacies: Families of Choice and Other Life Experiments.* London: Routledge.

Weston, K. (1997) *Families We Choose: Lesbians, Gays and Kinship.* New York: Columbia University Press. (Revised edition. Originally published 1991.)

Weinberg, M.S., Williams, C.J. and Pryor, D.W. (2001) 'Bisexuals at midlife: Commitment, salience and identity.' *Journal of Contemporary Ethnography 30,* 2, 180–208.

Whittle S. and Turner, L. (2007) *Bereavement: A Guide for Transsexual, Transgender People and Their Loved Ones.* London: Department of Health.

Whittle, S., Turner, L. and Al-Alami, M. (2007) *Engendered Penalties: Transgender and Transsexual People's Experiences of Inequality and Discrimination.* Manchester: The Equalities Review.

Young, E., Seale, C. and Bury, M. (1998) '"It's not like family going, is it?": Negotiating friendship towards the end of life.' *Mortality 3,* 1, 27–42.

Part III

Community Engagement and Support

Chapter 8

Polari's Life Story
Learning from Work with Older LGBT People

Lindsay River and Richard Ward

Introduction

Growing older is undoubtedly a layered experience; we age socially, bodily, cognitively etc. But some commentators argue that we are 'aged by culture' in ways that have little or no connection to our own subjective experience (Gullette 1997). From this perspective, ageing is something that is done to us rather than something that we 'do'. We can see this in the way certain discourses on old age group 'the elderly' together, promoting policies and forms of service provision that carry a host of assumptions regarding the 'likeness' of older people and that overlook and sometimes actively deny the differences between them. Such constructions of old age have particular force in times of economic hardship where the projected 'burden' of older generations is often deployed in support of financial strictures imposed on the welfare state. Notions such as the ageing time-bomb, described by Katz (1992) as 'alarmist demography', rely upon the homogenising of older people, requiring that they are viewed as undifferentiated, devoid of personal histories. These narratives shape the way that ageing itself is understood. Rather than movement through time, old age is seen almost as a place at which we arrive, a place that confers a certain (unwanted) status and from which unfair demands are made upon wider society.

Against this backdrop a rather different 'counter-narrative' has emerged that is critical of the way that older people are collectively labelled and judged and the consequent glossing over of important differences and inequalities in later life (e.g. Daatland and Biggs 2006, Gubrium and Holstein 2003, Ward and Bytheway 2008). Such arguments have significant implications for health and social care practice as they foreground the need to be mindful of diversity and hence to foster inclusive provision. In this context, a focus on biographies shifts us away from the idea of old age as fixed or static. Rather, it involves seeing ageing as movement through time with continuities and change, and the accumulation of experience, at an individual and collective level. In this chapter we reflect on the 'life' of an organisation that worked with and for older lesbians, gay men and bisexual people (and latterly with older trans people) in seeking to raise awareness of sexual diversity and promote good practice across housing, health and social care services to older people. As we will discuss, the work of Polari embraced this counter-narrative of ageing and worked to promote the inclusive delivery of mainstream services.

Our aims for the chapter are threefold: to offer an overview of the work and outputs from Polari, highlighting key messages from them; to identify certain enduring or perennial challenges in our work of raising awareness of the needs and perspectives of LGBT people; and to draw on the findings of Polari's work to offer recommendations and guidance for practitioners who may be considering how to develop 'LGBT-friendly' practice. A particular focus for this chapter is upon the active role that support and care services can play in the writing of individual biographies and in the broader prospects for minority groups and communities as they age.

About Polari

Polari the organisation took its name from the 'cant slang' (see Baker 2002) used by gay men, particularly during the period up to the Sexual Offences Act 1967 when homosexuality was criminalised (and where outward indications of a gay identity risked imprisonment, psychiatric intervention and public censure). The organisation ran for a total of 16 years and during this time undertook a series of projects and commissioned work with the explicit aim of improving conditions for older LGB people within mainstream services. Polari is unique in the UK for having worked over such a long time specifically with older LGBT groups and individuals, and following its closure in 2009 we felt it was important to document some of the lessons learned and insights gained so that they are not lost to current and future work in this field. Inasmuch as it is possible to talk of the 'life course' of an organisation, we intend to map Polari's own biography and consider how this was shaped by the lives and experiences of the people with whom it worked.

Polari came about in the early 1990s when a group of mainly working-age lesbians and gay men formed a small committee with the intention of investigating the housing needs of older LGB people.

Collectively, this group recognised a serious problem that dogged the efforts of older members of the LGB communities to gain recognition and for their needs to be met. On the one hand, the many organisations concerned with older people in the UK tended to overlook sexual minorities, and this applied not only to service providers but also to policy and research into welfare needs (Cronin 2006). At the same time, those organisations working with the LGBT communities tended to overlook older people, focusing instead upon younger generations. Again, this applied as much to research as to policy and practice. As later research came to show, commercial settings such as the 'gay scene' were also often experienced as overtly ageist with an atmosphere unwelcoming to older customers (Heaphy, Yip and Thompson 2003). Pugh (2002) described these conditions as creating a 'community without a generation', signalling the disenfranchisement of older LGB people who were often faced with few options or places to turn in times of need. At the time, these conditions called for a specific focus upon older LGB people and, many would argue, still do.

Over the years the voluntary committee membership changed, as did Polari's own agenda. The direction of the organisation and the work it undertook were shaped by the lessons learned from engagement with older LGBT contributors and participants along the way. In this respect, the life of Polari was closely intertwined with the lives of the people it worked with. In the next section we outline some of the work undertaken and endeavour to show how the learning that came from each piece of work helped to write Polari's own biography.

Polari's work and outputs[1]

Shortly after its inception, Polari commissioned a piece of research designed to identify the housing needs of older LGB people. At the time the committee was considering whether to set up an LGB-specific housing association and wanted to gauge levels of interest in the provision of housing support amongst older members of the LGB communities. The findings of the 'As We Grow Older' report (Hubbard and Rossington 1995) proved to have a defining influence on Polari's future agenda. While the research itself encountered the sort of problems that have become well known in research with LGBT communities,

---

1   All the reports mentioned in this section are accessible online at the Age of Diversity website: www.ageofdiversity.org.uk/documents.

such as difficulty in identifying those aged 70 years and over and under-representation of bisexual and black and minority ethnic (BME) participants, its findings prefigured some of the enduring themes that subsequently emerged from research on ageing and sexuality in the UK.

One strand of the research surveyed housing providers, including sheltered housing and care home managers from selected areas across the UK, the response from whom was extremely low. At this time, many providers in older people's services simply did not want to engage on issues of sexual identity and/or felt it was irrelevant to their service users. One care home manager simply remarked: 'All the residents are too old to have a sexual identity of any sort.' There was a clear sense that questions on sexuality were considered in some way inappropriate and that these providers felt they were being asked to venture into territory that they perceived as private to their service users. Despite this, the research noted the promotion of 'family-friendly' atmospheres in many services and the implicit prioritising of heterosexual perspectives that ran through these facilities and organisations.

Of the older LGB respondents, many expressed a sense of threat and fear when looking ahead to a time when they would require help or care (a theme that remains prominent in sexualities research, as demonstrated by many of the chapters in this book). Those who had entered sheltered housing or care homes reported hiding their sexuality, going 'back into the closet' in order to avoid discrimination from staff and fellow residents. One respondent in her seventies revealed: 'In the [sheltered] accommodation I live in, nobody knows I am lesbian. They mustn't. It is so gossipy and they pick on anybody who is different. It makes me very lonely.' Illustrating how admission to long-stay care can have an isolating effect for LGB service users, a gay man in his late eighties, wrote:

> Though of a comparatively high standard of accommodation, I don't think my care home is a particularly easy place for a gay man to live. They know about me but I have to be discreet, which I never used to be. Also my gay friends tend not to visit me any more, not being made to feel welcome and also feeling it could make life difficult for me.

Many of the other 131 respondents endured unsuitable housing conditions in the community and for some that included hostile and abusive treatment from neighbours.

The question of what people wanted in terms of possible future options for housing and care revealed something of the diversity within older LGB groups. For instance, some older lesbian respondents wished for women-only provision, while many older gay men wanted to see LGB-specific provision. Some respondents had a very clear idea of the housing provision they wanted to see, and welcomed being asked. For instance, one lesbian in her seventies wanted: 'Small bungalows – one bed, living room, etc. Secure and warm but not segregated, i.e. a village, but yet be part of a street, say several in one street so you can mix in hetero society as well,' while a gay man who responded to the survey wished for: 'city centre accommodation within the gay village [Manchester]'.

It was clear from this research that tensions existed amongst those surveyed as to the preferred forms of housing support, and that for many it was unfeasible that they should uproot themselves from their current neighbourhoods and networks in order to move to wherever such a service might be sited. Crucially, however, a large proportion of respondents wanted to see greater accessibility and fairness in mainstream services, with some expressing concerns about the potential ghettoising of older LGB people if targeted services were created. The outcome for Polari was to rethink its role; the group decided that its greatest impact could potentially be achieved through working strategically to promote change across existing housing, health and social care services, rather than seeking to provide a new service.

After further consultation in different parts of the UK, Polari successfully bid for funding to undertake a three-year participatory project aimed at facilitating a dialogue between older LGB residents, policymakers and service providers in three London boroughs: the Polari in Partnership Project[2] (PiPP) (Davies and River 2006). In our report on the project we endeavoured to give an honest account of the strengths *and* weaknesses, knowing that both would likely be instructive for future initiatives. For instance, in our project design we had underestimated the significance attached to opportunities for sociability among older LGB people. The project focused upon campaigning for change when many potential participants placed greater importance on making friends and building or extending their social networks. Moreover, by focusing upon just three London boroughs we effectively excluded many people

---

2   The experience of conducting this work has been written up in a paper that draws comparisons with another initiative with older LGB people that took place on the South coast: the 'Gay and Grey' project (see Ward, River and Fenge 2008).

who might have wanted to participate. In this respect we highlighted the importance of working across administrative boundaries, given that throughout the UK older LGBT people are rarely concentrated in certain areas and tend to be dispersed geographically.

The project employed a participatory action research design intended to foreground the role of older LGB people themselves. We discovered that many participants had long histories of negative encounters and relations with providers and as a result were reluctant to directly engage in a dialogue with them. A lifetime's accumulated experience had coloured their perspectives, especially of state-run services. We also found that some participants did not wish to 'out' themselves within their borough of residence but would consider getting involved in work with neighbouring boroughs. Nonetheless, the participatory design demonstrated the value of collective action, encouraging service providers to take notice often in a context where individual efforts to voice discontent in the past had been dismissed or ignored. Taking part in the project equipped participants with skills and confidence that they carried with them into future activities, in effect building social capital within older LGB networks.

A significant outcome from PiPP was that the project identified many older LGB people with chronic and enduring mental health conditions, often with negative experiences and histories as users of mental health services. This reflected the findings of a number of UK studies into the mental health of the LGBT communities, including recognition of the long-term impact of living with discrimination (McFarlane 1998) and greater vulnerability to more common mental health problems such as anxiety and depression within LGBT populations (King *et al.* 2003).

Polari subsequently went on to bid for funding to undertake a one-year investigation of the experiences and needs of older LGB mental health service users and their carers (see Wintrip 2009). The study built on the findings from PiPP and recognition that mental health in later life was not just a neglected topic within LGBT communities but possibly a hidden problem. Using a survey and interviews, the study revealed an overarching concern with safety that is central to decisions on accessing help and support when it is needed. Indeed, the study identified a number of older LGB people who had chosen not to seek help from mental health services.

For instance, one lesbian interviewee commented:

> I haven't used any [statutory] services since 1976. I stayed away because I was worried, I thought that if I went into hospital again I wouldn't get out. I didn't think I could have survived another imprisonment. So I was doing my best to manage outside of services, but I was really struggling.

We also heard from respondents whose first experiences of mental health services came at a time when homosexuality was treated as a mental disorder and psychiatric interventions involved torturous forms of aversion therapy (see King, Smith and Bartlett 2004). Not only had these experiences shaped lifelong perceptions of the health service, they had blighted the lives and well-being of the individuals concerned as well.

Participants described past and current experiences of service use where they endured discrimination and abuse from both staff and fellow service users. For instance, one participant recalled:

> I went through three days of beatings from other patients in the hospital whilst the staff did nothing. It only stopped when one of the other patients screamed at the nurses, 'Aren't you going to do anything about this?' One nurse just said, 'Well she's butch, she should be able to look after herself.'

Within mental health services, LGB users were reluctant to 'come out' as a consequence of feeling unsafe to do so, yet at the same time many avoided disclosing their mental health needs within LGB networks, anticipating a stigmatising response. For instance, one participant commented:

> I certainly feel like I can't talk about my mental health problems with my friends, straight or gay – gay a little bit more actually. This shocks me actually, I think they don't want to hear it because they don't know what to say, so I find myself not talking about it but feeling very false because I'm not who I am.

As we have discussed elsewhere, feeling unsafe to come out to fellow service users has meant that LGB people often do not have a voice in the mental health service user movement (see Ward, River and the Scottish Dementia Working Group 2010).

A final piece of work, begun under the auspices of Polari and completed by Lindsay River (2011) in her new role as convenor of Age of Diversity, concerned experiences of general practice. Based upon a survey of over 280 LGB respondents aged 50 years and over, the report revealed some striking variations in their experiences of seeking help from a GP. For instance, a higher proportion of lesbians than gay men reported negative experiences, and fewer reported positive encounters of practice. The reported experiences of BME and Irish respondents tended to be more negative than those of the other respondents. There were some commonalities; a large majority said that they had never seen anything referring to sexual orientation in their local practice. Many said that it would make them feel more comfortable and welcome if signs existed that general practices were aware of the existence of a local LGBT community. Many reported encountering a pervasive assumption of heterosexuality:

> As a woman it was assumed I was heterosexual – as a result I was constantly plied with requests to use birth control methods such as the coil, the Pill, etc. Now, as a disabled, older woman, it is taken for granted that I'm STRAIGHT'. (Lesbian in her fifties)

As with much of Polari's work the study revealed histories of discrimination and negative experiences. For instance, one gay man in his sixties reflected back on an early encounter with one clinic:

> The Portman Clinic wanted to 'treat' my homosexuality when I was referred there in the early 1970s for diagnosis of what turned out many years later to be multiple allergies. I told them 'I don't think you can help me' and walked out. Someone without my confidence about their sexual identity and as anxious as I was about an undiagnosed incapacitating illness could so easily have gone along with a treatment regime based on ignorance and prejudice, for which there was no evidence whatever of its effectiveness.

The survey also took account of more recent experiences and revealed how current examples of discrimination and bad practice can compound earlier experiences, having something of a cumulative impact. One lesbian respondent in her fifties wrote:

> Many bad experiences. Main one was disbelief, followed by changing the subject, to downright hostility. As a disabled

woman, the matter of my having any sexuality at all is a puzzlement to some medical practitioners. Mainly I meet with ignorance about what this might mean in terms of sexual health or other health issues.

Nonetheless the report also gave cause for cautious optimism. While many respondents detailed negative and discriminatory experiences associated with visiting their GP, both recent and historical, the report also contains evidence of much good practice and clear indicators that in some areas of primary care conditions and practice are improving:

> My GP has a wealth of experience in trans-gender issues, having had five previous couples on his books where one party was transitioning. His support to me as the partner of an FTM (female to male) has been one of the main things that kept me sane. Through the trust that we have built up between us, I have been able to discuss my own bisexuality, and to seek advice when I've indulged in unsafe sex. He has never judged, and has always put me at complete ease. (Bisexual man in his fifties)

> I was well supported in a very open way by our GP when my partner had a heart attack. There was no awkwardness when I needed to ask for a sample bottle to be brought back from the surgery by her! They just do not seem to make a thing of it. Had a really good discussion with the GP as to why lesbians might prefer female GP. (Lesbian in her sixties)

A majority of respondents were 'out' (i.e. had disclosed their sexuality) as gay, lesbian or bisexual to at least one person in their GP practice and/or would be happy to be asked about their sexual orientation, and this included a majority of the respondents aged 70 years or over. This finding supports Brighton-based research for the 'Count Me in Too' project (discussed by Browne, Bakshi and Lim in Chapter 10 of this book) where older LGBT people were found to be more likely to be 'out' to their GP than younger age groups. We see these findings as significant because they challenge the notion that older LGB people are more likely to want to hide their sexuality, and suggest instead that under the right conditions older people are prepared to identify themselves as lesbian, gay or bisexual.

Collectively, this work and the outputs from it serve as milestones in the life course of Polari and illustrate efforts made by the group to respond to the messages that emerged from each piece of work. In the next section we turn to consider some of the overarching issues arising from this body of work, and their implications for health and social care practice.

Implications for practice
Labelling
Many participants in Polari's project work (some in their seventies and eighties) were long-standing campaigners for equality and have struggled on various levels to be heard and taken seriously, not least by health and social care providers. Yet older cohorts of LGB people have been cast as hidden and invisible and this collective labelling has often served to excuse policy makers and providers from seeking to meet their needs. There is a need to look critically at the language that is used to represent such groups and the potential it has to compound poor provision.

Training
A prominent recommendation from almost all Polari's work has been the call for awareness-raising and training, especially for frontline staff. This is one area where the biographies and life experiences of older LGBT people can be utilised in order to educate and pose questions for practitioners. For example, building on the work of the PIP Project, Polari joined forces with AGLOW (Association of Greater London Older Women) to provide training to care workers in one London borough. The group performed sketches that were based upon the experiences of older lesbians – for example, acting out encounters with care workers making home visits and their differing responses to an older service user 'coming out'. These 'ethno-dramas' (Saldana 2005) proved a valuable way to raise questions about care practice and for trainees to consider the perspectives of older LGBT service users. It was revealing to us that most trainees had not been given any previous opportunity to acquire an understanding of LGBT issues and were grateful for the opportunity for open discussion.

Disseminating good practice
A particularly important consideration for practitioners is the writing up and dissemination of their work with older LGBT service users.

Where pockets of good practice exist these are often only shared at a local level, denying others the opportunity to learn from and build upon this work. Older people's services lack an evidence base for work with LGBT service users, and practitioners are uniquely placed to contribute to this. Where relevant, building relations with the academic community can support this and lead to both national and international recognition for innovative practice that may have positive implications for continued funding.

Fostering social networks

Polari's work has highlighted the vulnerability attached to social isolation for many LGB people in later life and the value of creating spaces and opportunities for peer support. By mapping local community resources, practitioners can build links between different sectors and organisations. While it is important that older people's services develop an LGBT-friendly culture, it is equally incumbent on LGBT groups and organisations to become 'age-friendly'. Knowledge transfer activities, including staff-swapping and collaborative service delivery, can build capacity on both sides.

Involving older LGBT service users

Practitioners have a role to play in ensuring that user-involvement initiatives are fully inclusive and that as a result older LGBT people are given the power to decide what types of knowledge and information about them is shared and disseminated within services and beyond. With this advice in mind, and as a postscript to the life of Polari, a new user-led (currently unfunded) organisation called 'Age of Diversity' has been formed (www.ageofdiversity.org.uk). Age of Diversity is run by and for older LGBT people and aims to recruit its membership from across the UK. Our hope is that as a collective force, increasingly it will succeed in making it difficult for policy makers, researchers and service providers to ignore or discount the distinct needs of older LGBT people.

Discussion and concluding comments

In some respects, the history of Polari offers a fairly representative queer life story, in that many of the challenges faced reflect those of the people it has worked with and for. As a group we struggled for recognition from policy makers and mainstream service providers. Our 'life expectancy' was shortened because of an absence of sustained support or funding, and after nearly two decades of campaigning, many of the issues we brought to light have still to be absorbed or taken up within mainstream health and social care. Nonetheless, observable changes are taking place and much can be done to speed the pace of that change. Having looked back over the life of Polari and highlighted some of the lessons we learned in the course of this work, we come now to ask what all this means in terms of a broader understanding of the issues associated with ageing sexualities. There are three points in particular that we would highlight in looking ahead to future work in this field.

1. The first issue, as pertinent now as it was to the small group that founded Polari, concerns the invisibility of LGBT perspectives to policy on old age, which we can understand as an instance or outcome of '*intersectionality*' (Crenshaw 1993). This is a term that has been used to describe how different systems of oppression are mutually reinforcing, and while thoroughly debated in the field of race and gender studies, an awareness of intersectionality has rarely been applied to how we think about ageing sexualities (Cronin and King 2010). In essence, it calls attention to the ways that discrimination on the grounds of age and sexual orientation coalesce producing particular effects, and indeed how many different factors such as gender, class, ethnicity and health status all impact on the life chances of older LGB people. As Cronin and King (2010) have argued, intersectionality theory is useful because it allows 'a greater understanding of complex biographies' [that are obscured by categorisations such as 'older LGB'] 'while still retaining a concern with wider dynamics of power' (p.877). We would argue that the notion of intersectionality is a useful one for providers in health and social care, not only for understanding issues of LGBT (in)visibility but also as a framework for bringing about change.

2. Another perennial challenge to our work and to winning the hearts and minds of those involved in services to older people relates, paradoxically, to the invisibility of heterosexuality. The sociologist Diane Richardson (2000) has argued that because heterosexuality is considered natural and normal, it is rarely 'seen' as a sexual identity in the way that 'non-normative' sexualities are made visible. What

this has meant to the work of Polari is frequent resistance and refusal on the part of providers to address issues of sexuality with older service users, but in a context where the perspectives and interests of heterosexual service users are implicitly and sometimes explicitly favoured or prioritised. This is a process known as '*heteronormativity*' and relates less to direct forms of discrimination in different settings and institutions than to the often more subtle ways that heterosexuality is simply assumed and upheld in the organisation and delivery of services. In our experience, heteronormativity has been a barrier to the promotion of more inclusive services and generates significant disadvantage and inequalities in services to older people. As such, it is helpful to look beyond questions of discriminatory practice, which are the focus of recent equalities legislation, to consider the more subtle ways in which certain perspectives and interests are privileged.

3. Our final point concerns the role played by health and social care services in the lives of older LGBT people both historically and in the present day. Some studies of the life course have put emphasis on how certain forms of disadvantage and inequality have a kind of cumulative quality, building over time so that people face even greater forms of disadvantage in later life (e.g. Dannefer 2003, O'Rand 1996). The earlier lives of many older LGBT people were shaped by what Mort (1987) has described as a 'medico-moral alliance' where the church, medicine, legislature and judiciary in the UK aligned themselves in the persecution of sexual minorities. Given what we have learned of the lives of LGBT people before the Sexual Offences Act 1967, we can certainly appreciate how such early experiences might ripple out across the rest of someone's life. So we have to consider whether the services to which people turn for help and support in later life are serving to compound these disadvantages or working to ameliorate them. For those working in health and social care it is useful to consider the biographies of the services they provide, and historically, the role they might have played.

As we have endeavoured to illustrate in our account of Polari's work, different groups, agencies and services can collaboratively write their own biographies by seeking the active participation of service users and letting their experience and interests shape the way ahead. In this way of working a very different story can be told for older LGBT people as they engage with health and social care. The telling and writing of Polari's biography underlined for us just how much conditions have changed, and in many respects improved, since the organisation's early days. It used to be hard not to tell a fairly negative tale of LGBT people's encounters with welfare services but the possibility for a more positive narrative is emerging. Undoubtedly the new equalities legislation has played a significant role in this, but ultimately it is due to the ongoing and collective efforts of older LGBT people themselves.

References

Baker, P. (2002) *Polari: The Lost Language of Gay Men.* London: Routledge.

Crenshaw, K. (1993) 'Mapping the margins: Intersectionality, identity politics and violence against women of color.' *Stanford Law Review 43*, 6, 1241–99.

Cronin, A. (2006) 'Sexuality in Gerontology: A Heteronormative Presence, a Queer Absence.' In S.O. Daatland and S. Biggs (eds) *Ageing and Diversity: Multiple Pathways and Cultural Migrations.* Bristol: Policy Press.

Cronin, A. and King, A. (2010) 'Power, inequality and identification: Exploring diversity and intersectionality amongst older LGB adults.' *Sociology 44*, 5, 876–892.

Daatland, S.O. and Biggs, S. (eds) (2006) *Ageing and Diversity: Multiple Pathways and Cultural Migrations.* Bristol: Policy Press.

Dannefer, D. (2003) 'Cumulative advantage/disadvantage and the life course: Cross-fertilizing age and social science theory.' *Journals of Gerontology Series B: Psychological Sciences and Social Science, 58*, 6, s327–37.

Davies, P. and River, L. (2006) *Being Taken Seriously: The Polari in Partnership Project – Promoting Change for Older Lesbians, Gay Men and Bisexuals.* London: Polari.

Gubrium, J.F. and Holstein, J.A. (eds) (2003) *Ways of Aging.* Oxford: Blackwell.

Gullette, M.M. (1997) *Declining to Decline: Cultural Combat and the Politics of the Midlife.* Charlottesville, VA: University Press of Virginia.

Heaphy, B., Yip, A. and Thompson, D. (2003) *Lesbian, Gay and Bisexual Lives over 50: A Report on the Project 'The Social and Policy Implications of Non-Heterosexual Ageing'.* Nottingham: York House Publications, Nottingham Trent University.

Hubbard, R. and Rossington, J. (1995) *As We Grow Older: A Study of the Housing and Support Needs of Older Lesbians and Gay Men.* London: Polari.

Katz, S. (1992) 'Alarmist demography: Power, knowledge and the elderly population.' *Journal of Aging Studies 6*, 3, 203–225.

King, M., Smith, G. and Bartlett, A. (2004) 'Treatments of homosexuality in Britain since the 1950s: An oral history. The experience of professionals.' *British Medical Journal 328*, 7437, 429–432.

King, M., McKeown, E., Warner, J., Ramsay, A. *et al.* (2003) 'Mental health and quality of life of gay men and lesbians in England and Wales.' *British Journal of Psychiatry 183*, 6, 552–558.

McFarlane, L. (1998) *Diagnosis Homophobic.* London: PACE.

Mort, F. (1987) *Dangerous Sexualities: Medico-moral Politics in England since 1830.* London: Routledge and Kegan Paul.

O'Rand, A.M. (1996) 'The precious and the precocious: Understanding cumulative disadvantage and cumulative advantage over the life course.' *The Gerontologist 36*, 2, 230–238.

Pugh, S. (2002) 'The Forgotten: A Community Without a Generation – Older Lesbians and Gay Men.' In D. Richardson and S. Seidman (eds) *The Handbook of Lesbian and Gay Studies*. Thousand Oaks, CA: Sage Publications.

Richardson, D. (2000) *Rethinking Sexuality*. London: Sage Publications.

River, L. (2011) *Appropriate Treatment: Older Lesbian, Gay and Bisexual People's Experience of General Practice*. London: Age of Diversity and Polari.

Saldana, J. (ed.) (2005) *Ethno-dramas: An Anthology of Reality Theatre*. Lanham MD: Altamira Press.

Ward, R. and Bytheway, B. (2008) *Researching Age and Multiple Discrimination*. London: Centre for Policy on Ageing and the Open University.

Ward, R., River, L. and Fenge, L. (2008) 'Neither silent nor invisible: A comparison of two participative projects involving older lesbians and gay men in the United Kingdom.' *Journal of Gay and Lesbian Social Work 20*, 1/2, 147–166.

Ward, R., River, L. and The Scottish Dementia Working Group (2010) 'Between Participation and Practice: Inclusive User Involvement and the Role of Practitioners.' In J. Keady and S. Watts (eds) *Mental Health and Later Life: Delivering an Holistic Model for Practice*. London: Routledge.

Wintrip, S. (2009) *Not Safe for Us Yet: The Experiences And Views of Older Lesbians, Gay Men and Bisexuals Using Mental Health Services in London*. London: Polari.

Chapter 9

Opening Doors and Opening Minds

Sharing One Project's Experience of Successful Community Engagement

Sally Knocker, Nick Maxwell, Mike Phillips and Stacey Halls

Introduction

Opening Doors is the largest funded project working exclusively with older lesbian, gay, bisexual and transgender people in the UK and is now in its fourth year. As of the end of June 2011, the project had 602 members: 433 men (including two female to male trans men) and 169 women (including seven male to female trans women). Opening Doors London is targeted at people living in the city, but has attracted interest and membership from outside the capital, and sometimes far beyond. As part of the UK lottery funding bid, the project was evaluated over two years by independent evaluators and some of the findings from the report are included here. Indeed, this chapter has been written collaboratively by the project team and the independent evaluators and we have sought to include insights from both sides.

The chapter will explore two key aspects of the project's successes. The first is the extent to which it *has* 'opened doors', reaching an unprecedented number of older LGBT members, and the range of services it provides to maintain this engagement. The second success story is the way in which the project aims to 'open minds', partly through producing a checklist/toolkit for social care providers designed to help promote and monitor good practice in relation to working with older LGBT people. The project's partnership with one London borough to implement this toolkit through a range of training initiatives will also be outlined. The main purpose of the chapter is to reflect on the lessons learned from Opening Doors' pioneering work, both in terms of its successes and its struggles, so that those considering similar work can learn from these experiences.

About Opening Doors London

The first three years of the project have resulted in the successful recruitment of large numbers of participants, the provision of a wide variety of activities and establishing of a number of broader partnerships. Working initially in five London boroughs, led by AgeUK Camden as the host organisation, the project recruited one men's development coordinator and one women's development coordinator. It later also recruited a befriending coordinator and a part-time campaigns officer post. A project coordinator has recently been appointed, as the project has secured continued funding from the Big Lottery. The sustainability afforded by this continued funding has been an important factor in our success.

The project has set up and organises a number of initiatives:

- monthly (separate) social groups for men and women, which include film nights and visiting speakers
- a telephone advice and 'signposting' (referral) service
- a befriending service for more isolated older people who are less able or confident to access group activities
- a monthly newsletter with information about forthcoming events
- community safety surgeries in partnership with the Metropolitan Police
- a range of group-based activities including Scottish/Latin dancing, computer classes, history talks, an arts project, walking groups, faith and culture talks and an oral history project
- lunch clubs, one for men, linked to a general older people's day centre, and one for women at a central London café.

In addition the project has run some specific time-limited projects including short-term psycho-educational groups facilitated by trained therapists and a partnership project with an arts focus with Gendered Intelligence, a charity working with transgender younger people, which resulted in an 'INTERarts' exhibition of works created.

Opening Doors has also been successful in setting up and running annual information fairs bringing together a range of information stalls from statutory and voluntary agencies and speakers, which has enabled health and social care professionals and older LGBT people to meet up and raise awareness of the specific needs and concerns of older LGBT service users. In 2010, AgeUK Camden also ran a conference entitled 'How to Reach Older LGBT Communities across London', attended by 130 people. It achieved a high national profile which included project members and staff featuring in the Radio 4 *It's My Story – Glad to be Grey* programme, reaching over a million listeners, while some of its lesbian members were interviewed on *Woman's Hour*.

The two-year evaluation of the Opening Doors in London project revealed that it is highly valued by its members, and produced many moving examples of how it has reduced isolation and provided a vital sense of community:

Opening Doors enables me to have dates in my calendar. (Evaluation survey respondent)

I believe the project has filled a gap in my life for which I do not know of any replacement. Social opportunities for older gay people are very limited. (Evaluation survey respondent)

Reaching older LGBT people

Many researchers and writers have commented on the challenges of gathering data from older LGBT people and particularly older lesbian women (e.g. Heaphy, Yip and Thompson 2003; see also Chapter 4). This is partly because 'difficulties remain because many older lesbians and gay men, who choose not to come out, continue to be invisible' (Concannon 2009, p.2).

The older LGBT community is not one easily defined, homogenous group. Opening Doors London is open to LGBT men and women aged 50 and above, and so the membership spans half a century of age. The experience of an LGBT person in their fifties will be hugely different from that of someone in their nineties, just as the experience of living an LGBT identity in London will be different from that of someone in a non-urban area. Similarly, social networks differ greatly from person to person and some are more open about their sexuality or gender identity than others. In a project set up with the intention of reaching people who are socially isolated, where someone is cut off from social networks and not 'out', a series of challenges exists in reaching those who would most benefit from the service.

So how do we reach people who are often considered 'hard to engage'? London particularly has one of the most thriving and busy commercial gay scenes in the world, yet with its focus on youth, the majority of Opening Doors members tell us that they rarely if ever go out on the gay scene. A significant 100 per cent of those attending an Opening Doors evaluation event agreed with the statement 'I feel uncomfortable on the scene now because of my age and fear being rejected' (Phillips and Knocker 2010). So, whilst advertising in the gay press (which is only available in gay venues or on the internet) or putting our leaflets in bars on the scene will attract younger LGBT people to volunteer, we still need to look for other avenues for project promotion that might be considered both 'age-appropriate' and 'LGBT-friendly'.

Overcoming obstacles

Promotional campaigns in public access areas such as general practice (GP) surgeries, libraries and community centres are certainly a good option, but also hold inherent engagement problems. A major obstacle is homophobic and transphobic attitudes from some staff and managers. We know that, on occasion, our resources get thrown away immediately on receipt with the response that 'I'm not putting that up in my centre'. The Equality Act 2010 and its Public Sector Duty Requirements go some way to help with this, and our covering letter to services gives a gentle reminder that publicly funded bodies are required to proactively consider the different barriers that may prevent some people accessing quality services, and we offer our help in their achieving this.

Another obstacle to overcome is stigma and discrimination amongst the wider public. Even where staff have displayed the Opening Doors London material, we have had reports of posters being ripped down and bundles of leaflets being removed by other service users. Our response to that is to give a good supply of promotional material, and replacing a poster every day soon becomes a weekly task until it gets left alone, and it becomes an accepted part of the service offered. We also provide training and awareness sessions to other services, either with Opening Doors staff providing more formal training or sending in one of our experienced Service User Ambassadors. This has included providing short talks to all the care management teams in the five main boroughs. But we have also received responses from other services seeking to justify the non-engagement of older LGBT people, from 'we don't have anyone like that in our centre' to 'I don't ask someone's sexuality because it might offend'. Where someone is thought to be LGBT, many service providers are uncertain how best to approach the subject. Sexual orientation monitoring remains a much debated topic, but our advice, covered in our *Supporting Older LGBT People: A Checklist for Social Care Providers* (see later in this chapter) is to ensure that LGBT resources are available and on display to *all* service users. This not only helps to create a welcome and supportive atmosphere in which LGBT people can seek appropriate services, but also educates non-LGBT people on the issues faced by the LGBT communities. An overarching 'mantra' for the Opening Doors work has long been that services need to 'come out' as LGBT-friendly before they can ever hope to engage fully with older LGBT service users. Over the three years of the project, we have seen greatly increased numbers of self-referrals from people accessing information in their local community centres and libraries, and more promisingly, an increasing number of health and social care professionals themselves referring clients to Opening Doors.

Spreading the word through existing members

Word of mouth proved an effective way to promote the service. There is an ongoing need to tackle the challenges of identifying 'hidden' older LGBT people accessing services, but the power of friends encouraging friends can never be underestimated. Providing a safe and welcoming atmosphere is the first step, so that people want to return. Many of the principles we follow here apply more generally to facilitating groups where opportunities for sociability and peer support are hoped-for outcomes. We ensure that there are supportive volunteers and other service users around to break the ice. Another approach is to give a structure to the meeting, such as a film night, which takes the emphasis off conversation and interaction for those who initially feel uncomfortable doing so. We provide first-name badges to people attending, making it easier to go up and say hello to someone. Variety, too, is important, particularly with greater numbers attending, so that there is something to cater to all tastes. Some attendees just want to come along and catch up with friends, so a social slot is good, with an LGBT-themed film or speaker for those who prefer more structure.

Location, location, location

Older LGBT people are widely distributed around London, so the 'where and when' need to be considered. With a 'catchment age' spanning 50 years, differing needs should be considered where possible, such as daytime meetings not being accessible to those who are working, and late evening meetings being problematic for those with transport or mobility issues, or who are simply wary of going out after dark.

The biggest group within Opening Doors London is the men's evening group in Hampstead, which regularly attracts between 40 and 50 men from across London and beyond, which is an indicator for us of the paucity of provision in other areas. As more people get to hear about the service, so more requests are being made for locally accessible groups. Perhaps as a consequence of having seen what can be achieved, and having built up the confidence to ask for appropriate services, more of our participants are questioning why it can't be done in their own borough or town.

One point to note here is that even if there were a locally accessible group in every area, many older LGBT people would prefer to travel outside of their area for fear of being 'outed' in their own communities. Where funders require a group to be in a specific locality, it is perhaps worth considering expanding the criteria for attendance to anyone 'who lives, works or socialises' in a given area. Close consideration should also be given to the venue. Some older LGBT people would be happy to attend a group within an LGBT venue (e.g. a gay pub), whilst others may fear being 'outed'. To a lesser extent, but still important, is the reluctance from some to be labeled as 'old', so holding meetings in established and known care settings for older people can be off-putting for some potential service users.

Group dynamics

In smaller groups personality issues and complex support needs can also come to the fore. Newcomers are welcomed by volunteers and introduced to others. However, inevitably tensions do arise and this can deter people coming to future groups, so sustaining numbers in smaller satellite groups has been a challenge. Some participants present with support needs that the project is less well equipped to meet. As with Polari's project work, Opening Doors has a high per centage of people with mental health problems, with 21 per cent of those surveyed in 2010 saying that they have had mental health issues in the last five years (Phillips and Knocker 2011).

The ingredients of successful engagement

There seems to be a range of possible explanations for Opening Doors' success in reaching so many people. The fact that it is a London-based project means that there is likely to be a higher density of LGBT people. Many of those interviewed as part of the evaluation of the project had previously lived in other parts of the UK and Europe and had come to London as young gay people, perceiving London as a more 'gay- and lesbian-friendly' place, with more obvious meeting places to connect with other LGBT people. For example, Jo, one of the women members of the project, had run away from an abusive family life in Liverpool and came and lived on the streets in her teens for a period before she linked up with another lesbian woman.

Another key reason for the success of Opening Doors is that it has had a strong social focus rather than a political or campaigning one as a starting point. The 'Polari in Partnership' project (see Chapter 8) working in three London boroughs from 2002–2005 was able to work on an ongoing basis with only 30 people. This was partly because the focus of the group was on engaging older LGBT people in consultation about local services. Davies and River (2005) state that 'some older lesbians and gay men did not want to be involved in meetings, and would have preferred more social opportunities to combat isolation' (p.18). The authors suggest that projects should organise more social activities first and it is then possible for a smaller group of activists to be drawn from the wider group. The messages the Polari project was hearing from people was that they had had enough to deal with at different times in their lives and so now wanted to have some fun. There is a lesson to be learnt here in benefiting from experiences from other projects where open and honest accounts of what works and doesn't work are shared.

Keeping things separate

There has been a huge benefit in having both women's and men's development coordinators in the project and in the fact that most of the men's and women's groups meet separately, with only occasional mixed events. There are different theories about why single-sex groups work better. We found that gender politics were an influence on patterns of association amongst the participants. Some of the women, with a history of feminist activism that stretches back to the 1960s and 70s maintained a commitment to a separatist agenda. The evaluation also identified a few gay men with strong feelings about mixing in a gay male-only environment. What is clear is that any new project starting out with only one worker is likely to have more difficulties recruiting members from the opposite sex, although we found that different 'rules' applied, according to the situation. Many Opening Doors members are happy to mix on the campaigning side of the project's activities and for larger events such as activities at Gay Pride.

'Sisters are doing it for themselves'?

Gender was also an important influence on how participants built networks and developed friendships over time. In the women's groups we noticed a tendency for women to come along to a few of the main groups, meet a friend or friends and then choose to meet those friends independently from the project. In our view this could be considered a success of the project and perhaps indicates that larger groups are not the preferred way of connecting for at least some of the women who joined the project. It highlighted for us the need to accommodate different patterns of sociability and approaches to the development of social networks.

From talking to the women who participate in Opening Doors, our experience has shown that many have their own networks already and perhaps don't need to be organised by others (a point highlighted in an earlier study by Heaphy *et al.* 2003). By contrast, many of the men have indicated that they like structured activities. We have also found that those women who are in an existing relationship are less likely to turn to the project, perhaps because their partnerships provide them with their main social and emotional support. Some women who have found a partner have, for example, stopped attending groups. So, overall we were able to identify different approaches to using the project that included people 'passing through', as well as more prolonged attendance, and this seemed to be influenced by gender differences.

It is clear that age is itself an influencing factor on how people have participated in the project. There has been feedback from members that they would prefer groups run by and for *older* women. As the women's development coordinator and some of the most dedicated volunteers are younger lesbians, there is an inevitable gap between the workers and participants, and as a team we are currently seeking to address this by recruiting older workers.

Opening Doors continues to face challenges in recruiting and sustaining the involvement of older lesbian women. It has recently set up an advisory group to support the women's development coordinator. We are currently considering running fewer of our regular small groups and putting more resources into larger events which combine sessions on issues of interest – for example, lesbian co-housing projects, and some creative and fun workshops. A key learning point for any new project is that age and gender issues are as important a consideration as differences in sexuality.

Opening Doors as a vital link to other services

Through involvement in Opening Doors a number of individuals who were previously very isolated or in need of more intensive support have been able to access a range of other services they had previously avoided or had not been aware of. This has included appropriate benefits and housing advice, health promotion initiatives and contact with social services.

One of the most successful partnerships that Opening Doors has developed is with the Metropolitan Police service. For a generation of people who have had some very difficult experiences with the police, particularly looking back to when homosexuality was criminalised, it has been hard to encourage LGBT people to report being victims of crime. Whilst advances have been made in the areas of tackling homophobic crime, the perceptions of many older LGBT people about how a complaint would be handled by police or other agencies remained sceptical. Opening Doors therefore took a proactive role in setting up regular community safety sessions at a central London pub, which were attended by the police LGBT liaison officers. These officers could then talk informally to group members, advise about their role and encourage people to report any crime or harassment, either directly to them or via the project's workers acting as intermediaries. There is evidence that more gay men in particular would now feel comfortable contacting the police, as one man who had been harassed in the past but had felt unable to report this experience explained: 'I feel more confident now that the police would take it [a complaint] more seriously' (Phillips and Knocker 2010, p.54).

The following example highlights the importance of reaching individuals who are feeling particularly vulnerable and isolated.

Case study

Rose is a 73-year-old lesbian living in a sheltered housing complex. She currently uses a number of voluntary sector services in her borough. Four years ago her neighbours found out about her sexuality and started to harass her. They sent spiteful letters, spread rumours around the housing scheme, and one neighbour even spat in her face and verbally abused her.

She went to the housing officer to report the abuse but the reply from the housing worker was that 'they have done all they can, they are concerned about the welfare of all residents, but they are unable to intervene'. Rose felt she had nowhere else to go and began to 'just live with it' as she put it.

Rose attended an Opening Doors women's group and informed us that it was the first time in several years that she felt safe and supported to talk about her personal life and history.

LGBT police liaison officers who spoke to the group were able to look into her case and put her in touch with a number of agencies who now offer her ongoing support.

Opening minds in social services

The work with the Metropolitan Police service has demonstrated the value of partnership in promoting greater confidence in services, traditionally perceived as hostile to many older LGBT people. This model has influenced the project's current efforts to engage more with social care providers, whose services need to be equally accessible to LGBT people. The employment of a part-time campaigns officer has enabled the Opening Doors project to become more proactive in its campaigning and awareness-raising role. A specific partnership with the London Borough of Hackney to develop an LGBT Kitemark and staff training to help implement improved practice is currently being launched. It is hoped that this will offer a useful template for work in other areas.

Background to this work

We received repeated indications from our members regarding their concerns over 'coming out' to care services. Some have already had bad experiences on the receiving end of care but many more fear the prospect of homophobic attitudes and responses. In a survey of members, 61 per cent of respondents said that they worried about receiving home care and 78 per cent said they feared the prospect of moving into sheltered housing or a care home, in case they were discriminated against on the grounds of their sexuality. However, three-quarters did say that they would 'feel comfortable to answer questions about [their] sexuality as part of an assessment for health or social services' (Phillips and Knocker 2011).

Yet, when the Opening Doors staff were visiting care manager meetings, one of the most common concerns was when and how to raise the issue of someone's sexual orientation, as staff fear causing offence. Another issue raised was how to work with staff members, and particularly hands-on care staff, with strongly held religious beliefs that include viewing homosexuality as sinful or taboo. Some Opening Doors members receiving home care services have reported being given religious texts by staff and being treated in an openly hostile and even abusive way. In one case the Opening Doors team have had to support a lesbian woman in a formal complaints process. However, there have also been positive examples of religious staff being open and accepting. These discussions have highlighted the need for the team to consider broadening its remit to providing more guidance and training to promote good practice, but also for the need for clearer policy guidance alongside targeted work in this area right across health and social care.

Developing a checklist for good practice

It was through feedback from both members and professionals that the team decided to develop some practical guidance for how organisations could take steps to develop more positive approaches to working with older LGBT people. AgeUK nationally had developed a 'ten steps' approach for encouraging local Age Concerns to develop best practice in LGBT inclusiveness, which offered a useful starting point.

Opening Doors London partnered with LB [London Borough of] Hackney Adult Social Care with the view that the commissioning process, with its regular monitoring, would be well placed to ensure that services delivered through adult social care are truly inclusive of the needs of older LGBT service users. The checklist was initially drafted in May 2010 and was sent to a membership of over 450 older LGBT people in London along with a form to provide detailed feedback. Three subsequent consultation events were held to discuss the draft checklist. In July, a workshop with representatives from Hackney Council discussed peoples' experiences, fears and desires regarding social care services. In August and September discussions at our men's and women's regular group meetings provided a further opportunity for our members to voice their concerns and suggest approaches to overcoming current barriers to receiving appropriate and inclusive service provision. Two-thirds of the respondents feared prejudice from care services, one fifth expressed fear of people from religious fundamentalist faith treating them in an abusive or otherwise discriminatory manner, and one third expressed fear of being forced to have care provided by someone of the opposite gender. Those who were consulted feared ending up having to 'play straight' or gave examples of not feeling comfortable in their own home. One gay male participant said: 'When social care staff are in my home I sometimes feel like a stranger because I have to hide photos, literature, etc. which use the words "gay".' Another example came from someone attending a day centre who felt marginalised and excluded during a reminiscence discussion that focused on weddings and first dates. Many reported never seeing anything in their local council's literature which acknowledged the existence of lesbian, gay or bisexual people and felt that, in the event of their being assessed for a service, the assessment would start 'from a position of assumed heterosexuality'.

All of this feedback was obviously a strong endorsement of the need to do some work with local councils to develop best practice guidance that it was hoped would ultimately lead to actual improvements in service delivery.

LB Hackney Adult Social Care have made a commitment to using the checklist to monitor how LGBT-friendly their services are and have contracted the Opening Doors project to provide tailored equality training to front-line staff teams in order to ensure that their staff are aware of the needs of older LGBT service users and are trained in engaging positively with these groups.

The checklist was formally launched in October 2011 with the aim that the successful working relationship enjoyed with LB Hackney will be replicated with other local authorities across London. A full copy of the checklist is available to download at www.openingdoorslondon. org.uk.

The *Checklist for Social Care Organisations Working with Older Lesbian, Gay, Bisexual and Transgender People* covers the following broad areas:

- organisation-wide ways to be LGBT-friendly
- ensuring that older LGBT people are supported by LGBT-friendly staff
- care management and social care assessment
- caring – care staff (homes, day care and in the home)
- resources and reading.

The tool provides very specific and practical examples for good practice – for example, the kinds of questions to ask a person to encourage them to be open in an assessment: 'Would you like to tell us who are the important people in your life?' rather than ask about a husband or wife; or 'Do you need support to keep up contact with anyone in particular? How do you like to spend your leisure time?' The checklist also highlights the importance of specific acknowledgement of homophobic abuse within safeguarding policies and guidelines. The 'checklist' format is designed to enable service providers to work through particular areas requiring action, and to have a clear sense of achievements as well as identifying areas still needing improvement.

The successful collaboration with the Metropolitan Police outlined earlier is offered as a potential template from which a similar partnership with social care services could be established. This would involve identifying an 'LGBT liaison' person within social services who can act as a contact point for those who are anxious about being referred to a care manager.

Taking the work forward

The checklist has now been launched and the next phase of the work is to implement it throughout the London Borough of Hackney's services, which includes delivering a series of half-day training courses to their social care services teams. It is a credit to Hackney's management team that they have taken on this piece of work, particularly at a time of unprecedented cuts and demands on core services. However, there remain some very big challenges, not least that there are obvious limitations in what a half-day training session can do to shift attitudes, particularly in the case of workers with entrenched homophobic opinions. There has been recent success in including older gay or lesbian speakers or Opening Doors 'ambassadors' on training courses or at events, as hearing personal stories helps to open minds in a way that more abstract or theoretical training and written case studies can never achieve. As a result we have come to understand the transformative power of using biographies and life stories for training purposes. Many care workers may think that they have never met a lesbian or gay person and so may subscribe to unhelpful or frightening stereotypes. It is important for workers to have an opportunity to talk about these fears and to develop a greater understanding of what it might be like for older gay and lesbian people who have faced a history of persecution and rejection from wider society.

Conclusion

The success of Opening Doors[1] provides a proven model for community engagement and an ever-increasing membership is helping to make older LGBT people more visible across London and beyond. Whilst involvement of older gay men has been particularly successful and continues to expand, there are ongoing challenges in reaching older lesbian women that highlight the importance of longevity for an initiative such as this. By securing a further three years' funding the project has been able to consolidate and expand its work, hopefully ensuring that it becomes a core service rather than just a short-term project, as is so common in LGBT initiatives. This was largely thanks to an unwavering commitment from the host organisation, AgeUK Camden, and a huge amount of detailed work to prepare a successful funding bid, which can be an onerous demand for smaller projects with limited resources.

Sustainability is not only vital to having a lasting impact and outcomes but makes economic sense too. As other initiatives have demonstrated, short-term funding means that a massive amount of labour and momentum is lost when the term of funding ends, to say nothing

---

1   To become a member or for general information about the work of Opening Doors London, go to www.openingdoorslondon.org.uk.

of the networks and connections that 'go cold' if not maintained. In being able to build a service over time the Opening Doors project has achieved a broader spread of successes, with the largest number of older LGBT people ever to have been engaged by such a project in the UK.

Opening Doors London plays a unique role as it combines direct work with older LGBT people with a developing campaigning arm. This is advantageous, as it ensures that its core awareness-raising messages are grounded in real people's experiences, which ultimately are more likely to open hearts and minds. Opening Doors has proved the demand for more specialist groups to meet the distinct needs of older lesbian, gay, bisexual and transgender people. Whilst there is a strong social focus to Opening Doors it has also been able to ensure that this client group, often labelled as 'invisible' by service providers, is more able to access other core public services when needed. In this sense Opening Doors can be seen to be supporting the citizenship of older LGBT people. It is hoped that the project's successes and challenges outlined here can offer inspiration and guidance to other fledgling older LGBT groups in the years ahead.

References

Concannon, L. (2009) 'Developing inclusive health and social care policies for older LGBT citizens.' *British Journal of Social Work 39*, 3, 403–417.

Davies, P. and River, L. (2005) *Being Taken Seriously: The Polari in Partnership Project – promoting change for older lesbians, gay men and bisexuals.* London: Polari. Accessible at: www.ageofdiversity.org.uk/documents.

Heaphy, B., Yip, A. and Thompson, D. (2003) *Lesbian, Gay And Bisexual Lives over 50: A Report on the Project 'The Social And Policy Implications of Non-Heterosexual Ageing'.* Nottingham: York House Publications, Nottingham Trent University.

Phillips, M. and Knocker, S. (2010) *Opening Doors Evaluation – The Story So Far.* London: Age Concern. Accessible at: www.openingdoorslondon.org.uk/resources.html.

Phillips, M. and Knocker, S. (2011) *Opening Doors Evaluation – The Story Continues.* London: AgeUK.

Chapter 10

Ageing in Gay Brighton

Kath Browne, Leela Bakshi and Jason Lim

Introduction

Recent work across the social sciences and within social policy has recognised the heterogeneity of lesbian, gay, bisexual and trans (LGBT) populations (see for example Browne and Lim 2010; Hines 2007; 2010; Kuntsman and Esperanza 2008; Taylor 2007). Such differences can be overlooked where research seeks to 'compare' particularly lesbian and gay people and lives to heterosexual people and lives, especially quantitatively. Recognising the diversity of experiences amongst those who identify as, or are recognised within the category, LGBT must also account for geographical variations (see Browne, Brown and Lim 2007). The places in which LGBT lives 'take place' are key to understanding inequalities and social differences based on gender and sexual identities. Therefore place, as well as time, acts to shape individuals' lives. Explorations of place-specific experiences and issues are required to shape the development of responsive services that can cater for locally specific, as well as national, populations.

This chapter focuses on older LGBT people, and in doing so highlights the importance of recognising difference, as well as commonalities, when addressing the needs of LGBT people. It draws on data from the research project 'Count Me In Too' which indicated that when working with older LGBT people, there are particular concerns around socialising and around housing. However, it should also be noted that the research did *not* find a plethora of statistically significant differences between LGBT people on the basis of age. Therefore the core messages from Count Me In Too about differences between and among lesbian, gay, bi and trans people regarding issues such as isolation, health, well-being and safety also apply to older LGBT people (see www.countmeintoo.co.uk for further details regarding these aspects of the research, information on how the project was undertaken, findings reports and summaries of findings). Further, this research found commonalities between older LGBT people and LGBT people of other age groups. Consequently, it could be argued that services will be better placed to meet the needs of older LGBT people if they also connect with and take into account broader LGBT strategies and communities that are not age-specific. Nonetheless, we also highlight some of the specific issues affecting older LGBT people, namely socialising and housing. Prior to this, the chapter will outline the context of Brighton (the supposed 'gay capital' of the UK) and the methods used in the Count Me In Too research.

Context and methods

Brighton has recently (since the 1990s) become renowned as the 'gay capital' of the UK, a 'cosmopolitan' place of tolerance and acceptance of diversity (http://gay.brighton.co.uk, accessed on 20 October 2010). Brighton has a relatively large gay scene, given the size of the city (its population from the 2001 census was 247,817), and a supposedly large LGBT population. (Some estimates put this at 15–20% although these figures are disputed.) Thus, Brighton is understood as – and has a reputation for being – a metropolitan 'gay Mecca' (see Browne and Bakshi 2011; Browne and Lim 2010; Browne, Bakshi and Lim 2011). This chapter uses the Count Me In Too research, a project that sought to explore differences between and among LGBT people and to identify areas of need. Count Me In Too offered insights into the imaginings of Brighton as the 'gay capital' and the lives of LGBT people in the city. More than this, it is a research project where LGBT people in Brighton shared their views and experiences, and worked with service providers and others to gather and present evidence that would promote positive changes for LGBT people. The initial research design and data analysis involved local LGBT individuals and voluntary and community groups and services, as well as statutory services. The data was collected between January and October 2006, using a qualitative and quantitative questionnaire completed by 819 respondents, that consisted of open and closed questions. The sample details are as follows:

- Sixty per cent (n = 492) of the sample were aged between 26–45, with 9.5 per cent (n = 78) over 55.

- Gay men made up 53 per cent (n = 431) of the sample and gay women/lesbians 34 per cent (n = 280), with 6 per cent (n = 47) identifying as bisexual.

- Of respondents aged over 55, 20 per cent (n = 16) identified as lesbian, 64 per cent (n = 50) as gay, and 3 per cent (n = 2) as bisexual, while 13 per cent (n = 10) were otherwise coded.

- Five per cent (n = 43) of the overall sample identified as trans.

- Twenty-six per cent (n = 11) of trans respondents are aged over 55, compared to only 8 per cent (n = 64) of non-trans people.

- Twenty per cent (n = 160) of the total sample earned an income of under £10,000. However, of those over 55, 32 per cent (n = 24) earn less than £10,000 per year.

The questionnaire was routed (meaning that respondents followed particular routes through the questionnaire according to how they answered certain questions), and one section specifically addressed those over 55 (classified in this study as 'older'). In this routed section older LGBT people were asked about their desires for housing and their experiences of being an older LGBT person in Brighton and Hove. This chapter discusses the qualitative and quantitative data that this section elicited, as well as the comparisons between 'older' LGBT people and others in the research.

Recognising the bias towards representation of a gay, white and 'affluent' grouping in LGBT questionnaire research, 20 focus groups were undertaken. These sought to connect with groups that the LGBT Community Steering Group understood as multiply marginalised, based on an intersectional understanding of social difference; the research subsequently found the cumulative effect of discrimination that is implied in the Equalities Act 2010 term 'dual discrimination' (see Browne, Brown and Lim 2010; Browne and Davis 2008; Taylor, Hines and Casey 2010) and that is often overlooked in questionnaire data. There were specific focus groups for older LGBT people, trans people, bi people, and LGBT people who identified as disabled, black and minority ethnic LGBT people. We also targeted people whose experiences of certain issues (such as mental health difficulties and hate crime) might have implications for their experiences of LGBT life. The focus group targeted specifically at older LGBT people was created in part by using contacts from a Brighton City Council survey of older LGBT people in supported housing.

The data for this chapter were re-analysed from that presented in a summary of findings regarding older LGBT people (see Browne and Lim 2009). When undertaking numerous cross tabs by age across the various findings reports, it became clear that age was not always associated with a significant difference between LGBT people. We have chosen to focus on particular areas of need and exclusion for this paper, to highlight specific issues that were raised by LGBT people in our research. Nevertheless, it is important to note that further research is needed to explore the similarities between different age groups, rather than presuming difference, and particularly to address areas of commonality between older LGBT people and younger LGBT people.

'Gay Brighton': Socialising in the 'Gay Capital of the UK'

Despite Brighton being labelled the 'gay capital' of the UK, 16 per cent (n = 12) of older LGBT people in this research said that it is 'difficult' or 'very difficult' to be an older LGBT person in the city. This compares to 5 per cent (n = 6) of those under 26, who think it is 'difficult' or 'very difficult' to be a 'younger' LGBT person in Brighton. Similar to other general research about older people, older LGBT people are more likely to fear crime in Brighton when compared to other age groups in the Count Me In Too research, and are more likely to avoid public displays of affection and going out. Thus, rather than being a 'gay Mecca' for all, for older LGBT people Brighton can still be seen as dangerous. There are two key ways in which the 'gay capital' is sold and experienced in terms of socialising: first, through Pride – an annual celebration of LGBT lives – and second, through 'the commercial scene', which is a range of bars and clubs that cater predominantly for a gay (and at times lesbian) clientele. Exploring older people's experiences of these spaces offers insights into the incorporation or otherwise of older LGBT people into 'the heart' of Gay Brighton.

Pride

It has been argued that Pride offers a 'break' from heterosexual lives and that it questions the ways in which heterosexuality is assumed to be the norm and the expected sexuality in everyday spaces (see Bell and Valentine 1995; Browne 2006). Such freedoms are apparently afforded to all LGBT people, and in this research 90 per cent (n = 724) of respondents have attended Pride in Brighton & Hove. Pride in Brighton & Hove is a key moment in the city's calendar and feeds into the understandings of the city as 'gay-friendly'. However, the park and parade events that often are equated with Pride can be noisy, busy and crowded, with alcohol and drugs being prominent in these spaces – factors which older people in Count Me In Too pointed to as exclusionary (see below). Research undertaken in 2004 found that the majority of those at the park event were aged below 30 (see Browne, Church and Smallbone 2005). In the Count Me In Too research, no 'younger' person (aged under 26) or person aged between 36 and 45 said they do not want to go to Pride, compared to 11 per cent (n = 8) of older people who said they do not want to go.

These findings are significant in terms of socialising and LGBT well-being because not only is Pride a moment that is supposed to be enjoyed by all of Brighton, it is also core to the 'joining together' of LGBT people and the sense of community that is supposed to occur during this event. In this way, Pride is often presented locally as 'gay Christmas' and a draw to the city. Moreover, it is pointed to as central to creating 'gay Brighton' in the mainstream as well as gay media. Not 'feeling part' of Pride can, then, have significant implications for feelings of belonging to LGBT communities, as well as for broader city engagement. Nonetheless, it should be noted that the majority of older LGBT people do want to go to Pride and had been attending in the years preceding 2006 when this research was undertaken.

Accessing and using 'the scene'

Brighton has built its reputation as the 'gay capital' through its commercial scene, consisting of bars, clubs and shops that are mainly targeted at gay men. This scene is crucial to Brighton's reputation as the 'gay capital' (see Browne and Bakshi 2011). However, the Count Me In Too research found that not all LGBT people enjoyed the scene (see also Browne and Bakshi 2011). Out of all the age groups, people over 55 are least likely (53%, n = 41) to agree that they enjoy LGBT venues and events, whilst those in the youngest age group (under 26) are most likely to agree with the statement 'I enjoy using LGBT venues and events' (84%, n = 103) (see Figure 10.1). People over 55 were also most likely to say that they do not use LGBT venues and events. These data were augmented by those in the older people's focus group who identified issues such as intergenerational contact, noise and ageism:

Rex: There are very few places you can go to like to talk, that are comfortable to talk in except maybe during the day. *There is always this dance music and all the rest of it, clubbing atmosphere and it is only conducive to a meat market atmosphere, which is what they are.* You don't go there to have intellectual conversation, do you, or talk about the future of the gay community or so on, have an opinion, exchange of opinions. *Certainly for our age group – well there is no [place], everything is alien.*

Liam: You choose the place to go to, you find somewhere that's reasonably friendly except that they sort of crank up the music. So it can be quite a quiet place until you know post 9 o'clock and then the music starts up. That's a particular pub [a pub named earlier] that I know from my experience is very welcoming for everybody so you get a complete range of the people in there. But lots of pubs I just wouldn't go into because as you say they are either really scene places –

Researcher: Is that just about music or are there other ways that you are not feeling welcomed?

Liam: Well it's an ageist thing. I mean in a sense that's one of the things that slightly annoys me, the gay scene is very much divided up into sections, young, whatever, if you are into bands. *In some pubs I've walked into and there's sort of, 'My god what's this old geezer doing coming in here,' it's got a feel about it.*

Researcher: How does that make you feel?

Liam: Uncomfortable and I don't go back, that's a simple answer, well I mark it down as another place not to go to.

Phillip: It just annoys me that you can't have pubs that are from the 18-year-olds up to the 80-year-olds. They just won't cover the spectrum, as you were saying, they just group you. Where I go in the [name of pub] they make anyone welcome there you know, but the youngsters don't go in there unless they specifically want to chase the older guys you know. It's the same in the other pubs you all sort [of stick] to your own scene. That's why it is like that, but if the landlords for the sake of using the word like that did sort of make their views known that everyone was welcome, then they probably would get a more full age spectrum. *[But they]*

*make it quite distinct that they only want youngsters so they can wind up
the music you know and get as much money out of them as they can you
know rather than, for our sort of generation the idea of going to the pub
was a little social gathering wasn't it? It was a social club.*

This quote from the Count Me In Too older people's focus group
illustrates how older LGBT people negotiated the Brighton gay scene,
where places to socialise could be found but were not always what
older LGBT people wanted. Ageism, as well as feeling 'out of place'
and unwelcome, were common experiences giving rise to feelings of
exclusion and marginalisation from some LGBT places, for older people.
Negotiating space and time in the way these respondents describe, older
LGBT people are at times able to find spaces that they enjoy, but in the
main the lack of intergenerational mixing, noise, and being seen as 'the
old geezer' militate against their inclusion in certain parts of Brighton's
gay scene. Young people's engagement in specific forms of consumption
and sexual practices was seen by older LGBT respondents as 'alien'
and, by implication, alienating. If the 'scene', often understood through
youth culture, is a symbol of LGBT belonging and presence in the city,
then being excluded from it may become significant, even if there are
other (LGBT) leisure spaces to go to. Pubs themselves can also have
different and changing meanings, associated with different experiences.
Phillip, for example, views the pub as a social club, suggesting that he
used to enjoy a different form of socialising within the pub than what
he sees occur today. Contemporary forms of socialising are perceived
to come from other people in the pubs and clubs, as well as from the
atmosphere that is created by landlords, managers and bar owners. The
participants note how different LGBT spaces are produced through the
specific features of pubs and clubs, like loud sound systems, so that an
understanding of belonging and exclusion in the city needs to take
account of the specific ways in which older people relate to the LGBT
spaces of the city.

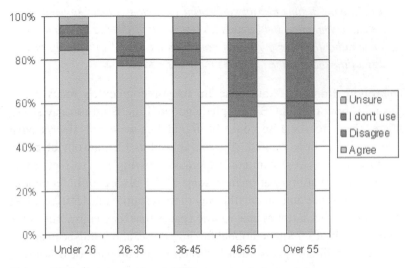

Figure 10.1: 'I enjoy using LGBT venues and events' by age

The reliance on the commercial scene in Brighton is put into context by the absence of other public community spaces. Whilst there are over 40 venues (pubs, clubs and shops) and a series of support services that offer 'drop-in' hours for specific groups (for example, LGBT people with mental health difficulties or young LGBT people), there are no not-for-profit, open-access spaces aimed at LGBT people. There is no drop-in space that specifically targets older LGBT people, although the Gay Elderly Men's social group meets regularly. The specific eligibility for involvement in this group is made obvious in its name, and there is a long history associated with the group's development and its break away from its lesbian counterpart, Lesbian Link (although Lesbian Link is not an age-specific group). The absence of 'non-scene' social spaces was noted by many of our participants, belying the possibility of engagement with 'gay Brighton' for those who didn't want to use gay commercial venues and bars (see also Browne and Bakshi 2011).

Socialising is a key aspect of belonging to LGBT communities. As we move on to consider housing, this chapter will explore fears not only of being excluded from the scene, but also regarding lack of support for expressing LGBT identities.

Housing

Having stable, secure, suitable and friendly housing is an important factor for health and well-being. Whilst the home has come under critical scrutiny with regard to the possibilities of enacting lesbian and gay identities and to the questions of belonging or not being 'at home' (see, for example, Gorman-Murray 2007, 2008; Johnston and Valentine 1995), much less attention has been paid to the materialities of housing. Yet the provision of – and access to – housing has been understood as key to understanding LGBT lives, and particularly the vulnerabilities of those 'on the margins', including younger LGBT people (see Browne and Davis 2008; Cull, Platzer and Balloch 2006). Consequently, exploring housing needs is important in understanding and engaging with older LGBT people's lives.

The 'Whole of Me' (Knocker 2006), a national LGB project, found that older LGBT people are two-and-a-half times nore likely to live alone than other older people (see also the more recent report by Stonewall 2011). There were also stark differences between older and younger LGBT people in our research in terms of housing composition, illustrating some key distinctions in experiences of the city, based on age:

- Respondents aged over 55 (49%, n = 37) were more likely to live alone than those under 26 (8%, n = 9, p = .0005). Only 8 per cent (n = 6) of those aged over 55 lived with lesbian and gay friends, compared to 20 per cent (n = 23) of those under 26.

- LGBT people aged over 55 (3%, n = 2) are less likely to live with straight/heterosexual people, when compared to those who are under 26 (22%, n = 26, p = .001).[1]

- Those aged over 55 (26%, n = 19) are less likely to live with a same-sex partner, compared to those aged 26–55 (45%, n = 275, p = .0005).

These differences may be due to ageing and household composition – i.e. as people get older they are less likely to live in shared accommodation. Nonetheless, shared households can also provide support, social outlets and other advantages.

The 'Whole of Me' research suggests that older LGB people have a significantly greater dependence on professional care services because they are twice as likely as older heterosexual people to be single, and

---

1   Those aged under 26 were significantly (p<.001) more likely to live with straight/ heterosexual friends than those over that age. This could point to a greater acceptance of LGBT people amongst younger people and greater integration, or it could indicate forced households due to the necessity of sharing and high housing prices in the city (see Browne and Davis 2008).

four-and-a-half times as likely to have no children to call upon in times of need (Knocker 2006). Similarly, in the 'Count Me In Too' research, when compared to other LGBT people, those over 55 (15%, n = 11) are more likely to live in social housing than those in the 26–35 age group (p<.0001). However, 67 per cent (n = 51) of older people in this research own their own homes. The majority of older (66%, n = 29) (and younger 74%, n = 86) people are happy with who they live with, but these figures are lower than for other age groups (p = .001). There may, therefore, be links between housing composition and satisfaction, and between housing composition and isolation. Indeed, older people are the age group most likely (37%, n = 28, p = 0.002) to say that at times they feel isolated in Brighton.

For older LGBT people, choosing where to live was a key issue, illustrating the importance of housing for belonging, well-being and isolation. Only 18 per cent (n = 14) of those aged over 55 believe that there is enough housing support for older people in Brighton; 39 per cent (n = 30) said that there is not enough. Table 10.1 illustrates the complexity of the desirability of housing/residential care. Whilst overall 63 per cent (n = 39) would be interested in 'sheltered housing /extra care housing/residential care specifically for the LGBT community', it can be seen that a smaller proportion of those aged over 66 share this desire. The numbers of people here are small, however, and therefore more research is needed to explore the desire for LGBT-specific supported housing. Nonetheless, these figures may be indicative both of the fear of ageing and what this might mean in terms of LGBT identities, and the converse concern regarding ghettoisation.

Table 10.1: Would you be interested in sheltered housing / extra care housing / residential care specifically for the LGBT community?

	Yes		No	
Age group	Number	%	Number	%
55–65	33	71.7	13	28.3
66–75	5	38.5	8	61.5
76+	1	33.3	2	66.7
All older age groups	39	62.9	23	37.1

It is not only older people who are concerned about the housing support they currently receive or might imminently need; LGBT people more generally, as they age, can begin to consider their options and the barriers that they perceive:

> It's a genuine fear that I have. I am fiercely independent. I am just over 40. If my health deteriorates a lot over the next 10 years I will be allowed to go into sheltered housing. My fear is that as I get older, as my family of origin die, I will be alone and I do fear going into care. I am amazed even when I worked in health that there are no nursing/care homes specifically for the LGBT community because I know because of my lifestyle I couldn't ever if I had to go into a str8 [straight] care, nursing home as I got older. (Questionnaire respondent)

For some LGBT people, the fear of getting older is associated with the prospect of going into 'straight' care – mainstream care where having freedom and opportunities to engage in activities that the respondent above associates with LGBT identity is not perceived to be possible. The options for LGBT people are limited, and the absence of provision of specific LGBT care, alongside a general assumption that care for older people is straight, gives rise to a deep-seated fear. Being 'fiercely independent' may be challenged not only by the physical need for support, but also by the difficulties of maintaining your 'lifestyle' in 'str8 [straight] care'. The desire for LGBT-specific residential accommodation for older people (see Table 10.1) was echoed throughout the qualitative data and was, in the main, supported by those who were yet to need it:

> Though I don't need it yet I feel specific old people's homes for gays and lesbians would meet a very real need. (Questionnaire respondent)

There seems to be an assumption amongst respondents who understood themselves as 'not yet older' that LGBT-specific care is desirable. This appears to be related to concerns about the ability to enact LGBT identities (or, in the example just cited, lesbian and gay). Undoubtedly, checking and addressing older LGBT people's satisfaction with housing should be a priority for services and providers, and so too should enhancing reputations and images of care and support for LGBT people who fear the prospect of what is to come.

In contrast to those who have yet to become 'older' (in their understanding of their life stage), those in the older people's focus group expressed interest in – but also concerns about – LGBT-specific provision. This suggests that as people age, the idea of LGBT-specific housing may be considered in a more nuanced way, offering further insight into the data in Table 10.1. The 'options' were considered in discussions about the tensions and benefits of living in mixed communities, compared to living in 'gay ghettos':

Alf: It also occurs to me that you know at some stage in the future I'm, it might be better for me to live in some sort of sheltered accommodation or whatever, but one of the things that I like about where I am is that I am actually in a mixed community, there are young people, there are older people, there are kids, you know what I mean, there is everybody around me. *I don't want to be hived off into a little ghetto of elderly gay people.*

Jude: Brighton Council has got policy, unofficial, putting the same sort of people together all over their town right, so if you are trouble makers you go to Moulsecoomb or upper part of Whitehawk, if you've got mental health issues or learning difficulties you go [into] little…enclaves more or less, they are situated in the town all over the place. Where are they going to group people together if they go for housing and help?

Researcher: Would you want to be grouped together?

Jude: No. *I want to mix with everybody.*

Alf: *I mean as long as I feel safe, I'd much rather that was the general situation.*

Jude: Yeah exactly.

Paul: Well *I'm living in your worst nightmare* [laughter]. Stuck out in the far end of Moulescoomb with everybody waiting to… God's waiting room sort of thing. I'm the youngest one there.

('Count Me In Too' older focus group)

Fear of what will happen when LGBT people age and the 'community' they will be put in is clear throughout these narratives. Jude emphasises the need for LGBT-friendly and safe options for older LGBT people.

These perceptions of safety are related to particular areas of the city. Older LGBT people in this research voiced concerns about areas of deprivation and large estates with a high proportion of social housing (Moulsecoomb and Whitehawk), especially in relation to perceptions (rightly or wrongly) of an association between such areas and hate crime against LGBT people (see Browne and Davis 2008; Browne and Lim 2008; Browne *et al.* 2011; also Taylor 2009). Paul highlights the undertone of the comments made regarding both sheltered accommodation and the area of deprivation where he lives, Moulsecoomb, describing his situation as 'your worst nightmare'. Fears about safety exist in tension with the desire not to be ghettoised and spatially excluded. Alf doesn't want to be in a ghetto of older gay people, but neither is he asking for a community of LGBT people with a mixture of age groups, nor a non sexuality-specific community for older people, but for a 'mixed community'. This suggests that for some older LGBT people wider opportunities for interaction are preferable to identity-specific provision, whether that be around age or gender/sexual identity. This discussion illustrates that LGBT-specific accommodation as the *only* place for older LGBT people to live is not seen as desirable because it restricts individual choice and prevents interactions with other people.

As we have seen in the discussion above, age is a crucial factor in determining whether LGBT people feel welcome in these spaces, so 'money' and the absence thereof cannot solely account for the marginalisation of older LGBT people. Similarly, it is clear that there are *no* options for specifically LGBT-friendly accommodation, even for those who want it and could afford it. The provision of 'str8 care' is all that is available in both the private and the public sector. Among those who asked for housing options that would respect their LGBT lives, some did not need to rely on the public sector; their housing needs could, in theory, be provided by the commercial sector.

Regardless of housing provider, there were calls for support for sustained community networking so that older LGBT people could contribute to and benefit from each other's support and skills:

Ian: I was listening to a programme this morning, it was on but it was about the development of health visitors in Salford back in God knows when, you know, 1920 or whenever it was. They decided that it would be absolutely impossible for lots of well-meaning middle-class women to go into working-class homes and dispense advice, and I can understand that. So what they did was to work out a system of employing, to start with anyway, employing working-class women to become advisors to their community. So they sort of built up a network and eventually that become almost like an unofficial network so everybody could, was in touch with one another, giving advice about children, about health. It seems to me that something like that for people of our age would be rather good, but I mean that it was generated from us [older LGBT people] and that we have a network of people who at least kept in [touch], you know, fortnightly.

('Count Me In Too' older focus group)

Ian's comments relate to the isolation that older LGBT people can feel and point to the specificity of older LGBT people's need for social networks that offer appropriate support and opportunities for socialising. This chapter has evidenced the way in which many older LGBT people feel excluded from particular spaces on the scene, the implications of lack of public, accessible and friendly LGBT meeting spaces, and the difficulties many older LGBT people face in expressing their sexual/gender identities because of where they live. We suggest that these issues can result in and from isolation and are the undertone of Ian's plea for sustained community networking – networking that offers appropriate support and that mobilises the skills, experiences and values shared within LGBT communities. Such networks could be deployed in ways that work to improve older LGBT people's lives by empowering a diverse range of older LGBT people. Supporting the generation of networks by 'us' requires that services and policy makers recognise the value of, and resources within, LGBT communities and offer proper (and fully financed) support to undertake meaningful changes (see also, Browne *et al.* 2011). More than this, they should value and address the diversity among LGBT people, as well as the range of experiences, lives and opinions of older LGBT people.

Conclusion

The Count Me In Too research found that despite the imagining of Brighton as tolerant, open and accepting, there were key issues for LGBT people that needed to be addressed. These issues were not always or necessarily age-specific, but there can be little doubt that older LGBT people in the city experience issues of multiple marginalisation. Overall, then, when developing provision that caters for older LGBT people, effective practice will cater for the diversities, including taking into account that lesbians, gay men, bi people and trans people will have specific needs and issues within this grouping. Such provision should also take account of common experiences arising from subscription to identities that differ from the 'norm', recognising the importance of belonging and inclusion in LGBT communities.

The chapter will now conclude by drawing out specific points regarding socialising and housing, and by outlining the implications of these findings for practitioners.

Pride and the commercial gay scene play an important part not only in understandings of Brighton as the 'gay capital', but also in creating feelings of belonging to LGBT communities. Yet the Count Me In Too data points to the differential ways in which older LGBT people feel included within 'gay Brighton' and the social spaces that create it. Older people in this Brighton-based research wanted to be part of LGBT events and scenes, but often felt 'out of place' because of their age. Discrimination and the limited inclusivity of the scene was an issue for older people and, as we have shown elsewhere, many other groupings within the LGBT collective (see Browne and Lim 2010; www.countmeintoo.co.uk). Thus the presumed 'benefits' of living in 'gay Brighton' may not be accessible to all older LGBT people, nor the symbolically youthful, sexualised scenes welcoming and inclusive of them. More work is needed to explore what it is that older people want from LGBT social space. What would or could make spaces friendly and attractive to older LGBT people when they are not a homogenous group? Indeed, as has long been recognised, the category of 'older' encompasses various generations, such that different groupings of older LGBT people have different experiences of visibility, secrecy, criminalisation and support. Therefore we cannot assume that the next generation of older LGBT people will want the things that the current generation of older LGBT people call for. Nuanced and ongoing explorations of the complexities of older LGBT people's lives are key to making sense of – and providing for – this grouping as the UK population ages.

Not only are there differences between the housing experiences of the general population and LGBT people (see Knocker 2006), there are also differences among LGBT people, including differences by age. Housing choice can become a key concern as LGBT people age, even in the supposed 'gay capital'. These concerns include older people's housing and the prospect of growing old without suitable accommodation that enables LGBT people to express their sexuality regardless of their ability to pay for housing and care. There is a need for further research into the housing needs and desires of older LGBT people, as well as of LGBT people who are 'yet to become old' but fear getting older because of discrimination or lack of appropriate provision and support in relation to their gender and sexual identities. We have identified key factors that include living in a way that enables an LGBT 'lifestyle'; feeling safe enacting these gender/sexual identities; and the tensions and benefits of living in mixed communities, compared to 'gay ghettos'. Practitioners and providers should give attention to whether people feel safe or, conversely, restricted in expressing their identity, and to the composition of the communities that they enjoy living in or would like to live in. Further research might also consider whether the differences between those aged under 65 and those over 65 regarding LGBT-specific care provision and housing represent a generational difference in outlook (i.e. when those under 65 get older, they will not reproduce the views of their elders), or arise from differing experience (e.g. those over 65 are more likely to live in a care home or sheltered accommodation, and once they do so, they come to value mixed accommodation; and when those under 65 start moving into such accommodation, their views may also shift in this way).

Finally, in dealing with the isolation that can result from exclusion from social scenes and inadequate experiences of housing and associated support, it was clear that LGBT groups and peer networks could offer productive possibilities for improving the lives of older LGBT people. These should be developed, supported, worked with and encouraged by practitioners in collaboration with LGBT groups, networks and commercial scenes.

References

Bell, D. and Valentine, G. (1995) *Mapping Desire: Geographies of Sexualities*. London: Routledge.

Browne, K. (2006) '(Re)making the other: Heterosexualising everyday space.' *Environment and Planning A 39*, 4, 996–1014.

Browne, K. and Bakshi, L. (2011) 'We are here to party? Lesbian, gay, bisexual and trans leisurescapes.' *Leisure Studies 30*, 2, 179–196.

Browne, K. and Davis, P. (2008) *Housing: 'Count Me in Too' Additional Analysis Report.* Spectrum and the University of Brighton. Available at www.spectrumlgbt.org/cmiToo/downloads/CMIT_Housing_Report_April_08.pdf%20. Accessed on 22 September 2011.

Browne, K. and Lim, J. (2008) *Community Safety: 'Count Me in Too' Additional Analysis Report.* Spectrum and the University of Brighton. Available at www.spectrum-lgbt.org/downloads/CMIT/CMIT_Safety_Report_Feb08.pdf. Accessed on 22 September 2011.

Browne, K. and Lim, J. (2009) *Count Me in Too: Older People Summary Findings Report, February 2009.* Spectrum and the University of Brighton. Available at www.realadmin.co.uk/microdir/3700/File/CMIT_OlderPeople_16Feb09_v3-1.pdf. Accessed on 23 September 2011.

Browne, K. and Lim, J. (2010) 'Trans Lives in the "Gay Capital of the UK".' *Gender, Place and Culture 17*, 5, 615–633.

Browne, K., Bakshi, L. and Lim, J. (2011) '"It's something you just have to ignore": Understanding and addressing contemporary lesbian, gay, bisexual and trans safety beyond hate crime paradigms.' *Journal of Social Policy 40*, 4, 739–756.

Browne, K., Brown, G. and Lim, J. (2007) *Geographies of Sexualities: Theory, Practices and Politics.* Aldershot UK and Burlington US: Ashgate.

Browne, K., Brown, G. and Lim J. (2010) 'Sexual Life.' In J. Vincent, J. Del Casino, M.E. Thomas, P. Cloke and R. Panelli (eds) *A Companion to Social Geography.* Oxford: Wiley Blackwell.

Browne, K., Church A. and Smallbone, K. (2005) *Do it with Pride Report.* Community and University Partnership Programme, University of Brighton and Brighton and Hove City Council. Available at: http://eprints.brighton.ac.uk/5867/1/Do_it_with_Pride_report.pdf. Accessed on 22 September 2011.

Cull, M., Platzer, H. and Balloch, S. (2006) *Out on My Own: Understanding the Experiences and Needs of Homeless Lesbian, Gay, Bisexual and Transgender Youth.* University of Brighton. Available at: www.communities.gov.uk/documents/housing/pdf/outonmyown.pdf. Accessed on 22 September 2011.

Gorman-Murray, A. (2007) 'Reconfiguring domestic values: Meanings of home for gay men and lesbians.' *Housing, Theory and Society 24*, 3, 229–246.

Gorman-Murray, A. (2008) 'Queering the family home: Narratives from gay, lesbian and bisexual youth coming out in supportive family homes in Australia.' *Gender, Place and Culture 15*, 1, 31–44.

Hines, S. (2007) *Transforming Gender: Transgender Practices of Identity, Intimacy and Care.* Bristol: Policy Press.

Hines, S. (2010) 'Queerly Situated? Exploring Negotiations of Trans Queer Subjectivities at Work and within Community Space.' In S. Hines (ed.) *Gender, Place and Culture.* London: Routledge.

Johnston, L. and Valentine G. (1995) 'Wherever I Lay My Girlfriend That's My Home: The Performance and Surveillance of Lesbian Identities in Domestic Environments.' In D. Bell and G. Valentine (eds) *Mapping Desire: Geographies of Sexualities.* London: Routledge.

Knocker, S. (2006) 'The whole of me: Meeting the needs of older lesbians, gay men and bisexuals living in care homes and extra care housing.' Age Concern England. Available at www.scie-socialcareonline.org.uk/repository/fulltext/104375.pdf. Accessed on 22 September 2011.

Kuntsman, A. and Esperanza, M. (2008) *Out of Place: Interrogating Silences in Queerness/Raciality.* York: Raw Nerve Books.

Stonewall (2011) *Lesbian, Gay and Bisexual People in Later Life*. London: Stonewall. Accessible at: www.stonewall.org.uk/documents/lgb_in_later_life_final.pdf.

Taylor, Y. (2007) *Working Class Lesbian Life: Classed Outsiders*. New York: Palgrave Macmillan.

Taylor, Y. (2009) *Lesbian and Gay Parenting: Securing Social and Educational Capital*. Basingstoke: Palgrave Macmillan.

Taylor, Y., Hines, S. and Casey, M. (2010) *Theorizing Intersectionality and Sexuality*. Basingstoke: Palgrave Macmillan.

Chapter 11

Meeting the Needs of LGBT People Affected by Dementia

The Story of the LGBT Dementia Support Group

Roger Newman and Elizabeth Price

Introduction

This chapter considers LGBT perspectives on dementia and the organisation of dementia care. Our focus is the journey taken by one of the authors, Roger Newman, from the role of carer to that of activist and campaigner. Out of sheer frustration and at times real anger at the way LGBT people were overlooked in dementia services, Roger founded the LGBT Dementia Support Network. In its time the Network established itself as a unique and internationally acclaimed model of support to LGBT people affected by dementia, as well as serving to raise awareness of LGBT perspectives in a field still dominated by a medical model of the condition, which has failed to respond effectively to the diverse needs of those affected. As the Network observed in its publicity material: 'Gay or Straight: Dementia doesn't discriminate.' Our intention for this chapter is to share something of the struggle to establish the Network and to highlight some of the challenges we met during the life of this project before we were reluctantly forced to close. Our hope is that others in the field of dementia care will feel inspired to take up from where the Network left off.

ROGER'S STORY OF CARE

It is 20 years since my then partner was diagnosed with pre-senile dementia. It was a condition I knew nothing about, let alone its description 'Alzheimer's disease'. I assumed he had a rare condition and I certainly knew no other gay men who had anything similar. Moreover, my experiences of dealing with health professionals and service providers suggested that they were also in the dark when faced with a gay carer and a gay man with the condition, so each experience of dealing with them and coping with their responses brought new challenges, not to say frustrations, as they assumed my needs would simply be the same as they were for 'straight' spouses.

The diagnosis occurred when there were no laws protecting LGBT people from discrimination and there was not even a suggestion that there might ever be a law which legally recognised a partnership between two people of the same sex. So, even being rewarded with the title of 'carer' seemed like a step forward.

During the eight years of caring, I can honestly say, however, that no service provider related to me in a straightforward or empathic way. My partner's doctor refused to see me, even though we had taken out mutual powers of attorney; his designated social worker failed to respond to numerous phone calls because, they said, I was 'simply a concerned friend'; following his sectioning he was tested for HIV without any reference to me; after his diagnosis I was told to leave him to the hospital and to go away and simply forget about him; and, after a few weeks in a mental health ward, I discovered that he had been moved to a residential home without reference to me. I read, I think correctly, that each act of apparent mistreatment, rejection, misunderstanding, dismissal and the neglect of both my partner's and my own feelings, was as a direct result of a lack of appreciation of the ways in which our sexual identities impacted on our experiences of dementia. Even now, I can hardly believe how resilient I had to be in order to deal with each unexpected challenge. My only support was from local gay friends who had no greater knowledge of dementia than I did, but were there for me simply because they were good friends.

Background

It is estimated that, by the year 2050, there will be as many as 1.5 million people with dementia in the UK (Alzheimer's Society 2011). The condition has been described as 'the modern epidemic of later life' (Bond and Corner 2001, p.95) and the social and economic effects of the condition are attracting increasing attention from policy makers, academics, practitioners and the general public. The nature of dementia, and the way it impacts on those diagnosed and their families and friends, mean that many of the people with a diagnosis will be supported, at some point, by partners, spouses, family members or friends, though it should also be stressed that many people with dementia are also likely to live alone. The experiences of the carers of people with dementia have been well documented and are increasingly important markers for policy development in dementia care.

The concept of 'carer', however, tends to be limited to a somewhat stereotypical view of who and what a carer is and does. This 'carer' is female and operates largely within the circumscribed frame of the biological family unit. She is, often, an adult daughter who is perceived to be the archetypal caregiver though, in her absence, adult children may also assume primary caring roles (Collins and Jones 1998). So, whilst dementia is currently newsworthy and very much a contemporary political pre-occupation, an understanding of the experience of dementia, or caring for a person with the condition, is limited to a model which relies heavily on the biological family unit. There is, therefore, little known about the experiences of people who care outside this framework.

This chapter aims to highlight one person's drive to widen conceptualisations of 'who cares' for people with dementia, and of how carers may be supported. The focus is on the experience of Roger Newman who worked with the Alzheimer's Society in the UK to form the Lesbian, Gay, Bisexual and Transgender (LGBT) Support Group. The remainder of the chapter is organised primarily around Roger's account of his journey from carer to activist and beyond. In presenting this narrative we hope to argue that, in a world increasingly focused on the personalisation of care, a more nuanced and diverse understanding of the experience of dementia care is necessary in order to ensure effective social policy and service provision.

Dementia and dementia care: LGBT perspectives

It is very difficult to estimate the number of LGBT people who have dementia or, indeed, the numbers of their family and friends who may support and care for them. Estimates of the per centage of LGBT people in the UK (for there are no entirely reliable figures) range from 1.4 per cent in the Integrated Household Survey, to 2.4 per cent for the DTI Fair Treatment at Work Pilot Survey as noted in the 'Measuring Sexual Identity: Evaluation Report' (ONS 2010). Other research suggests a much higher figure. The Final Regulatory Impact Assessment: Civil Partnership Act 2004, for example, quotes a figure of 5–7 per cent.

These widely differing estimates reflect the various methods used to elicit this information. What they also suggest, of course, is the inherent difficulty in eliciting an accurate figure. An average of these figures would suggest that around 4 per cent of the UK population may be LGB or trans. This, in turn, indicates that there may be some 30,000 LGBT people in the UK living with dementia (added to which must be a corresponding number of carers/supporters). This sizeable population remains, however, largely invisible to both policy makers and practitioners.

The reasons for this apparent invisibility are complex, but perhaps relate to the ways in which issues of LGBT sexuality have been consistently absent from mainstream research agendas in the fields of medicine, sociology and gerontology. In addition, the diagnosis of dementia itself serves to obliterate, in the public consciousness at least, other defining personal features and social identities, apart from those highlighted by the condition. There is also, in dementia care itself, a tendency 'to relegate certain issues, which are often difficult and challenging, to the margins of academic and professional discourses' (Innes, Archibald and Murphy 2004, p.11). It should be stressed, of course, that LGBT people are easily 'hidden', lacking the more obvious identifiers of other minority groups, and this is, of course, sometimes by design – the decision to make oneself known to others (coming out) may be a life-changing decision for any LGBT person, and issues of perceived safety and expectations of confidentiality are critical in this decision-making process.

Unsurprisingly, therefore, the small amount of research done with LGBT people who have dementia (and their carers) to date suggests that practitioners in dementia care are unaware of how to respond appropriately to LGBT service users (Manthorpe and Price 2003; Price 2005, 2007, 2010, 2011; Ward 2000; Ward, Pugh and Price 2011), and that service users manage additional anxieties related to their sexualities that would not, ordinarily, be pre-occupations shared by heterosexual carers. Lesbian and gay carers, for example, are required to proactively manage disclosures of sexuality to service providers who may come into their homes to provide or arrange care. People's experiences of providing care for a person with dementia and their interactions with service providers are, as a result, overlaid with a pervasive anxiety around how these disclosures will be responded to and shared. Moreover, biological family relationships that may have been damaged or fractured by family members' responses to a person's sexuality require varying degrees of re-negotiation when a member of the family requires care (Price 2011). Research to date suggests that caring for a person with dementia, as a gay man or lesbian woman, presents a range of challenges and associated well-founded anxieties that are, arguably, unique (Price 2010). It was in response to such challenges that Roger's work with the Alzheimer's Society began.

MOVING FORWARD AND BUILDING SUPPORT: ROGER'S STORY CONTINUES

My experiences as a carer and the heartfelt sense that conditions for LGBT people affected by dementia could be much improved led me to set up the LGBT Dementia Support Group. The formation of this group is not simply a matter of historical interest, however, since the process identifies and reflects key issues that are fundamental to recognising and meeting the needs of LGBT people affected by dementia. Initially, such needs were signposted via my frustration with the consistent use of non-inclusive images in publications produced by the Alzheimer's Society. I wrote a letter to the Society in which I pointed out that photographs used for the Society's publicity materials showed Caucasian people surrounded by loving, supportive spouses and, presumed biological, families. I enquired if I was, perhaps, the only person caring for someone with dementia who wasn't married, or who was the same gender as the person with dementia they cared for.

The issue of visible inclusivity remains problematic to this day and should be a concern for all those involved in publicity, advertising and public relations in the field of healthcare. It is important to understand that those of us who are members of minority groups are always looking for signs that we are 'included'. Failure to show such signs send a message that our needs are neither considered nor met, and even, perhaps, that we are not welcome at all. Service providers have a professional responsibility to ensure that each time a policy, a publication, or the formation of a new group and its programme is produced, it should clearly demonstrate inclusion and diversity as an intrinsic constituent of its philosophy. This is easily achieved and actually requires relatively little thought or extra resources. Simply displaying images of same-sex couples in public areas may be sufficient to demonstrate the fact that a service provider recognises that not all service users, or their carers, are heterosexual. Not to do so is, I believe, a sign of professional laziness and, perhaps subconscious discrimination.

The LGBT Support Group of the Alzheimer's Society was co-founded by myself and three others, though sadly by this time, my partner had died after going missing from his residential home and being found dead on a nearby beach. Following our initial advances the Society became increasingly proactive in championing the LGBT cause, and much of this was, I feel, due to the fact that raising awareness of the issue gave LGBT staff within the organisation the impetus to 'come out' and support the three of us who were now the basis of a steering group aiming to create a Gay Carers' Network. We knew that the Alzheimer's Society was, at that point, the only major national charity with a group specifically aimed at supporting lesbian and gay carers. The Society itself was still a relatively new one and was keen to be seen to be inclusive. Indeed, it was not long after the formation of an LGBT group that the London area office appointed a member of staff to head up black and minority ethnic work amongst carers, signalling a chain of events regarding the recognition of the diverse needs of people affected by dementia.

After launching the phone helpline in the Society's newsletter, we waited in hope for our first call – and we waited some more! However, one evening we were shocked at hearing the phone ring: our first client phoned, and so began a service and a journey of discovery. I think that, to a certain extent, members of the support group had harboured an unconscious assumption that the needs of lesbian and gay carers would simply mirror those of the heterosexual population, but with an added factor of the gay or lesbian carer experiencing discrimination from service providers. However, after listening to the first callers, we soon realised that LGBT carers' situations may be far more complex than this – we had not accounted for the fact that lesbian and gay relationships may be qualitatively different from those of the heterosexual population, and so any caring issues inevitably reflect those differences. Some of our callers were in contact for years, sometimes our relationships lasted the entire duration of their cared-for person's dementia. We thus developed friendships and bonds which were, I would argue, deeper and more intense than those experienced in many other helpline situations.

The challenges carers were facing included an inability on the part of service providers to understand and use appropriate language when working with lesbian or gay service users; a widespread acceptance of gay and lesbian stereotypes and myths about the nature of gay and lesbian people's relationships, and a general lack of awareness of, and frank disregard for the importance of 'the family of choice' in the lives of lesbian and gay people. For our own part, we soon realised — although with hindsight it should have been obvious — that lesbian callers might prefer to speak to another lesbian woman, but we had only one lesbian group member. It had also not registered with us that, statistically there were more women with dementia, and also that lesbian members of families might be almost pushed into the caring role because 'they were single and therefore more free to do the work' (we had to face that particular issue on a number of occasions). In 2002 the potential for expanding our work led to a successful bid to Comic Relief for funding. We were able to appoint a worker who worked to raise awareness within the 200 Alzheimer's Society branches about the needs of lesbian and gay carers.

At our inception, it was obvious that the work of the Network would be complete only when the Society's understanding and ownership of our needs was so total that no separate statements or publications related to the needs of LGBT people would be necessary. Eventually, we realised that the only way to tackle this was to be more closely involved with branches in the knowledge that meaningful local support could only effectively take place if the branches of the Society recognised and understood LGBT issues. There were some very positive responses from some branches. A lesbian woman rang the helpline, but lived many miles from her phone contact. We decided to phone the local branch manager to seek his help. His response was disarmingly honest but also heartwarming. He told us frankly that he had originally been quite homophobic when the Network was created but, having attended one of our awareness-raising sessions, he now understood more and consequently felt he could now 'cope'. He took our caller under his wing, and we felt assured that even if he might get the language wrong, or show some misunderstandings, his heart was certainly in the right place and, more significantly, he now felt confident and prepared to ask for help if he sensed he was getting out of his depth. For us, this was an encouragingly good model for other branches to follow, and later there were other cases where the same approach was used.

THE CHALLENGES WE FACED

Despite building an international profile and receiving a great deal of attention across Europe, America and Australasia, we still faced challenges. One of our callers, who was caring for both parents, after informing his GP that he was gay, was told that he couldn't possibly provide adequate care because of his 'multiple partners' (a gross and bigoted supposition). Fortunately, we were now not having to deal with many responses like that, but just as frustrating, and becoming more frequent, was the response to our work from service providers, who produced a somewhat defensive stance, saying that they couldn't quite understand why a separate LGBT support group was necessary when it was a point of principle within their provision that they treated everyone equally, whoever they were. In other words, they appeared to be responding to an accusation of discrimination when, actually, we were simply asking them to practise what they preached about personalisation as it related to LGBT people and, more especially, older LGBT people. What our callers were telling us was that coupled with the challenges of caring for someone with dementia was another challenge of coming out to service providers. Older LGBT people bring to the present a whole range of experiences, sometimes extremely painful, of being an LGBT person in a hostile public environment. Therefore, dealing with us as LGBT people requires an enlightened approach, and not to employ such an approach will only compound a condition like dementia, and not alleviate it.

The group published some extremely effective posters which proclaimed 'Gay or straight, dementia does not discriminate', and though these were rarely to be found in Alzheimer's Society Branch offices, they were to be found in social work offices throughout the country. Indeed, the words on the poster became the title for LGBT speakers' input into dementia conferences both in the UK and abroad, and it was clear that the needs of LGBT people with dementia and their carers were, in many places, now more firmly on the agenda. Perhaps as a consequence, the calls to the support group began to change – there was a clear sign that LGBT carers were more ready to use the knowledge of their sexuality as the key to receiving the best possible care; for example, a lesbian woman phoned on behalf of friends who simply wanted to know how to approach the act of 'coming out' to service providers. There was also clear confirmation that most LGBT people do not necessarily form partnerships appropriate for civil registration; rather they construct what have been referred to as 'families of choice'. Therefore, the support offered by the LGBT Support Group was sometimes related to a relationship which might not be known, neither to the family of the person with dementia, nor to the service provider. Additionally, there was a refreshing increase in calls from service providers who simply wanted to get their delivery to LGBT clients exactly right and wanted further advice regarding how to achieve best practice. There still, of course, remained those heartrending calls, so typical within the world of dementia care, from people who had been in partnerships for many years and now had to face the apocalyptic reality of their loved one's impending decline into dementia. The support offered at these times was perhaps not very different from that of other dementia helplines, except that we offered the opportunity for one gay person to talk with another.

The challenges we faced as a group continued when, one Saturday afternoon, our first trans caller, who was caring for her mother, rang the helpline. The group had somewhat blithely declared that it was an LGBT support group, but our knowledge, understanding and expertise in working with the trans community had been neither researched nor tested. We had assumed that our approach would essentially be no different from that with LGB callers. This first trans caller presented us with a familiar issue of the demanding task of caring for a parent with dementia, but the personal issues arising from her own transgender identity and experiences and her parent's original attitude to her transition were clearly key features too. The group had to acknowledge that advice and further research was necessary to ensure best practice on this issue and help from 'a:gender' (an organisation providing support to trans people) was sought. Members of that group were contacted with the aim of discovering something about the incidence of dementia amongst trans people and asking for pointers to present and future challenges for trans carers. We planned to include a trans person in the support group, but, sadly, the demise of the support group as a whole curtailed that important innovation. The group ended when the resources offered by our host were redirected elsewhere and it became impossible to continue. However, many of the issues we identified and the needs we were able to meet did not simply evaporate – in highlighting them in this chapter we hope that dementia service providers and practitioners will feel encouraged to take these forward in their own work.

Summary points

There is growing recognition that, due to demographic changes, older LGBT people make up a sizeable proportion of the LGBT community as a whole, and might eventually be a majority. Some very successful organisations already exist to meet their needs, and recognition of the reality of dementia within their ranks has led to the creation of initiatives such as befriending and buddying projects. In the absence of specifically LGBT nursing or residential homes, and with insufficient service providers declaring themselves to be 'LGBT-friendly', the challenge facing LGBT organisations in the future will be to 'own' the problem and respond appropriately. LGBT people clearly demonstrated the ability and willingness to mobilise their considerable resources during the HIV/AIDS crisis in the 1980s and 90s, and the realities of an ageing community now require a similarly fervent response in the context of dementia.

Although the LGBT Support Group has ceased to exist, its story, and that of Roger in particular, reflect a number of issues that have significance beyond the life of the group itself. The challenges Roger faced when caring for his partner inspired him with a determination to address the inequity and frank discrimination he and his partner experienced. His determination was such that the Alzheimer's Society eventually bowed to the pressure to engage with the fact that not all carers are heterosexual, and that not all people with dementia have a biological family they might rely on for help and support – whether such awareness is systemic in dementia care services remains a moot point. As such, it was one man's stubborn determination, rather than a corporate sense of responsibility, that kick-started the Society's interest in the experience of LGBT carers for people with dementia.

There is still much to be done, of course, in terms of recognising the arguably unique ways in which LGBT people experience the various challenges associated with dementia. A life lived as a sexual dissident may bring a particular flavour to these experiences, though, of course, it should not be assumed that an LGB or trans identity presupposes a predetermined and easily recognised set of fixed 'needs' that can be learned and met through a casual engagement with the principles of anti-oppressive practice. Recognising and meeting individuals' needs is, of course, far more complex, and what we argue for here is an awareness and a nuanced appreciation of the ways in which an LGB or trans identity may combine with dementia to produce a very particular mix of experience, need and expectation. The policy context in the UK, however, suggests that this objective is far from being realised. Whilst the personalisation agenda offers a very real opportunity to appropriately recognise and engage with issues of diversity for people with dementia and their carers, the much vaunted Dementia Strategy has little to say about issues of diversity in general, and LGBT issues in particular.

We conclude this chapter with a short vignette in which we have attempted to combine a number of challenges and issues that have become apparent to support group members over the years. Michael's story is designed to allow the reader an opportunity to think through and consider appropriate responses to LGBT people who have dementia, and those who care for and support them.

Michael: A case study

Michael was 85 years old and lived alone in a small seaside town in the South of England. Michael was gay and in the past had indicated that, other than his close friends, he would prefer no one to know this.

Michael had been having trouble with his memory and, when visiting some friends, appeared to have forgotten how to get home. He was found by the police in the local bus station in a confused and clearly distressed state. Following this incident, his mental health deteriorated further and he was eventually admitted into residential care, as it was felt that he was unable to care for himself safely at home. Michael had no contact with his biological family, so his social worker made this decision in his best interests.

Michael did, however, have a small network of close friends who all lived some distance away. They expressed concern about Michael having been admitted into care, but none was able to offer an alternative living situation. One friend contacted Michael's social worker to ask if he could be moved to a care home nearer to his friends and this was duly arranged.

The social worker thought it was best if they shared information about Michael's sexuality with the staff at Michael's care home, as she felt this would allow a more individualised service response to Michael's needs. Despite this, however, Michael's sexuality was never referred to by staff in the home. He was not asked about his past friendships and relationships and his room was devoid of references to his past life. One staff member said she felt uncomfortable working alongside images of two men embracing, so she removed some of the photographs from Michael's room – it was felt that Michael's confusion was so profound that he would probably not miss them.

Other members of staff felt this was inappropriate, but still found it difficult to engage with Michael. He was not included in reminiscence groups, as he seldom seemed to have anything to contribute – even when he had tried to talk about his past life, other residents seemed very uncomfortable with his references to same-sex relationships and experiences. It just seemed easier all round not to mention Michael's past life.

As time went on, Michael became very withdrawn and depressed (staff put this down to a worsening of his dementia). His friends found it increasingly difficult to engage with him when they visited, and, as a consequence, their visits gradually stopped. Michael died a year after being admitted to the residential home.

Questions to consider

1. Do you feel the social worker made the correct decision to inform Michael's service providers that he was a gay man? What effect do you think this disclosure may have had?

2. The concept of 'family' is very important in the context of care-giving relationships. What does the word 'family' mean to you – how would you define a family?

3. How do you think the residential home could have managed residents' negative perceptions of Michael?

4. Could you suggest some ways in which it might have been possible to ensure Michael's past life was validated?

5. How could you encourage Michael's friends to continue to visit him when his dementia became more challenging?

References

Alzheimer's Society (2011) *Dementia: What we're fighting for.* Annual Report 2010/11, London: Alzheimer's Society. Accessible at: http://alzheimers.org.uk/site/scripts/download_info.php?fileID=1202. Accessed on 11 May 2012.

Bond, J. and Corner, L. (2001) 'Researching dementia: Are there unique methodological challenges for health services research?' *Ageing and Society 21*, 95–116.

Collins, C. and Jones, R. (1998) 'Emotional distress and morbidity in dementia carers: A matched comparison of husbands and wives.' *International Journal of Geriatric Psychiatry.* *12*, 12, 1168–1173.

Innes, A., Archibald, C. and Murphy, C. (2004) 'Introduction.' In A. Innes, C. Archibald and C. Murphy (eds), *Dementia and Social Inclusion.* London: Jessica Kingsley Publishers.

Manthorpe, J. and Price, E. (2003) 'Out of the shadows.' *Community Care* 3–9 April, 40–41.

Office for National Statistics (2010) *Measuring Sexual Identity: Evaluation Report.* Available at: www.ons.gov.uk/ons/rel/ethnicity/measuring-sexual-identity---evaluation-report/2010/index.html. Accessed on 11 May 2012.

Price, E. (2005) 'All but invisible: Older gay men and lesbians.' *Nursing Older People 17*, 4, 16–18.

Price, E. (2007) 'Pride or prejudice; gay men, lesbians and dementia.' *British Journal of Social Work 38*, 7, 1337–1352.

Price, E. (2010) 'Coming out to care: Gay and lesbian carers' experiences of dementia services.' *Health and Social Care in the Community 18*, 2, 160–168.

Price, E. (2011) 'Caring for Mum and Dad: Lesbian women negotiating family and navigating care.' *British Journal of Social Work 41*, 7, 1288–1303.

Ward, R. (2000) 'Waiting to be heard – dementia and the gay community.' *Journal of Dementia Care 8*, 3, May–June, 24–25.

Ward, R., Pugh, S. and Price, E. (2011) *Don't Look Back: Improving Health and Social Care Service Delivery for Older LGB Users.* Available at: www.equalityhumanrights.com/uploaded_files/research/dont_look_back_improving_health_and_social_care.pdf. Accessed on 11 May 2012.

Conclusion

Making Space for LGBT Lives in Health and Social Care

Richard Ward

This book has quite a specific focus. By asking our readers to consider the perspectives of older lesbian, gay, bisexual and trans people we are drawing attention to a minority within a minority. Furthermore, we have focused attention upon the relationship that these groups and individuals have to health and social care services, and upon the many challenges attached to appropriately meeting their needs therein. This is, then, a book with a fairly specialised interest, and much of what it contains supports the development and enhancement of particular skills and understanding that may well be absent from more generic texts or training on later life and ageing. In part, the targeted nature of the discussions in this book reflects a move away from the idea that ageing and later life is something that we can capture through a single grand narrative, or indeed that there are certain assumptions or expectations that we can hold about later life that apply uniformly to older people. Instead, what drives this book is recognition that twenty-first-century ageing is a diverse affair marked by a burgeoning array of pathways or roadmaps to our later years. Such diversity is something that health and social care practice should embrace, even facilitate, and at the core of this book lies an emphasis upon the use of biographical approaches as a possible means to achieving this.

Nonetheless, the chapters collected in this volume are also intended to support readers to think more broadly about questions of collectivity and identity. This book considers the merging of sexuality and ageing in a context where much of the existing debate on sexuality *still* overlooks ageing and where both academic and practice-related considerations of old age have failed to consider sexuality as anything other than an 'add-on' to how we understand and make sense of the ageing process. This oversight has led to the social and cultural invisibility of older LGBT identities and a failure in both policy and practice to take account of the needs of LGBT people as they age. It is a persistent omission, and by that we mean it happens knowingly. In this respect, the preoccupations of this book speak to a much larger set of challenges for the welfare system, including questions of how care and support can uphold difference and respond to the multiplicity of demands that emerge from a diverse older population, while overcoming discrimination that may exist at all levels. By asking our readers to consider the intersection of ageing and sexuality we hope to have shown how this strengthens an understanding both of ageing and of sexuality, thereby supporting a more sophisticated approach to social difference in practice. Our focus upon a particular minority also provides a template for considering more general questions and challenges attached to developing services and working cultures that are fair, inclusive and at least somewhat free of bias and the unwanted privileging of certain interests over others.

Developing biographical practice

The call to consider biographical approaches within services to older people is far from new. Such work is the result of a now well-established 'narrative turn' across the social sciences and its subsequent take-up as a therapeutic 'tool' in many different areas of health and social care. There are many published examples of biographical methods in work with older people (see our list of 'Selected Resources for Working with Older LGBT Groups and Individuals' at the end of the book) as well as an array of more theoretical explorations of the meaning of narrative and its relationship to selfhood and subjectivity. The recent establishment of the UK-wide 'Lifestory Network' (see http://lifestorynetwork.org.uk) and initiatives such as the 'My Home Life' programme for care homes (see http://myhomelifemovement.org) provide clear evidence of the shift toward using biographical approaches in work with older people as a central tenet of care practice. Yet, to date, many such initiatives have failed to take account of older LGBT service users or to recognise the implications for care providers of creating LGBT-friendly cultures of care. This book therefore makes a timely contribution to the broader project of developing biographical practice as part of the equalities agenda for health and social care.

Biographical narratives have also played a central and long-standing role in the history of gay liberation and the evolving rights-based campaigning activities of the LGBT communities. The queer sociologist Ken Plummer (2001) has observed that:

> Until roughly the 1970s, if any life stories were to be told of 'homosexuality' they were usually to be told by doctors or moralists, and were couched in the most negative terms – since homosexuality was seen as a sickness, a pathology and a crime. (Plummer 2001, p. 94)

It is no coincidence then that much of the output from the early days of the gay liberation movement in both the US and the UK involved the sharing of life stories and common experiences and a consequent reclaiming and reframing of LGBT identities (see, for example, Kennedy and Davis 1993, Porter and Weeks 1991, Lesbian Oral History Group 1989, and the Gay Men's Oral History Group 1989).

Hence, the telling of life stories has a status and significance within the LGBT communities that is closely intertwined with a history of emancipation and the struggle for recognition and rights. Such narratives have been central to the process of developing a collective awareness, as Riessman (2008) notes in her discussion of the power of biographical narrative for minoritised groups: 'Major resistance movements of the twentieth century were born as individuals sat together and told stories about small moments of discrimination. Commonalities in the stories created group belonging and set the stage for collective action' (Riessman 2008, p.9).

Crucial to this process, as Plummer (2001) has pointed out, is that a community emerged to listen to these stories and spaces were created that allowed their telling. Very much at the heart of this book lies a call for health and social care practice similarly to create the spaces for LGBT lives to be told, with practitioners serving in the role of what Plummer has described as 'coaxers, coaches and coercers', skilfully and sensitively eliciting these stories to the benefit of their tellers. Knowing something of the backdrop to these narrative traditions in the LGBT communities is, then, a useful consideration for practitioners. It illustrates the connection between personal biographies, a collective community history and broader structural change. Indeed, in the context of health and social care, where limited evidence currently exists of good practice in working with LGBT service users, work with a biographical focus is one of the few areas where some form of an evidence base exists (see Chapter 6 in this book for some examples of this work), with many commentators recommending such approaches precisely because they support an understanding of the connection of personal experience to broader collective histories of discrimination and oppression.

So, formalising efforts to reflect upon a life lived and the meaning it holds has its origins in both the development of a humanistic model of care to older people, and the emergence of contemporary LGBT communities. In taking up such approaches in health and social care it is vital that this work does not become disconnected from its roots, and that practitioners understand the continuities that exist and the meanings they hold when using biographical approaches in care. This means avoiding the relegation of biographical work to the status of another administrative task in the 'processing' of older service users. Many readers will be familiar with the standard tick-box profiles used in assessments and care reviews that are so often filed away in an office drawer, rarely to be consulted or updated. This is an exercise in information-gathering that, as Stephen Pugh points out in Chapter 2, 'Care Anticipated', is so far removed from the 'real' work of learning about the meanings that people attach to life events and how they make sense of the lives they have lived. For some areas of practice in particular, using a biographical approach means dispensing with the type of thinking associated with more positivist and realist traditions that assume a straightforward link between an objective reality and the representation of it. In many respects biographical ways of working owe more to the arts and humanities than to the scientific objectivity of the natural sciences, and thereby represent something of a departure from the type of evidence-based practice currently so lauded in many areas of medicine and healthcare. Instead, we are led to consider the constructive qualities of storytelling, and to recognise the contingency of identities and their fluid and negotiable nature, something that Jane Traies underlines in Chapter 4 as she plots the changing identities of the older lesbian participants in her research. And while hard-line scientists may cast this work as little more than an aesthetic exercise in representation, we would argue that it goes to the heart of who we are, that there is an ontological quality to the telling of lived experience that is constitutive of our identities in the here and now.

Surface, space and flow

On reviewing the chapters gathered together in this volume, one of the more striking features to emerge is the frequent reference made by our contributors to questions of place and space. This includes highlighting the importance of particular spaces and places to the lives of older LGBT people and also the use of spatial metaphors as a way of conveying different aspects of the ageing process or biographical practices. From roadmaps and roadblocks to notions of queer space and discursive spaces for meaning-making and identity-building, it appears that space as well as time is crucial to how we think about ageing and how we make sense of the lives we have led. With this in mind we felt it was appropriate to continue the spatial metaphors when it came to thinking about some of the main messages from the different chapters in relation to health and social care practice. We are using the metaphors of surface, space and flow to support discussion of three key considerations for practitioners when it comes to developing inclusive practice. These are, first, issues of *access to a service* for minority groups and communities; second, questions of the *appropriateness of a service* to diverse service users, once accessed; and finally, concerns surrounding the *outcomes of a service* and the extent to which these outcomes differ between various groups and individuals. All three aspects can be monitored in an effort to gauge how inclusive a particular service or field of practice is, but what are some of the specific considerations when it comes to working with older LGBT service users?

Surface

One of the main strands to run through the book is a concern with how LGBT people imagine their future selves and, in relation to this, picture possible scenarios for the use of health and social care. To an extent this theme of imagined futures reflects a pragmatic response to the difficulties for researchers of recruiting older LGBT people (especially the 'oldest old'), and those currently making use of services. Such individuals remain hard to identify, not least because many consider 'coming out' when accessing services to be unwise or unsafe. But these explorations of imagined futures raise some important questions about how health and social care services look from the outside – their surface, so to speak – and illustrate the type of beliefs and perceptions about service providers that circulate within the LGBT communities.

Clearly, providers across all sectors need to consider how a service looks, not only from 'the inside' for a current user, but from the outside, from the perspective of potential future users – to what extent do LGBT people see themselves reflected in these surfaces? As Browne and colleagues (Chapter 10) conclude from their research conducted in Brighton, certain areas of provision would do well to enhance their reputation with the LGBT communities in order to address issues of access and take-up by these groups. Existing research has shown that many LGBT people anticipate that they will be discriminated against when using care services (Hunt and Dick 2008; Whittle, Turner and Al-Alami 2007) and this anticipation is itself a barrier to accessing services. One important consideration, flagged by a number of chapters in this book, is the extent to which healthcare and medicine are implicated in the history of LGBT discrimination and oppression. As River and Ward argue in Chapter 8, different branches of health and social care have their own biographies, and practitioners need to acknowledge how this might intersect with the lives of individual service users. Mental health services are a key example, given their role in the 'treatment' of homosexuality and transvestism through to the early 1970s. While the different therapies deployed at this time, and their longer-term effects, have been well documented in histories of the gay community (e.g. Mort 1987), it remains uncertain to many LGBT service users just how far modern psychiatric services and mental health nursing have gone in taking responsibility for this dubious history or the impact that such therapies have had on people's lives. Indeed, as Louis Bailey points out in Chapter 3 on trans ageing, psychiatry still assumes an unwarranted and at times damaging authority over the lives of trans people, requiring a diagnosis of mental illness as the sole route to gender reassignment surgery, in effect pathologising trans identities in ways that many trans people find unhelpful.

The imagined futures theme in this book also confirms that there are certain specific concerns that reoccur frequently in research with LGBT groups regarding health and social care provision. Prominent amongst these is the prospect of entering residential care. From some of the earliest UK-based research conducted by Polari over 15 years ago to current research reported for the first time in this book, admission to a care home is shown to be a frightening and, for some, unthinkable future prospect. Yet research tells us that older LGBT people are more likely than their heterosexual peers to rely upon formal care services as they age, not least because they are less likely to have children and more likely to live alone (Stonewall 2011). We need to consider the 'surfaces' of these care settings and how they might be made less threatening to the LGBT communities. For instance, Stein and Almack draw some useful comparisons between the US and the UK in Chapter 7 and highlight instances of good practice based upon a North American model, but so far there are few signs of change this side of the Atlantic. Ultimately, it seems that for many people looking to their future care needs it is the prospect of sharing their life experience and having common histories that they hold as important, as Stephen Pugh identifies in Chapter 2. For anyone who believes in the idea that biographical narratives provide a means by which to connect the self to the social world that we inhabit, it would seem perfectly reasonable to fear the prospect of living in an environment where no space exists to share such narratives. So, one question this book raises is, to what extent does space exist for LGBT people to tell their life stories in residential and other forms of care, and how might space be created in order for future LGBT residents to do so?

Another prominent concern to emerge from this book regards what is known as 'body work'. In short, this is the 'hands-on' type of care and support that involves the touching and handling of the body by a paid caregiver. For many LGBT people, imagining the receipt of body work is, as Stephen Pugh notes, a 'sticking point' to the acceptability of formal care. Body work involves the politics of touch, the provision of care under conditions where an often naked older person receives physical help from a clothed younger person. The intimacy and vulnerability of this situation is one where many LGBT people fear prejudice may come to the fore in ways that would be hard to challenge or resist. Indeed, existing research shows that some care workers struggle with the prospect of providing such care to older LGBT people (Archibald 2010). Despite being such a commonplace and day-to-day feature of care of older people, body work remains under-researched, and as such there are few pointers for good practice, or evidence that might allay the fears of service users and providers alike.

Having considered the 'surface' of health and social care services, particularly in terms of how they appear for those imagining future needs, we turn now to consider how services are experienced and to ask questions about the different types of spaces that might be opened up in order to make a service appropriate for older LGBT people.

Space

For a book concerned with biographies and the passage of time it might seem odd to concentrate on issues of space, but the chapters collected here show that thinking spatially, in different ways, is useful for health and social care provision. This includes, as Kath Browne and colleagues (Chapter 10) point out, recognising the significance of different spaces to older LGBT people, as well as their sense of being 'out of place' in certain types of environment as they age. And, as Rebecca Jones (Chapter 1) demonstrates through her research with bisexual participants, it is about the power of opening up creative spaces that allow people to think about and describe their lives in ways not otherwise available to them in their day-to-day routines.

Perhaps one of the more straightforward messages concerning space comes from the chapters on community engagement that highlight the significance of the material spaces associated with services and different areas of practice. Many LGBT people actively look for signs and indicators that their identities are acknowledged and respected by service providers, and report that such indicators inform their thinking about disclosing their sexuality to that provider. As Roger Newman (Chapter 11) notes in his account of caring for his partner with Alzheimer's, when such outward and visible signs do not exist, it has an alienating and distancing effect. Far from being a token gesture, using images, emblems, flags and the like is viewed positively by many older LGBT people. Such small acts add to the sense of safety that is crucial to how people perceive the services they use. Through attention to the physical environment practitioners can influence the preparedness of LGBT service users to identify themselves, meaning that services can be made more appropriate to their needs. When a service provider claims that older LGBT service users 'don't exist' within their service, they are in effect revealing that no LGBT service users feel sufficiently safe to identify themselves within that service and, until those conditions change, are likely to remain the 'unknown service user'.

Turning to the question of biographical practice it is also helpful to think in a more figurative sense of how such work opens up a particular space in health and social care settings. Biographical work creates space for meaning-making and is often carved out against a rather different set of discourses and practices where the emphasis is upon quantitative, scientific types of knowledge. Taking a person's temperature or blood pressure involves recording information that is seen to relate directly and unproblematically to that individual, but the elicitation and use of biographical detail opens up a very different space providing the opportunity to build a narrative and to make sense of the present through the context of the past. In their exploration of the biographical narratives of gay men living with HIV, Wright and colleagues (Chapter 5) show how the dramatic and unexpected life-changing introduction of new therapies required these men to make sense of this profound change to their lives. The biographical interviews they participated in offered a discursive space for this work of reconstructing a sense of self, with clearly therapeutic qualities. These spaces are also educative for practitioners. As Stephen Pugh (Chapter 2) argues, based on his own research using an anticipatory biographical approach, such narratives can offer insights and understanding for those who coax and coach them from service users and are an important source of knowledge about LGBT lives that can help practitioners to better understand the complexities of how ageing and sexuality intersect in people's lives.

Flow

Finally we turn to the question of flow, that is, how LGBT service users journey through a service, and the crucial question of whether the outcomes for them are comparable to the outcomes for their heterosexual peers. Service use is never a static affair; people may 'pass through' a service when time-limited or temporary help or care is required, or their needs may alter over time, requiring a flexible and adaptive response. It is here that biographical work has a central role to play: from the first point of assessment through to possibly the end of a person's life, biographically oriented practice can ensure that the input of care supports continuity rather than serving to disrupt personal narratives. Stein and Almack's contribution to this book (Chapter 7) underlines that there are certain points or situations, such as at the end of life or in bereavement, when people are at their most vulnerable and appropriate care is paramount. Here, a positive outcome might be a 'good death', and the authors offer some important insights into what that could entail for LGBT service users, demonstrating along the way the value of considering different systems of care.

One of the messages from a number of the chapters in this book is the importance of past experience for how people perceive and use services in the present. And it is helpful for practitioners to know something of these histories in order to understand people's attitudes in the here and now. As River and Ward (Chapter 8) reveal from the work of Polari, negative outcomes from earlier service experiences, such as discrimination or the unthinking assumption of heterosexuality on the part of service providers, have an important shaping influence on subsequent decisions over whether or not to access help from formal services, and how people present themselves once making use of them. In certain areas of service provision it would seem that sometimes quite recent experiences of discrimination or abuse from fellow users and from staff mean few older LGBT people feel safe enough to identify themselves, and this shapes both their passage through a service and the outcomes from it. As a number of the contributors to this volume make clear, questions of visibility and the difficulties of identifying LGBT service users represent a barrier to the tailoring of services at an individual level. Used sensitively, it may well be that biographical approaches can be used to create a more acceptable context within which service users can identify themselves to providers, but research is needed to support this. However, services should not require individual users to 'come out' before seeking to tackle heteronormative working cultures or giving consideration to ways in which existing practices may prioritise certain perspectives over others.

The chapters detailing LGBT-led community work offer valuable instances of how mainstream providers can work towards more positive outcomes for LGBT service users, often through collaboration with community-based organisations and initiatives that serve as intermediaries. Projects such as Count Me in Too in Brighton and the London-based work of Polari and Opening Doors demonstrate the value of participatory approaches with older LGBT people working collectively for change. These initiatives involve a more gradual 'flow' as older LGBT people are supported to develop the skills and confidence to bring about change to the services they use. As Knocker and colleagues (Chapter 9) reveal of the work by Opening Doors, the project has attracted a 'critical mass' of older LGBT people who are actively engaged in supporting mainstream providers to adapt and reorganise themselves in order to be more accountable to LGBT users. In this respect, more negative past experiences are being used to inform positive change so that the outcomes for future LGBT users will be improved. Ultimately, the question of flow relates to how well health and social care services work together to support LGBT users to identify their own route-map to later life.

As many of the chapters in this book illustrate, service provision can represent a roadblock in someone's life, or it can offer a vehicle for the road ahead. It is our contention that biographical approaches can facilitate the delivery of appropriate support and educate providers to work with diverse service users in ways that help them to plot the road ahead.

Critical biographical practice

In this final section we turn to consider some of the more critical notes sounded in the course of this volume regarding the use of and limits to biographical approaches in a health and social care context. It is, after all, important that biographical work is underpinned with a critical understanding and an appreciation that it is by no means a panacea to the challenges of inclusive practice. One crucial consideration relates to questions of the body and embodied experience that come to the fore, not least in Louis Bailey's chapter on the life course and trans identities (Chapter 3). Eliciting biographies and their associated meanings can be a singularly disembodied activity where the role of the senses, and of those aspects of experience that might not easily be captured in language, are lost or at best underplayed. As Bailey shows, for many trans people their bodies play a central role in their life stories, with physical changes signalling social upheaval and the reconstruction of their identities in a new gender or as gender-neutral. The experience of transitioning creates a very different sense of the life course as people enter a second puberty and are faced with learning new ways of being and interacting with the world about them – in certain ways, life restarts. It seems, then, that in some important respects the experiences of trans people as they age cause us to stop and think about the limits of the narrated or storied life when the embodied aspects of day-to-day living are so crucially important to identity and the rewriting of the roadmap into later life. Indeed, Chapter 3 leads us to ask how the body might be brought more directly into biographical practice in ways that would better facilitate the telling of a trans life.

Another critical perspective is offered by Kath Browne and colleagues in Chapter 10 as they draw attention to the key role that place and space play in the lives of older LGBT people. In their very nature, biographical narratives are concerned with time and its passage, and the role of place in the formation and maintenance of identities throughout our lives can be obscured as result. Yet Browne and colleagues show that our sense of self derives from the places that we belong to and is disrupted when we are made to feel out of place or excluded from settings such as the youth-oriented commercial gay scene of Brighton, where older customers are rarely catered for. Similarly, Chapter 10 considers the role of housing and the way that domestic arrangements can shape who we are able to be, as much as how we are able to live. We need to consider how biographical practice can better take account of the role that places and spaces play in people's lives, as well as the role we play as 'place-makers' creating certain environments through our collective activity, such as the queer spaces associated with Pride and other LGBT celebrations.

The telling of a biographical narrative can also be a highly individualised activity that emphasises personal growth, challenges and accomplishments but obscures the role that others have played and continue to play in our lives. In this respect, the work of Ann Cronin and Andrew King, who have elicited and explored the joint narratives of older LGBT caring couples, is particularly important (see Chapter 6 and Cronin and King 2010) in showing that lives and identities are fundamentally relational. Their work challenges traditional conceptions of care as that which is given by a caregiver to a care-recipient by showing the interdependent nature of many LGBT caring relationships. As biographical practice develops we need to consider the value of such relational approaches in order to better understand the networks in which people are embedded and which sustain them.

Finally, we need to consider those occasions when a story cannot or will not be told. For instance, there are occasions, as Rebecca Jones highlights in Chapter 1, when the appropriate language or frameworks simply do not exist in order for people to properly express themselves. For many bisexual people the gay/straight binary is an inadequate foundation upon which to develop notions of a future self. Here, as Jones demonstrates, creative responses using alternative media in 'non-normative' spaces may assist. As Jane Traies points out in Chapter 4 on older lesbians, there are also occasions when people wish to hide and remain hidden, and under these circumstances an invitation to reveal aspects of their life story may be seen as threatening or intrusive. Perhaps, then, one of the most important issues to highlight regarding biographical practice is that everyone is entitled to *decline* to tell their story, especially in the context of their use of health and social care. And the most important skill for the biographical practitioner may be the sensitivity to recognise when a story needs to remain untold. We each 'own' our life stories, and in health and social care practice there are important ethical considerations attached to how stories told are used and circulate beyond the reach of the person that they originate from.

Nonetheless, even with such caveats in mind, biographical approaches remain a valuable resource for working positively with older LGBT people and as a means to develop a more egalitarian and inclusive culture in health and social care, even against the backdrop of financial strictures and service cuts currently reshaping the welfare system. As Cronin and colleagues argue in Chapter 6, done well, biographical practice can help to negotiate and balance the need to provide tailored and personalised support at an individual level with an appreciation and recognition of the broader inequalities that particular minorities face as a group. With this in mind, we end with the words of Ken Plummer, whose work on biographical practices and the study of LGBT identities helped to inspire this book and the seminar series from which it originated. He speaks with some authority on the power of the storied life:

> In short, life stories can bridge cultural history with personal biography. What matters to people keeps getting told in their stories of their life [...] And going still further, life stories can ultimately be used to illustrate the workings of a wider community or whole society. Unique lives can make bridges to wider social concerns and help illuminate the 'myths we live by'. At the most general level, then, life stories may be seen as helping us see ourselves, others, life around us, and ultimately the universe. (Plummer 2001, pp.242–3)

References

Archibald, C. (2010) 'A Path Less Travelled: Hearing the Voices of Older Lesbians: A Pilot Study Researching Residential Care and Other Needs.' In R.L. Jones and R. Ward (eds) *LGBT Issues: Looking Beyond Categories.* Edinburgh: Dunedin Academic Press.

Cronin, A. and King, A. (2010) 'A Queer Kind of Care: Some Preliminary Notes and Observations.' In R.L. Jones and R. Ward (eds) *LGBT Issues: Looking Beyond Categories.* Edinburgh: Dunedin Academic Press.

Gay Men's Oral History Group (1989) *Walking after Midnight: Gay Men's Life Stories.* London: Hall Carpenter Archives.

Hunt, R. and Dick, S. (2008) *Serves You Right: Lesbian and Gay People's Expectations of Discrimination.* London: Stonewall.

Kennedy, E.L. and Davis, M.D. (1993) *Boots of Leather, Slippers of Gold: The History of a Lesbian Community.* London: Routledge.

Lesbian Oral History Group (1989) *Inventing Ourselves: Lesbian Life Stories.* London: Hall Carpenter Archives.

Mort, F. (1987) *Dangerous Sexualities: Medico-Moral Politics in England since 1830.* London: Routledge and Kegan Paul.

Plummer, K. (2001) *Documents of Life. 2: An Invitation to a Critical Humanism.* London: Sage Publications.

Porter, K. and Weeks, J. (eds) (1991) *Between the Acts: Lives of Homosexual Men 1885–1967.* London: Routledge.

Riessman, C.K. (2008) *Narrative Methods for the Human Sciences.* Thousand Oaks, CA: Sage Publications.

Stonewall (2011) *Lesbian, Gay and Bisexual People in Later Life.* London: Stonewall.

Whittle, S., Turner, L. and Al-Alami, M. (2007) *Engendered Penalties: Transgender and Transsexual People's Experiences of Inequality and Discrimination.* London: *The Equalities Review*, in association with Press for Change and Manchester Metropolitan University.

Glossary

- **Gender** – usually used to denote differences between the sexes that are thought to be socially constructed rather than biological.

- **Gender dysphoria** – distress caused by a conflict between your gender identity and the sex you were assigned at birth.

- **Gender-neutral** – identifying as neither male nor female.

- **Genderqueer** – an umbrella term for anyone who does not identify with the male/female gender binary.

- **Heteronormativity** – the privileging and naturalizing of dominant versions of heterosexuality.

- **Polyamory** – having more than one loving and/or sexual relationship at one time, with the knowledge and consent of all involved.

- **Polygender** – as with 'genderqueer' this term refers to those who do not identify with the male/female binary and includes people who identify as having a mix of male and female or as neither male nor female.

- **Queer** – a term that has been 'reclaimed' from earlier discriminatory usage, it is used by the many different groups and individuals adversely affected by heteronormativity as a self-identifying description, but is still considered to be offensive by some.

- **Trans** – inclusive term for wider transsexual, transgender and sometimes also transvestite community.

- **Transgender person** – someone with a non-traditional view of their sexual or gender identity.

- **Transsexual person** – someone who has moved or is moving from one sex/gender category to another.

Selected Resources for Working with Older LGBT Groups and Individuals

Reports

Age Concern England, Opening Doors (2001) *Good Practice Guidance and Resource Pack on Working With Older Lesbians and Gay Men.* Age Concern England Leaflet GPG115. Available with other resources at www.futureyears.org.uk/issues/lgbt_elders, accessed on 19 June 2012.

Age UK (2006) *The Whole of Me: Meeting the Needs of Older Lesbians, Gay Men and Bisexuals Living in Care Homes and Extra Care Housing: A Resource Pack for Professionals.* Available at www.scie-socialcareonline.org.uk/repository/fulltext/104375.pdf, accessed on 19 June 2012.

Care Quality Commission (CQC) (2008) *Guidance for Inspectors on How We can Promote the Rights of People Whatever Their Sexual Orientation.* London: Commission for Social Care Inspection.

Centre for Policy on Ageing (CPA) (2009–10) *Ageism and Age Discrimination in Health and Social Care: Reviews of the Literature.* Available at www.cpa.org.uk/information/reviews/reviews.html, accessed on 19 June 2012.

Commission for Social Care Inspection (2008) *Putting People First: Equality and Diversity Matters: Providing Appropriate Services for Lesbian, Gay, Bisexual and Transgender People.* Available at www.scie-socialcareonline.org.uk/profile.asp?guid=afabc8bf-0daa-42f3-a58f-da7d71012037, accessed on 19 June 2012.

Gibbons, M., Manandhar, M., Caoimhe, G. and Mullan, J. (2008) *Recognising LGB Sexual Identities in Health Services: The Experiences of Lesbian, Gay and Bisexual People With Health Services in North West Ireland.* Available at www.hse.ie/eng/services/Publications/topics/Sexual/LGBExperienceHealth_Services.html, accessed on 19 June 2012.

Grant, J.M. (2009) *Outing Age 2010.* Washington, DC, US: National Gay and Lesbian Task Force Policy Institute. Available at www.thetaskforce.org/downloads/reports/reports/outingage_final.pdf, accessed on 19 June 2012.

Help and Care Development (2006) *Gay and Grey in Dorset: Lifting the Lid on Sexuality and Ageing. A Research Project into the Needs, Wants, Fears and Aspirations of Older Lesbians and Gay Men.* Available at http://lgbtbristol.org.uk/lgbtwp/wp-content/uploads/2011/07/GayandGreyreport.pdf, accessed on 19 June 2012.

Hunt, R., Cowan, K., Chamberlain, B. (2007) *Being the Gay One: Experiences of Lesbian, Gay and Bisexual People Working in the Health and Social Care Sector.* London: Stonewall.

Institute of Medicine of the National Academies (2011) *The Health of Lesbian, Gay, Bisexual, and Transgender People: Building a Foundation for Better Understanding.* Washington, DC: The National Academies Press. Available at www.nap.edu/openbook.php?record_id=13128, accessed on 19 June 2012.

Kitchen, G. (2003) *Social Care Needs of Older Gay Men and Lesbians on Merseyside.* Get Heard/Sefton Pensioners Advocacy Centre, Southport.

Levenson, R. (2003) *Auditing Age Discrimination: A Practical Approach to Promoting Age Equality in Health and Social Care.* Kings Fund, London.

LGBT Movement Advancement Project and SAGE (2010) *Improving the Lives of LGBT Older Adults.* New York: LGBT Movement Advancement Project and SAGE. Available at http:// sageusa.org/resources/resource_view.cfm?resource=183, accessed on 19 June 2012.

Meads, C., Pennant, M., McManus, J. and Bayliss, S. (2009) *A Systematic Review of Lesbian, Gay, Bisexual and Transgender Health in the West Midlands Region of the UK Compared to Published UK Research.* Report number 71, WMHTAC. Birmingham: Department of Public Health and Epidemiology, University of Birmingham.

MetLife Mature Market Institute (2010) *Still Out, Still Aging: The MetLife Study of Lesbian, Gay, Bisexual, and Transgender Baby Boomers.* Westport, CT: MetLife Mature Market Institute. Available at www.metlife.com/assets/cao/mmi/publications/studies/2010/ mmi-still-out-still-aging.pdf, accessed on 19 June 2012.

Mitchell, M., Howarth, C., Kotecha, M. and Creegan, C. (2009) *Sexual Orientation Research Review 2008.* Manchester: Equality and Human Rights Commission.

Power, L., Bell, M. and Freemantle, I. (2010) *A National Study of People Over 50 Living with HIV.* London: Joseph Rowntree Trust. Available at www.jrf.org.uk/publications/over-50-living-with-HIV, accessed on 19 June 2012.

River, L. (2006) *A Feasibility Study of the Needs of Older Lesbians in Camden and Surrounding Boroughs.* London: Polari. This and other useful reports from Polari can be viewed at: www.ageofdiversity.org.uk/documents.

Scott, S.D., Pringle, A. and Lumsdaine, C. (2004) *Sexual Exclusion: Homophobia and Health Inequalities: A Review.* Available at www.scie-socialcareonline.org.uk/profile. asp?guid=e7522d2c-c48c-408c-a00e-0096af017dc5, accessed on 19 June 2012.

Whittle, S. and Turner, L. (2007) *Bereavement: A Guide for Transsexual, Transgender People and Their Loved Ones.* London: Department of Health. Available at www.dh.gov.uk/en/ Publicationsandstatistics/Publications/PublicationsPolicyAndGuidance/DH_074259, accessed on 19 June 2012.

Leaflets/short briefings

AgeUK (2010) *LGB: Planning for Later Life.*

AgeUK (2010) *Factsheet: Transgender Issues in Later Life.* Available at www. openingdoorslondon.org.uk/resources/AgeUK_Transgender_issues_in_later_life.pdf, accessed on 19 June 2012.

DoH (2007) *An Introduction to Working With Transgender People: Information for Health and Social Care Staff.* Available at www.dh.gov.uk/en/Publicationsandstatistics/Publications/ PublicationsPolicyAndGuidance/DH_074257, accessed on 19 June 2012.

Fish, J. (2007) *Reducing Health Inequalities for Lesbian, Gay, Bisexual and Trans People: Briefings for Health and Social Care Staff.* Series of briefings providing easy-to-read guidance for health and social care commissioners, service planners and frontline staff. Available at www.dh.gov.uk/en/Publicationsandstatistics/Publications/ PublicationsPolicyAndGuidance/DH_078347.

Irish Hospice Foundation Bereavement Resource Centre (2009) *Coping with the Death of Your Same-sex Partner: Information for LGB People.* Available at www.glen.ie/page. aspx?contentid=49&name=glen_publications, accessed on 19 June 2012.

Mayock, P., Bryan, A., Carr, N. and Kitching, K. (2009) *Supporting LGBT Lives: A Study of the Mental Health and Well Being of Lesbian, Gay, Bisexual, and Transgender People.* Available at www. glen.ie/page.aspx?contentid=49&name=glen_publications, accessed on 19 June 2012.

Musingarimi P. (2008) *Health Issues Affecting Older Gay, Lesbian and Bisexual People in the UK: A Policy Brief* UK (ILCUK). Available at www.ilcuk.org.uk/files/pdf_pdf_70.pdf, accessed on 19 June 2012.

Prism (2008) *How to be LGBT Friendly.* Available at www2.wlv.ac.uk/equalopps/how_to_ be_lgbt_friendly.pdf, accessed on 19 June 2012.

Royal College of Nursing and Unison (not dated) *Not 'Just' a Friend: Best Practice Guidance on Health Care for LGB Service Users and Their Families.* Available at www.rcn.org.uk/__data/ assets/pdf_file/0014/20741/notjustafriend.pdf, accessed on 19 June 2012.

Ward, R. and Jones, R. (2010) *How Can Adult Social Care Services Become More Accessible and Appropriate to LGBT People?* Outline 16. Dartington: Research in Practice for Adults (RiPFA). Available at www.ripfa.org.uk/publications/outlines, accessed on 19 June 2012.

Life story and biographical approaches

Frank, A.W. (1997) 'Illness as moral occasion: restoring agency to ill people.' *Health 1,* 2, 131–48.

Gubrium, J.F. (1994) *Speaking of Life: Horizons of Meaning for Nursing Home Residents.* New Brunswick, NJ: Aldine Transaction.

Gubrium, J.F. and Holstein, J.A. (eds) (2003) *Ways of Aging,* Oxford: Blackwell.

Lesbian Identity Project (2011) *Lesbians on…Living Our Lives.* Bradford: Lesbian Identity Project (LIP). (Fourth and final volume from the LIP lesbian oral history project. Available from LIP Women's Oral History Group, c/o The Equity Centre, Perkins House, 1 Longlands Street, Bradford BD1 2TP).

National Lesbian and Gay Survey (1992) *What a Lesbian Looks Like: Writings by Lesbians on their Lives and Lifestyles.* London: Routledge.

Neild, S. and Pearson, R. (1992) *Women Like Us.* London: Women's Press.

Neimeyer, R.A. (2005) 'Re-storying Loss: Fostering Growth in the Posttraumatic Narrative.' In L.G. Calhoun and R.G. Tedeschi (eds) *Handbook of Posttraumatic Growth: Research and Practice.* Mawha, NJ: Lawrence Earlbaum.

Quam, J.K. (1997) 'The Story of Carrie and Anne: Long-term Care Crisis.' In J.K. Quam (ed.) *Social Services for Senior Gay Men and Lesbians.* New York: Harrington Park Press.

Housing, health and social care research with older LGBT people

Addis, S., Davies, M., Greene, G., MacBride-Stewart, S. and Shepherd, M. (2009) 'The health, social care and housing needs of lesbian, gay, bisexual and transgender older people: A review of the literature.' *Health and Social Care in the Community 17,* 6, 647– 658.

Bayliss, K. (2000) 'Social work values, and anti-discriminatory practice and working with older lesbian service users.' *Social Work Education 19,* 1, 45–53.

Bevan, D. and Thompson, N. (2003) 'The social basis of loss and grief: Age, disability and sexuality.' *Journal of Social Work 3,* 2, 179–194.

Clover, D. (2006) 'Overcoming barriers for older gay men in the use of health services: A qualitative study of growing older, sexuality and health.' *Health Education Journal 65,* 1, 41–52.

Concannon, L. (2009) 'Developing inclusive health and social care policies for older LGBT citizens.' *British Journal of Social Work 39,* 3, 403–417.

Elford, J., Ibrahim, F., Bukutu, C. and Anderson, J. (2008) 'Over fifty and living with HIV in London.' *Sexually Transmitted Infections 84,* 6, 468–472.

Fenge, L. and Fannin, A. (2009) 'Sexuality and bereavement: Implications for practice with older lesbians and gay men.' *Practice 21,* 1, 35–46.

Fenge, L., Fannin, A., Hicks, C. and Lavin, N. (2008) *Social Work Practice with Older Lesbians and Gay Men.* (Post-qualifying social work practice.) Exeter: Learning Matters Ltd.

Langley, J. (2001) 'Developing anti-oppressive empowering social work practice with older lesbian women and gay men.' *British Journal of Social Work 31,* 6, 917–932.

Lee, A. (2007) '"I can't ask that!" Promoting discussion of sexuality and effective health service interactions with older non-heterosexual men.' In K. Clarke, T. Maltby and P. Kennett (eds) *Social Policy Review.* Bristol: Policy Press.

MacKenzie, J. (2009) 'The same but different: Working with lesbian and gay people with dementia.' *Journal of Dementia Care 17,* 6, 17–19.

Manthorpe, J. (2003) 'Nearest and dearest? The neglect of lesbians in caring relationships.' *British Journal of Social Work 33,* 6, 753–768.

Price, B. (2009) 'Exploring attitudes towards older people's sexuality.' *Nursing Older People 21,* 6, 32–39.

Price, E. (2005) 'All but invisible: Older gay men and lesbians.' *Nursing Older People 17,* 4, 16–18.

Price, E. (2008) 'Pride or prejudice? Gay men, lesbians and dementia.' *British Journal of Social Work 38,* 7, 1337–1352.

Price, E. (2010) 'Coming out to care: Gay and lesbian carers' experiences of dementia services.' *Health and Social Care in the Community 18,* 2, 160–168.

Pugh, S. (2005) 'Assessing the cultural needs of older lesbians, and gay men: Implications for practice.' *Practice 17,* 3, 207–218.

Robinson, W.A., Petty, M.S., Patton, C. and Kang, H. (2010) 'Ageing with HIV: Historical and intra-community differences in experience of aging with HIV.' In J.T. Sears (ed.) *Growing Older: Perspectives on LGBT Aging.* London: Routledge.

Smailes, J. (1994) '"The Struggle has Never Been Simply about Bricks and Mortar": Lesbians' Experience of Housing.' In R. Gilroy and R. Woods (eds) *Housing Women.* London: Routledge.

Turnbull, A. (2002) *Opening Doors: The Needs of Older Lesbians and Gay Men.* London: Age Concern. (A review of the literature; part of Age Concern's 'Opening Doors' project.)

Palliative Care and Hospice

Altilio, T. and Otis-Green, S. (eds) (2011) *Oxford Textbook of Palliative Social Work.* New York: Oxford University Press, Inc.

American Academy of Hospice and Palliative Medicine: www.aahpm.org.

Center to Advance Palliative Care: www.capc.org.

Hospice and Palliative Nurses Association: www.hpna.org.

McPhee, S., Winker, M.A., Rabow, M.W., Pantilat, S.Z and Markowitz, A.J. (eds) (2010) *JAMA Evidence: Care at the Close of Life: Evidence and Experience.* New York: McGraw-Hill Professional.

National Hospice and Palliative Care Organization: www.nhpco.org. For comprehensive consumer education about advance care planning, including state-specific advance directives (US), see NHPCO's Caring Connections: www.caringinfo.org.

St Christopher's Hospice: www.stchristophers.org.uk.

Social Work Hospice and Palliative Care Network: www.swhpn.org.

Notes on Contributors

Kathryn Almack is a Senior Research Fellow at the University of Nottingham. Her current research addresses the dynamics and diversity of people's friendship and family networks towards end of life. Within this field, she is researching the concerns, needs and experiences of older lesbian, gay, bisexual and transgender (LGBT) people.

Louis Bailey is a co-founder of the Trans Resource and Empowerment Centre (TREC) and represents TREC as a strategic executive partner of the National LGB&T Partnership (Department of Health). Dr Bailey's research concerns the medical history of gender variance and issues of trans life course and ageing.

Leela Bakshi took part in the 'Count Me In Too' project, initially as a participant and subsequently as part of the research team, leading to a role as an 'activist researcher'. She is co-author, with Kath Browne, of the book *Where we Became Ordinary? Lesbian, Gay, Bisexual and Trans Lives and Activism.* (2012 UNDER REVIEW).

Kath Browne is a principal lecturer at the University of Brighton. Her research interests encompass sexual identities, marginalisations and equalities, and gendered lives and sexed bodies. She has been lead researcher on 'Count Me In Too' since 2005. The book from this work is due in 2013.

Jose Catalan is a psychiatrist with many years' experience in HIV-related mental health problems. He has published extensively, and held senior academic posts at Oxford University and Imperial College London. He is a general hospital consultant psychiatrist at Chelsea and Westminster Hospital, London.

Ann Cronin is a sociologist of gender, sexuality and ageing. Together with Andrew King she has recently completed an Economic and Social Research Council (ESRC) funded knowledge exchange project in conjunction with Tower Hamlets Borough Council to improve services for older LGBT adults. She has contributed publications to *Sociology, International Social Work, Ageing and Society*, and is the author of numerous book chapters.

Stacey Halls is the women's Development Cordinator for the Opening Doors project, additionally undertaking campaigns and policy work. The campaigning role combines ensuring that older LGBT issues are on the agenda across London and providing statutory sector training to help facilitate more inclusive and welcoming services.

Rebecca L. Jones is a lecturer in health and social care at The Open University and chairs the Centre for Ageing and Biographical Studies. Her main academic interests are ageing, sexuality, and sexuality in later life.

Andrew King is Senior Lecturer in Sociology at Kingston University, London. His research interests encompass the intersection of ageing, sexuality and citizenship. With Ann Cronin he recently completed an Economic and Social Research Council (ESRC) funded knowledge exchange project to improve services for older LGBT adults in Tower Hamlets. He is widely published in high-impact academic journals and numerous book chapters.

Sally Knocker is a consultant trainer with Dementia Care Matters with over 20 years' experience as a writer and trainer in older people's care. An independent evaluator of 'Opening Doors London' she wrote AgeUK's resource pack 'The Whole of Me' and a Joseph Rowntree Foundation 'Perspectives' paper, based on extensive interviews with older LGB people.

Jason Lim is a lecturer in human geography at Queen Mary, University of London, UK. His research has considered intersections of sexualities, race, ethnicity and gender in everyday practice. He has worked with Kath Browne, Leela Bakshi and others to research LGBT needs and experiences in Brighton and Hove, UK.

Nick Maxwell is the men's Development Coordinator for Opening Doors London since January 2008, playing a key role in the development and successful expansion of the project. Coming from a nursing and counselling background, Nick has also held various posts within the LGBT sector dealing with LGBT health and homophobic/transphobic casework.

Roger Newman is a retired teacher from Margate, Kent. Resulting from his experiences of caring for his partner, David, he co-founded the LGBT Carers Group of the Alzheimer's Society. He is a member of national committees of AgeUK; a trustee of the Older People's Advocacy Alliance; and a co-founder of the East Kent Independent Dementia Support organisation. In 2007 he was awarded the MBE for services to charity.

Gareth J. Owen is a research fellow at the Peninsula College of Medicine (University of Exeter). His research interests include suicide prevention, service user involvement in research, and the lived experience of health and illness. Before completing a PhD in sociology he worked for many years as an HIV/AIDS specialist social worker.

Mike Phillips is a freelance trainer and consultant who is passionate about releasing potential through learning and development. He has delivered training across London, the UK and internationally. Mike has over 20 years' experience working in health and social care (including HIV, mental health and dementia) in various management and senior management roles. Recently, he was one of two independent evaluators of the Opening Doors London project.

Elizabeth Price is a senior lecturer in social work at the University of Hull. In practice, she worked with people with long-term mental health problems, and most recently with people diagnosed with dementia. Her research interests centre largely on sexualities and the experience of chronic illness.

Stephen Pugh is a senior lecturer at the University of Salford. His PhD explored the identities of older lesbians and gay men prior to 1967 and their subsequent experience of ageing. A qualified social worker, Steve is a trustee of AgeUK Salford and independent chair of Salford City Council's Adult Safeguarding Board.

Lindsay River, a queer writer, researcher and performer, came out in 1965 and has campaigned on LGBT rights since 1972. From a background in community health rights and development work with older people she became Director of Polari until its closure in 2009. She started Age of Diversity (ageofdiversity.org.uk) to carry on campaigning.

Ian Rivers is Professor of Human Development at Brunel University London and Visiting Professor in the Faculty of Health, Social Care and Education at Anglia Ruskin University. For nearly 20 years he has researched LGBT issues, and particularly discrimination. His latest book is entitled *Homophobic Bullying: Research and Theoretical Perspectives* (Oxford University Press: New York 2011).

Gary L. Stein, JD, MSW is an associate professor at the Wurzweiler School of Social Work – Yeshiva University, New York. He was a Fulbright Specialist in the UK in 2010. His interests include palliative care, bioethics, and LGBT healthcare. He received a gerontology award for his 2011 article on LGBT perspectives regarding long-term care ('Lesbian and gay elders and long-term care: identifying the unique psychosocial perspectives. and challenges.' *Journal of Gerontological Social Work 53*, 5, 421–435.

Mike Sutherland is a qualified social worker now lecturing at the Robert Gordon University, Aberdeen, and for The Centre for Excellence for Looked After Children in Scotland. He has researched the (in)visibility of LGBT issues in residential child care in Scotland and the US. He identifies as gay, male, and a parent of gay offspring.

Jane Traies retired from a career in education in 2001 and became a full-time student in 2008. Her MPhil dissertation, (completed in 2009, http://etheses.bham.ac.uk/497/) examined the cultural invisibility of older lesbians. She is currently a postgraduate student at the University of Sussex, researching the lives and experiences of lesbians over 60. (www.womenlikethat.co.uk)

Richard Ward is a researcher employed by the University of Manchester and the Greater Manchester West Mental Health NHS Foundation Trust. A qualified social worker, his research interests are in dementia and care in later life. He is currently leading an ESRC-funded study into appearance, body work and dementia care. (http://thehairandcareproject.com/)

Robin Wright has lived with HIV diagnosis for 20 years. He has a background in the performing arts, songwriting and music production. He obtained a Counselling Diploma in Adlerian and Individual Psychology while working in the HIV voluntary sector. His current interests include therapeutic body work, digital and interior design, HIV research and patient advocacy.

Subject Index

Author Index

Adam, B. 22
Adelman, M. 72, 116
AgeUK 58, 125, 126, 127
Al-Alami, M. 53, 201
Almack, K. 115, 116, 117, 125, 202
Altpeter, M. 28
Alzheimer's Society 184
Andrews, M. 100
Arber, S. 64, 98
Archibald, C. 46, 68, 76, 78, 109, 186, 202

Bailey, L. 12
Baker, P. 136
Bakshi, L. 70, 166, 169, 172
Ball, P. 22
Ball, S. 105
Balloch, S. 173
Barker, J.C. 72, 76
Barker, M. 23, 26
Bartlett, A. 141
Bayliss, K. 109
Beck, U. 36
Beckerman, N.L. 114, 117
Bell, D. 168
Bellamy, G. 115, 117
Bergeman, C.S. 93
Berger, R.M. 23
Biggs, S. 135
Blando, J. 116
Blaxter, M. 91
Bond, J. 184
Bonuck, K.A. 115, 116, 117, 122
Boulton, J. 41
Bowes-Catton, H. 26
Brashers, D.E. 89
Brookdale Center on Aging 116, 125
Brown, G. 167
Browne, K. 166, 167, 168, 169, 172, 173, 177, 178
Browning, C. 22
Bulbeck, C. 22
Bultena, G.L. 22
Bury, M. 87, 118
Bytheway, B. 22, 30, 135

Carlsson, M. 115
Carricaburu, D. 87
Casey, M. 167
Castillo, L.S. 121
Church, A. 169
Collins, C. 185
Combs, R. 55
Concannon, L. 152

Coon, D.W. 103
Corner, L. 184
Cowan, K. 67
Crenshaw, 146
Cronin, A. 1.2, 104, 105, 109, 111, 116, 137, 146, 207
Cull, M. 173
Cunningham, K. 85

Daatland, S.O. 135
Dannefer, D. 147
D'Augelli, A.R. 23
Davies, M.L. 89, 115
Davies, P. 139, 156
Davis, M.D. 198
Davis, P. 167, 173, 177
de Vries, B. 116
Deeks, S.G. 85
Department of Health 40, 56, 115
Dick, S. 201
Dodds, C. 93
Doka, K. 119
Donovan, C. 105, 118
Dorfman, R. 105
Dyer, R. 68

Eaglesham, P. 103
Economic and Social Research Council 9
Eliason, M.J. 117
Emlet, C.A. 86
Esperanza, M. 165

Fannin, A. 108
Fastenberg, D. 121
Fenge, L. 139
Fish, J. 23, 59, 72, 75
Forbes, K.E. 22, 28
Frank, A.W. 91

Gasgoyne, K. 85
Gauntlett, D. 35
Gay Men's Oral History Group 198
General Medical Council 122
Gergen, K.J. 87
Gergen, M.M. 87
Giddens, A. 36, 91
Ginn, J. 64, 98
Glacken, M. 115
Goltz, D. 22, 23, 24
Gordon, T. 22
Gorman-Murray, A. 173
Grant, J.M. 115
Grant, V. 115